THE NOT SO GOOD BOOK

WHAT DOES THE
'HOLY BIBLE'
REALLY TEACH?

By Brian Bolton

Foreword by Dan Barker

Published by the Freedom From Religion Foundation
PO Box 750 | Madison, WI 53701
FFRF.org | 608.256.8900

Library of Congress Data
Bolton, Brian
The not so Good Book: what does the 'Holy Bible' really teach? / Brian Bolton.
ISBN: 978-1-877733-18-5
Library of Congress Control Number: 2021916776

Editor: **Amit Pal**
Proofreaders: **Dan Barker, Annie Laurie Gaylor**
Graphic Designer: **Jake Swenson**
Cartoonist: **Steve Benson**
Photographer: **Lewis Kincheloe**

Table of Contents

Author

Brian Bolton is a Life Member of the Freedom From Religion Foundation and has published articles in Freethought Today for the past thirty years. He has sponsored FFRF's annual essay competition for graduate students since 2010. The executive wing of Freethought Hall bears his name. He endowed the Anne Nicol Gaylor Faculty Fellowship in Secular Studies and the Brian F. Bolton Faculty Fellowship in Secular Studies at the University of Wisconsin in 2021. He endowed the Brian F. Bolton Distinguished Professorship in Secular Studies at the University of Texas in Austin in 2020.

He is a retired academic psychologist with a background in mathematics, statistics, and psychometrics. His contributions in psychological measurement, personality assessment, and rehabilitation psychology have been recognized by universities and psychological societies. A summary of his academic recognition and contributions is included at the back of the book.

Note: The author does not receive royalties from sales of the book. All proceeds go to FFRF for the defense of church/state separation and the promotion of freethought philosophy and the secular worldview.

Foreword

By Dan Barker

One of the hardest things in the world to say is, "I was wrong."

As an evangelical preacher, my entire life had been built on the firm conviction that the bible is a reliable source of knowledge and morality. More than that, it was *the* truth: God's direct, inerrant word to humanity. "All scripture is inspired by God," the author of 2 Timothy tells us. Or as the NIV translation puts it: "God-breathed." "The prophets," I learned in 2 Peter 1:21, "though human, spoke from God as they were carried along by the Holy Spirit."

The first song I performed on the piano—at a recital when I was about nine or ten, taking lessons from Mrs. Beard, the pianist at Parkcrest Christian Church—was the hymn "Wonderful Words of Life."

> Sing them over again to me, wonderful words of life;
> Let me more of their beauty see, wonderful words of life;
> Words of life and beauty, teach me faith and duty:
> Beautiful words, wonderful words of life.

I thought the bible was God speaking directly to me. It was "a lamp unto my feet, a light unto my path" (Psalm 119:105). I remember sitting in the pew beside my parents singing:

> How firm a foundation you saints of the Lord,
> is laid for your faith in his excellent Word!

We used to have bible drills at Parkcrest. A group of us children would stand in front of the church holding our King James Bibles at the ready. The Sunday School teacher would call out a verse—say Micah 6:8—and the first child to read the passage out loud was the winner. I got really fast at memorizing the order of the books, honing a skill I still find useful.

Of course, the verses were pre-selected by the teacher. I'm sure we were never asked to find Psalm 137:9:

> Happy is the one who seizes your infants
> and dashes them against the rocks.

Or Hosea 13:16:

> Their little ones shall be dashed in pieces,
> and their pregnant women ripped open.

Imagine young teenagers reading out loud from the Song of Solomon:

> Your breasts are like two fawns, like twin fawns of a gazelle. . . .
> Your stature is like that of the palm,
> and your breasts like clusters of fruit.
> I said, "I will climb the palm tree; I will take hold of its fruit."
> May your breasts be like clusters of grapes on the vine (7:3–8).

If these are truly "wonderful words" from God, why should children need to be shielded from them?

Years later, as a minister, I would be the one cherry-picking and spoon-feeding. Across generations, the bible has been raised to such a revered loftiness that it has become like a god itself. The idea of *challenging* the "excellent Word" was unthinkable. Literally. It never entered my mind.

That's the power of indoctrination—not that you think you can defend your faith, but that it never occurs to you that it might need defending.

Well, it eventually occurs to some. When I took off the stained-glass–colored glasses of loyalty, I ended up painfully admitting that I had been mistaken.

When Oprah Winfrey asked me on TV in 1984 why I no longer believe in God, I replied: "The bible is an unreliable document, and it is a very uninspiring document. My heart cannot accept what my mind rejects."

"You went for 17 years as a minister to not believing in God?!" Oprah asked. "What does that say about you?"

"That means I was wrong," I replied.

If you ask me to explain more, I will reply that you are holding the answer in your hands. Brian Bolton is one of those inquisitive thinkers and thorough researchers who has accepted the challenge to do exactly what the preachers ask: He has opened the bible and read it for himself. Every word of it.

There are two kinds of "bible study." One is devotional and the other is critical. One uses scripture to probe the mind. The other uses the mind to probe scripture. When most Christians engage in bible study, they are not studying the bible at all. They are worshipping it. The method employing critical thought that Brian uses is not negative; it simply does not prejudge. It means being willing to follow the facts wherever they lead. As you read this book, it will become clear that Brian is using the only approach that yields true understanding: reason, not faith.

The bible does have some useful advice: "Test all things; hold fast to that which is good" (1 Thessalonians 5:21). With an open and perceptive mind, that is exactly what Brian Bolton has done. He has carefully tested and found that there is precious little in the wonderful words of life that we can truly hold fast to.

In *The Age of Reason*, Thomas Paine came to the same conclusion: "Whenever we read the obscene stories, the voluptuous debaucheries, the cruel and torturous executions, the unrelenting vindictiveness, with which more than half the Bible is filled, it would be more consistent that we called it the word of a demon than the word of God." My book, *GOD: The Most Unpleasant Character in All Fiction,* confirms Richard Dawkins's assessment in *The God Delusion* that the God of the bible is a "capriciously malevolent bully."

People are free to worship this character, of course, but shouldn't they know what it is they are worshipping? It is my hope that after reading Brian Bolton's stunning and honest analysis, believers who are mature, rational and kind will summon the courage to say: I was wrong.

Note: The chapters in this book were written over a quarter of a century for various publications. Consequently, you will find some occasional repetition. Each chapter is intended to stand alone, but combined with other chapters in the same section, it adds up to a complete picture. Some of the biblical passages are examined more than once, but usually from a different perspective. Think of it like listening to a favorite song, symphony or opera where themes are reinforced in a fresh context.

Because of the editing requirements of the various publications that have printed Brian's articles, you will see that while most of this book contains exact biblical citations, sometimes they have been removed, likely for space reasons.

—Dan Barker, co-president of the Freedom From Religion Foundation and author of many books, including *Losing Faith in Faith: From Preacher to Atheist* and *Godless*.

Introduction

The irrefutable conclusion that emerges from the thirty-nine chapters in this volume is that the Holy Bible is *not* the "Good Book" that believers consider it to be. In fact, it is a horrific compilation of unmitigated violence, disgusting obscenities, fraudulent history, and terrible advice. Ronald Reagan once said: "Within the covers of the bible are the answers for all the problems men face." Almost 200 years earlier, after a careful analysis of the text, Thomas Paine declared that it would be more appropriate to call it "the word of a demon than the word of God." The second opinion is fully supported by the evidence presented in this collection.

I have organized the thirty-nine chapters into nine primary categories of bible truth. The topics addressed begin with fundamentalist Christian dishonesty and end with unscientific biblical creationism. Between are included seven major subjects: godly hate, godly murder, Jesus's contradictory commands, Christian nationalism, decalogue deceit, prayer failure, and godly execution and feticide. The book covers basic topics of interest to scriptural skeptics, as well as curious bible believers.

Every assertion and comment that I make comes straight from "God's sacred revelation." The reader may reasonably ask which version of scripture I depend upon. There are scores of modern English translations of the bible and all derive, directly or indirectly, from the same set of "autographs." These are considered to be the best representations of what the original manuscripts actually contained, based on scholarly research by specialists in the field of textual criticism.

For the Old Testament, the universally accepted source document is the latest edition of Biblia Hebraica, and for the New Covenant, it is the latest edition of the United Bible Societies' Greek New Testament. Some supplemental texts are usually consulted, such as the Dead Sea Scrolls and Latin Vulgate, and all versions acknowledge idiosyncratic flexibility in their final translation decisions.

In my work, I have relied on seven translations: the *King James Version* (1611), *New King James Version* (1982), *Living Bible* (1971), *New International Version* (2011), *New Living Translation* (2015), *Contemporary English Version* (1976), and *Today's English Version* (1976). At times, I have also used the *Revised Standard Version* (1952) and *New English Bible* (1970).

Contrary to common assumption, the much revered *King James Version* was not an original translation, but rather a scholarly revision of William Tyndale's (1525) English translation and succeeding versions. The controversial, but very popular *Living Bible*, is one minister's simplified paraphrase of the *KJV*. Still, one way or another, all modern English translations of the bible derive from the same basic sources, and this is why there is a substantial degree of convergence in the various renderings of scripture. When inconsistencies do occur, the rational resolution is almost always to accept the consensus.

A unifying theme running through all thirty-nine chapters is the reactionary viewpoint known as Christian fundamentalism. As explained in the chapters in section I, fundamentalists claim that the bible is without error or inerrant, a perfect statement of factual and moral truth expressed in God's revelation to humankind. It must be emphasized that these radical bibliolatrists should not be called evangelicals, a term that subsumes all Christians, but instead are correctly designated fundamentalists, a label that uniquely identifies them.

I wrote thirty-eight of the chapters comprising the volume after retiring from a thirty-five-year career as an academic psychologist, which is summarized in my biographical statements. (Thirty chapters were written during the last six years.) My post-retirement focus on the bible actually began in the early 1980s as an avocational pursuit, provoked by the alarming resurgence of Christian fundamentalism at that time. Jerry Falwell, Pat Robertson, and Jimmy Swaggart have since been replaced by the current generation of Christian hypocrites, including Tony Perkins, Franklin Graham, and Mike Huckabee.

This collection of contemporary essays constitutes an arsenal of weaponry for use by atheists, humanists, and freethinkers in exposing the horrors of the Holy Bible. The volume was compiled to serve as a source book for all Americans who consider fundamentalist Christian zealots to be a threat to religious freedom in the United States. My hope is that readers will utilize these facts about the bible as ammunition in the ongoing battle against the extremists who want to implement a fundamentalist theocracy or Christian Caliphate in America.

—Brian Bolton

Acknowledgments

I want to express my thanks and gratitude to five people who helped prepare the manuscript for publication. Amit Pal was the chief editor who assured consistency in format and style. Annie Laurie Gaylor proof read all chapters in the initial editing process. Jake Swenson supervised the design and layout for the book. Steve Benson contributed the original cartoons which lead each section. Dan Barker proofed the final text and verified all bible references. Again, thanks to everyone for the excellent work on this project.

Special appreciation is given to these organizations: American Atheists, American Humanist Association, Center for Inquiry, and Freedom From Religion Foundation, for permission to reprint articles from these periodicals: American Atheist, American Rationalist, Free Inquiry, Freethought Today, The Humanist, and Skeptical Inquirer. The citations are listed in the Original Publication Sources section at the back of the book.

I. Fundamentalist Biblical Dishonesty

ONE
Basic Bible Facts Ignored by Fundamentalists

Three favorite expressions that saturate the pious language of Christian fundamentalists are "biblical values," "biblical principles," and "biblical worldview." For example, the stridently anti-marriage-equality restaurant chain Chick-Fil-A asserts that its operation is based on biblical values because it condemns birth control, divorce, and same-sex marriage—plus it's closed on Sundays. Similarly, Dave Ramsey's franchised Financial Peace University purports to be a "biblically based curriculum that teaches people how to handle money God's way."

Thousands of other so-called Christian businesses derive their values, principles, and worldviews from a highly selective and thoroughly misleading reading of scripture, disregarding all of the terrible material that predominates in holy writ. One common theme stresses the "biblical three Rs": repentance, redemption, and reconciliation. But the true overarching theme is actually punishment, punishment, punishment.

To be effective defenders of the secular perspective, humanists must be prepared to attack the Christian viewpoint at its point of greatest vulnerability, which is the bible itself. Rather than just playing defense against the endless assaults by fundamentalist zealots, it is essential to go on the offense, armed with knowledge about the errors, terrors, and contradictions that permeate "God's word."

This chapter summarizes nine categories of basic facts that should be useful to humanists who find themselves entangled in bible discussions. Of course, there is no substitute for actually reading the so-called "Good Book," which is exactly what many Christians do not do. "Good Book" is a monstrous misnomer for this detestable compilation of holy horrors. These nine categories are roughly ordered chronologically, from the beginning to the end of the scriptural story.

Nephilim and the Noachian Deluge

The bible's preeminent massacre is the Noachian Deluge, or the Great Flood, outlined in Genesis Chapters 6, 7, and 8, where God drowned everyone except eight people in a monumental, worldwide flood. God's motivation was the wickedness and depravity of humankind, but he also did it for a reason that's hardly ever acknowledged: the cross-breeding of human women with divine beings from the spirit world. These unions produced giant mutant offspring called Nephilim (Genesis 6:4).

The giants show up again after the Deluge (they're also called Anakim, Anak, Emim, or Rephain) a dozen times (Numbers 13:28, 33; Deuteronomy 1:28, 2:10–11, 3:11, 9:3; Judges 1:20; Joshua 12:4, 13:12, 15:8, 17:15, 18:16; and 2 Samuel 21:15–21).

Universal Jihad and Biblical Law

In the Hebrew (Old) Testament, the most serious violation is that of worshipping heathen gods or idols, which is reiterated a total of 332 times. This unforgivable misbehavior requires the death penalty, which is repeated more than eighty times through explicit decree, murderous action, or threatened elimination. Because God's severe punishments are inflicted tirelessly on his incorrigible children, it can be concluded that Hebrew history developed to a great extent around the first of the Ten Commandments: "Thou shalt have no other gods before me." In other words, God conducted universal jihad against infidels in a manner no different from that of the Islamic State. Deuteronomy 13 is a concise statement: Family members who recommend worshipping other gods must be executed, and all residents of a town where leaders encourage worship of other gods must be killed and everything burned. This will satisfy God's fierce anger, and he will have mercy and compassion for those adherents who undertook the murderous action in his name.

How is this any different than Sharia law? Maybe the advocates of official bans on Sharia in the United States (already approved in eight states and all irrelevant as well as unconstitutional) should also propose biblical-law bans, which should be supported by atheists under the guise of an equal protection argument.

Biblical Truth and Impossible Claims

The Hebrew Testament reports events that are simply unbelievable because of the impossibly large numbers involved or the incredible nature of the episodes described. Well-known examples are the six-day creation, the worldwide flood, and the parting of the Red Sea. These events obviously did not occur for the reason that they contradict everything we know today about the natural world. Here are some other examples: half a million Israelite troops were slaughtered in a single day (2 Chronicles 13:15–17); 22,000 oxen and 120,000 sheep and goats were sacrificed to God (1 Kings 8:62–63); 1,160,000 troops were garrisoned in Jerusalem (2 Chronicles 17:13–19); 675,000 sheep, 72,000 oxen, 61,000 donkeys, and 32,000 young girls were taken as booty after the massacre of the Midianites (Numbers 31:31–35).

The temple constructed under King Solomon was far too large and opulent to have been built in one person's lifetime (2 Chronicles 3–9). Speaking of unrealistic longevity, seven patriarchs lived longer than 900 years and another two dozen lived between 120 and 895 years (Genesis 5, Genesis 8, and other books). Samson killed 1,000 Philistines with a donkey's jawbone (Judges 15:15), Elijah ascended into heaven on a whirlwind (2 Kings 2:11), Joshua prayed for the sun and moon to stand still and they did (Joshua 10:12–14), and Jonah was swallowed by a great fish and was coughed up alive on the beach three days later (Jonah 1:15–17, 2:10). These and many other episodes could not possibly have happened and, moreover, their recitation as divinely inspired truth casts doubt on the credibility of all other remarkable bible claims.

Patrilineal Guilt

Perhaps no biblical contradiction is more difficult to comprehend than God's refusal to frame a consistent policy concerning the punishment of children for the sins of their parents. On one hand is God's policy that punishment for sin continues from parents to their descendants (Exodus 20:5; 2 Samuel 12:13–18; 1 Kings 13:34, 14:10, 21:25–29; 2 Kings 25:7). Directly contravening this principle, on the other hand, God declared that children should not be punished for the sins of their fathers and that all people must pay the penalty for their own sins (Deuteronomy 24:16; 2 Kings 14:6; 2 Chronicles 25:4; Jeremiah 31:29–30; Ezekiel 18:2–4).

Three gruesome examples illustrate God's preferred policy. Achan's children were stoned to death along with him (Joshua 7:13–26), the children of three disobedient men were buried alive with their fathers (Numbers 16:25–34), and when Daniel's false accusers were eaten alive by lions, so were their children (Daniel 6:24).

Redemption and the Blood Sacrifice

The Hebrew Testament contains twenty chapters in four books that specify, in exacting detail, how animals are to be sacrificed to the glory of God. The sacrificial animals (oxen, sheep, goats, turtledoves, and pigeons) are killed and their blood is sprinkled or smeared on the altar, then the carcasses are burned. While the typical ritual sacrifice involves a few dozen animals, some require the killing of thousands or even tens of thousands of animals, and God derived great pleasure and enjoyment from these barbaric sacrifices.

The blood sacrifice of a human is the central theme in Christianity. God's sacrifice of his only son, who is often labeled "the lamb of God," is referred to in twenty Christian (New) Testament verses as "redemption through his blood" and "redeemed with his precious blood" (e.g., Romans 3:25, 1 Corinthians 11:25, 1 Peter 1:19, 1 John 1:7, Revelation 1:5). Jesus himself also endorsed animal and human sacrifice (Matthew 5:23–24, Mark 10:45, Luke 5:12–14).

The sacrament of holy communion is really just vicarious cannibalism: "Whoever eats my flesh and drinks my blood has eternal life, and I will raise them up at the last day" (John 6:54). God sure has a bloodthirsty disposition.

Executing Atheists

The bible requires the death penalty for sixty specified crimes, including worshipping or sacrificing to heathen gods; worshipping idols; worshipping the sun, moon, or stars; consulting mediums, soothsayers, or astrologers; cursing God; Sabbath-breaking; adultery; murder; kidnapping; stealing; homosexuality; perjury; striking one's parents; rebelling against one's parents; unchasteness (if you're a daughter); prostitution (if you're a priest's daughter); proclaiming false prophecy; and having sexual relations with both a woman and her mother (all three must be burned alive).

Jesus generally endorsed Mosaic Law, and he specifically supported the death penalty for the sin of cursing one's parents (Matthew 15:4; Mark 7:10). Paul supported capital punishment for a variety of violations, including ungodliness or nonbelief. He referred to the irreligious as God-haters (Romans 1:26–32, 1 Timothy 1:8–11). While atheism certainly constitutes disobedience or blasphemy in the Hebrew Testament, it's not until Paul's declaration in the Christian Testament that it's named as a capital crime.

Most people don't know that God requires the death penalty for violations of the first nine of the Ten Commandments (Exodus 20:1–17). Opponents of Ten Commandments displays on public property should stop quarreling with the fundamentalists and instead adopt the strategy of demanding that the mandated penalties for violators be listed prominently alongside the commandments themselves. How is it not blasphemy to list them without naming God's ordained punishments? After all, such selective citing of biblical text willfully disrespects the sacred integrity of God's holy word.

Biblical Bigotry and the Blood Libel

The Christian Testament is absolutely clear about the question of who killed Jesus. In Acts 2 through 10, Peter stated repeatedly the same thing that Stephen (Acts 7:52) and Paul (1 Thessalonians 2:14–15) also said: the Jews killed Jesus. This allegation is consistent with what Matthew claims Jews said about themselves: "His blood be on us and on our children" (Matthew 27:25). Known as the blood libel, this corporate acceptance of guilt has been regarded by some as biblical justification for anti-Jewish bigotry today. Fortunately, the collective blame on all Jews was lifted—at least from Catholic doctrine—in 1965. More recently, Pope Benedict XVI reiterated the absolution in a 2011 book.

And what did Jesus have to say about Jews? "You are children of your father, the Devil" (John 8:44).

Peace, Violence, and Poverty

How can Jesus be the Prince of Peace (Isaiah 9:6) when he incorporated extreme violence into several of his stories? Jesus told his disciples that he will return unannounced and cut the unfaithful into pieces and send them to hell (Matthew 24:51, Luke 12:46). He also said that when he returns for the last judgment he will order the wicked people brought before him to be executed, and he will crush unbelievers to dust and relegate them to hell (Luke 19:27, 20:9–18).

Jesus is also portrayed as a dedicated servant of the poor (Matthew 25:31–46, Luke 14:13–14). However, Jesus's forceful command to help "the least of those among you" is totally contradicted by his support for right-wing economic ethics: "To those who have much, more will be given; from those who have little, even that will be taken away" (Matthew 13:12, 25:29, Mark 4:25, Luke 19:26). Is this the proof we need that the bible really is Donald Trump's favorite book?

Eternal Punishment Awaits Most People

The gospel makes it perfectly clear that Jesus was thoroughly obsessed with hell, a concept that he invoked in seventy-three verses. In three definitive statements, he said that the vast majority of humankind will go to hell (Matthew 7:13–14, 22:14, Luke 13:23–24). This pessimistic declaration is justified because Jesus knew that very few people could satisfy his sixteen moral mandates.

To be saved, believers must: obey Jesus's teachings (Matthew 7:26–27), give up everything (Luke 14:33), not accumulate material wealth (Matthew 6:19–21), desert home and family (Mark 10:29–30), reject interpersonal violence (Matthew 26:52), forgive others (Mark 11:25–26), not divorce a spouse (Mark 10:9–12), help the poor (Matthew 25:31–46), not pray in public (Matthew 6:5–6), not swear an oath (Matthew 5:34–37), mutilate oneself to atone for sins (Mark 9:43–47), cast out demons and speak in tongues (Mark 16:17–18), not publicly deny Jesus (Luke 12:8–9), not falsely prophesy (Matthew 7:22–23), have the faith of a child (Luke 18:16–17), and not commit blasphemy against the holy spirit (Mark 3:28–29).

There is no stronger evidence against the claim that the bible is the inerrant word of God than the bible itself. The most effective arguments against the false assertions of believers come straight out of holy writ.

Addendum: Fundamentalist Is the Correct Label

Journalists and writers use a variety of terms to describe the hardcore zealots of the Christian community, including Religious Right, Christian conservatives, Christian extremists, Christian nationalists and Christian supremacists.

But the most often (mis)used label is evangelicals. In fact, the only accurate descriptor for these radical Christian fanatics is fundamentalists. Furthermore, "evangelical" is the wrong term—for the simple reason that all Christians are by definition evangelical, as explained below. The words evangelical and gospel both derive from the same Greek root, *euangelion*, which refers to disseminating the good news or glad tidings of the Christian salvation story to all people.

This universal obligation incumbent on all Christians is reiterated five times as Jesus's Great Commission, which is stated near the end of the four canonical gospels and in the first chapter of Acts (Matthew 28:19; Mark 16:15–16; Luke 24:46–47; John 20:21–23; Acts 1:8).

It follows that all Christians must be evangelicals, as instructed by Jesus in his final command to his disciples. The predominant feature of evangelicalism is the missionary impulse to convert the world to faith in Jesus, including Mainstream Protestants.

In contrast, the term fundamentalist applies only to a small subset of Christians. The basic definition of fundamentalism was propounded at a historic conference in Niagara Falls, New York, in 1895, and subsequently elaborated in a series of twelve pamphlets published between 1910 and 1915. (For more details, see chapter five.)

The two primary postulates of fundamentalism are the claim that the bible is the inerrant word of God, a perfect expression of his divine will, and the assertion that all people who reject Jesus as Messiah will be punished throughout eternity, exactly as Jesus described.

In summary, "fundamentalist" is the correct label for these radical Christian zealots who want to inflict their unbiblical theopolitical beliefs on everybody else. Moreover, evangelical is the wrong word to describe these fanatics, because it does not identify the unique feature of fundamentalism—the claim of biblical inerrancy.

Journalists, writers, and editors should insist on the appropriate terminology in identifying this dogmatic, closed-minded minority of the Christian population.

Call them what they really are: fundamentalists!

TWO
Why Do Fundamentalists Lie About the Bible?

Fundamentalism emerged from respectable traditions of revivalism and evangelicalism in the last decades of the nineteenth century and quickly acquired a thoroughly independent identity. Specifically, fundamentalism was a reaction to liberal Protestant theology, which was attempting to accommodate Christianity to scientific, intellectual, and theological developments occurring at the time.

The doctrinal foundation of fundamentalism was expounded in a dozen pamphlets published in the second decade of the twentieth century. Titled *The Fundamentals*, the tracts covered a range of topics, including a defense of inerrancy, an attack on biblical scholarship, and polemics against Mormonism, Catholicism, and Christian Science.

The central dogma of fundamentalist theology is the absolute inerrancy of scripture. Subsidiary postulates include the deity of Jesus, the virgin conception, the substitutional atonement for sin, the authenticity of miracles, the reality of bodily resurrection, and the imminent Second Coming.

Contemporary Fundamentalism

During the last half of the twentieth century, fundamentalists became increasingly aggressive in translating their supposedly bible-based views into theopolitical action. In the first two decades of the twenty-first century, fundamentalist political commitment accelerated further with elected officials becoming spokespersons for various unwarranted scriptural claims.

For example, two conservative members of Congress, Mike Pence and Rick Santorum, became cheerleaders for the creationist fraud known as Intelligent Design. Intelligent Design was vigorously promoted as the biblical rescue strategy, after earlier versions of "creation science" were rejected by the scientific community, the federal courts, and mainline Christianity. Intelligent Design subsequently suffered the same fate.

Two prominent Midwestern state governors endorsed the false claim that America was founded on biblical principles. Then-Iowa chief executive Terry Branstad wrongly proclaimed that "the bible is recognized as the one true revelation from God." And Ohio Governor John Kasich advocated the establishment of a federal government office to promote biblical values around the world.

The Texas Republican manifesto places the bible at the center of American democracy, asserting that the US Constitution is based on the bible, as are other founding documents, and more generally that Judeo-Christian scripture established the foundation for America's legal, political, and economic systems. These claims have been thoroughly refuted by historians, legal scholars, and authorities in politics and government. Yet, fundamentalists repeat the false assertions endlessly, on the assumption that naïve Americans will eventually accept them.

Fundamentalist Bibliolatry

An increasing number of state legislatures have attempted to mandate bible study classes in public schools, while in other states local school boards have tried to do the same. Also, several legislatures have proposed a "Year of the Bible" or attempted to designate the bible the "state book." Of course, it was conservative idol Ronald Reagan who first proclaimed as president a national "Year of the Bible" more than three decades ago.

These assorted claims and proposed actions are symptomatic of a debilitating condition called bibliolatry, which refers to an emotional attachment to a text that is alleged to have sacred value by virtue of being divinely inspired. While the term typically refers to the Holy Bible, bibliolatry may also apply to any of the world's two dozen other venerated books, such as the Bhagavad Gita, Book of Mormon, or the Koran.

The terminology of bibliolatry includes three concepts that assist scholars in understanding fundamentalists' reverential attitude toward scripture. First, a *biblist* believes the bible represents the only true religious faith. Second, a *bibliolatrist* believes devoutly in the literal truth of the bible. Third, a *biblicist* strictly adheres to bible teachings.

It can be concluded from their pronouncements and behavior that fundamentalists are *biblists and bibliolatrists* of the highest order, but they fail completely as *biblicists*. The last contention will be thoroughly documented in this chapter. Before proceeding to a review of the relevant evidence, I will elucidate the postulate of biblical inerrancy.

Scriptural Inerrancy

The foundational premise of fundamentalism is the claimed absolute accuracy of the Holy Bible. All other theological propositions that derive from scripture depend wholly on the doctrine of biblical inerrancy. This means that every statement, action, and event is authorized and caused by omnipotent God. In other words, the bible is literally true in every verse, passage, and narrative statement. There are no errors, no ambiguous assertions, and no disguised metaphors. Scripture is the God-breathed, verbally inspired, perfect word of the Judeo-Christian deity (Matthew 4:4; 2 Timothy 3:16).

Because fundamentalists assert that every word in the bible comes straight from the mouth of God, it is essential that rational critics tentatively accept this claim as true and work within the framework of biblical inerrancy. By doing so they are able to expose the contradictions and hypocrisy in the fundamentalist political and cultural worldview without attacking the underlying theological premise of fundamentalism.

The puzzling question that naturally arises is why fundamentalist bibliolatrists adopt and tenaciously defend theopolitical positions that are not supported by or are even flatly contradicted by God's perfect word? Before considering the question of why fundamentalists lie about what the bible says, I will document the assertion that they do, in fact, lie about what Holy Writ actually says and doesn't say.

Ten Theopolitical Issues

Fundamentalists have promulgated uncompromising political positions on ten major sociocultural subjects in which they disregard or contradict God's perfect word. These are: abortion rights, animal welfare, capital punishment, decalogue displays, family values, Jesus's teachings, public prayer, same-sex marriage, slavery endorsement, and sworn oaths.

Abortion Rights

For the past half a century, Christian fundamentalists have fought against women's reproductive rights, specifically by claiming that God opposes abortion. Their standard propaganda includes admonitions such as "God loves the unborn," "Abortion kills children," "Pray to end abortion," "Lord forgive us," and "Abortion is a stench in the nostrils of God."

Nothing could be further from the truth. In fact, God does not oppose abortion. Rather, he is history's greatest abortionist. God is the most prolific "baby killer" and "murderer of unborn children" of all time. How do we know? The bible says so. Here is a summary of the scriptural evidence.

1. The biblical synonym for abortion—miscarriage or miscarry—occurs in four passages (Exodus 21:22, Exodus 23:26, Numbers 5: 21–27, Hosea 9:14). None prohibits or condemns abortion, and in three passages God himself causes abortions as punishment for disobedience.

2. Four passages in scripture describe ripping open pregnant women with swords (2 Kings 8:12, 2 Kings 15:16, Hosea 13:16, Amos 1:13). These gruesome murders of pregnant mothers-to-be with their unborn fetuses are reported as routine events in God's personal diary.

3. Four massacres of all living people in various populations, including pregnant women with their unborn fetuses, who did not receive exemptions, were carried out by God as punishment for sinfulness or as systematic ethnic cleansing (Noachian flood, Sodom and Gomorrah, Conquest of Canaan, twenty major slaughters) in which all inhabitants were killed.

4. Of the more than one dozen passages that refer to the developing fetus in the womb, none prohibits or condemns abortion, nor do they affirm the nonexistent fundamentalist constructs of "right to life," "sanctity of life," or "fetal personhood." God's word also tells us that life begins with the first breath and that those never born are the truly fortunate ones.
5. Notable for its absence from scripture is an eleventh commandment, "Thou shall not abort a fetus." Furthermore, although the bible specifies a total of sixty crimes that require the death penalty, abortion is not among them. The late Oklahoma senator Tom Coburn once declared that physicians who perform abortions should be executed (he was a doctor). As explained below, antiabortion terrorists have acted in accord with Coburn's belief.
6. Two basic facts from reproductive medicine extend the allegation that God is history's greatest abortionist. At least one-third of all fertilized eggs ("persons") do not implant in the uterine wall and are immediately destroyed. Two million fetuses ("persons") are spontaneously aborted in the United States annually. Both categories of occurrences are the handiwork of the fundamentalists' "pro-life" God.

Fundamentalist Christians' highest theological priority is banning abortion in the United States and severely punishing women who have abortions, in conjunction with their patriarchal program of controlling every aspect of women's lives. Not only does the bible not support their antiabortion zealotry, their God is actually a pro-abortion deity who hates women and their unborn fetuses. Why don't the fundamentalists simply acknowledge the biblical truth about abortion?

Finally, the ultimate expression of blatant fundamentalist hypocrisy is that the extremists have anointed themselves "pro-life," while simultaneously murdering a dozen and maiming seventeen innocent people they labeled killers and murderers. Antiabortion terrorism, which has been the subject of eight books, also includes assault, arson, kidnapping, firebombing, harassment, and endless threats of violence, all carried out at women's health clinics in the exalted name of the Prince of Peace.

Animal Welfare

In 2015, a committee of fundamentalist Christian leaders issued a ten-page statement on responsible animal care that declared broad support for widely accepted tenets of modern animal welfare. The statement was touted by the Humane Society of the United States as a major contribution to the animal welfare movement, saying that it "has the potential to create enormous good."

The authors assert that their carefully crafted precepts of compassionate animal care are "informed by scripture, sourced in our Creator God, and always rooted in his Holy Word." Their recommended principles are: (a) Humans should give animals the respect they deserve, because all animals have inherent God-given value, (b) Human cruelty toward animals is sinful and an affront to God, and (c) Humans are obligated to work for the protection and preservation of all of God's animals.

Remarkably, and disingenuously, each of these principles of humane treatment of animals invokes God's name, suggesting that the biblical deity endorses the concepts set forth in the three-part ethical formulation. To the contrary, the simple fact is that compassionate care for animals is thoroughly contradicted by God's horrific mistreatment of animals, as summarized in the following points.

1. Animal sacrifice is the central requirement in God's obscene theology of worship of himself. The specification of inhumane procedures and descriptions of gruesome events are presented in 202 verses or passages in fifty-six chapters of fifteen books of scripture.
2. The stipulated features are: sacrificial animals must be free of defects, their blood is splashed on the altar or consecrated individuals, and their carcasses are burned producing an aroma that is especially pleasing to the Lord.
3. While the typical ritual sacrifice entailed killing a few dozen animals, some involved hundreds or thousands or more. Scripture stresses that God derives immense pleasure and enjoyment from these barbaric sacrifices of innocent animals.
4. Blatant animal cruelty is another indicator of God's uncaring attitude toward animals. Well-known illustrations are the hamstring-

ing of horses, the stoning and burning of a miscreant's livestock with him, and the drowning of a herd of pigs.

5. God often used wild animals as vehicles of execution to punish disobedient Israelites and their enemies. His favorite killing instruments were lions, but he also employed bears and venomous snakes.
6. Our best friend, the dog, is mentioned forty times in scripture and none of the references is positive. Dogs are typically portrayed as disgusting scavengers that lick bodily sores and the blood of slaughtered adversaries and eat corpses.
7. The Passover Lamb occupies a special place in Christian mythology as the slain Lamb of God who was the redemptive blood sacrifice killed to take away the sins of the world and proclaimed by 100 million angels.

The statement's authors cited eighty-seven bible verses or passages as the sources for their principles of compassionate animal care, but not one comes from the voluminous content summarized in the seven preceding points. Why did they omit this scriptural truth? Because they opted to lie about God's Word and promote a socially acceptable view of animal welfare concerns.

Capital Punishment

Fundamentalists' unwavering support for the death penalty is fully endorsed by the bible. Their designated capital offenses always include premeditated murder ("a life for a life") and often subsume kidnapping, armed robbery, or child abuse. Having or performing an abortion is classified as a capital violation by a minority of fundamentalists.

The problem for the advocates of inerrancy is that scripture mandates execution for a total of sixty specified "crimes." Many of these entail transgressions of rules of religious ritual and dietary practice that are generally not applicable today. However, at least two dozen infractions occur on a regular basis in contemporary America.

Why don't fundamentalists demand that adulterers, apostates, astrologers, blasphemers, false prophets, fornicators, God-haters, homosexuals, idolaters, mediums, parent cursers, perjurers, rapists, rebellious sons,

Sabbath-breakers, sorceresses, unbelievers, and unchaste daughters be summarily executed, just as God's word requires?

And why don't these pious bibliolatrists insist that only biblically approved execution methods be employed? These include: stoning (e.g., Achan, Naboth), burning alive (e.g., Sodom and Gomorah, Nadab and Abihu), stabbing or impaling (e.g., King Eglon, Haman), drowning or suffocating (e.g., Noachian Deluge, Korah, Dathan, and Abiram), attacks by wild animals (e.g., forty-two disrespectful boys, Daniel's false accusers), beheading (e.g., Sheba, John the Baptist), ripping open bellies (e.g., pregnant women of Tiphsah and Gilead), and throwing from heights (e.g., Edomite men, Jezebel).

Finally, fundamentalists fail to acknowledge God's strong preference for collective punishment in implementing the death penalty. This terrible principle of injustice requires innocent associates of transgressors to be killed with them. Three gruesome examples are: Achan's children being stoned to death with him, three disobedient fathers' children being buried alive with them, and the children of Daniel's false accusers being eaten alive by lions with their fathers.

Decalogue Displays

Judge Roy Moore became a fundamentalist demigod in 2001 when he installed a two-ton granite Ten Commandments monument in the Alabama Judicial Building. Two years later it was removed after a federal judge ruled "Roy's Rock" to be unconstitutional and Moore was thrown out of office.

Every year, numerous state legislators and county commissioners across America attempt to place the decalogue on public property. Why do they persist with this fundamentalist fetish? The stated justification is that the Ten Commandments are "a reflection of our history and of our country's Judeo-Christian Heritage."

However, none of the decalogue shrines currently located on public property includes the full text of Exodus 20:2–17, which runs about 300 words. Instead, all extant displays present an abbreviated seventy-five-word version which omits some highly embarrassing content from the edicts:

1. The second commandment contains God's explicit promise to

punish the innocent descendants of those who violate the injunction against idolatry.

2. The fifth commandment to honor one's parents appeals to the selfish interests of offspring, when this sacred duty should be motivated by family values.
3. The fourth and tenth commandments both approve of the detestable (and biblically endorsed) institution of slavery.
4. The tenth commandment classifies a man's wife as one of his possessions, just like slaves and livestock.

It should be noted that the first commandment acknowledges the existence of multiple competing gods, which is the prerequisite assumption of polytheism. Furthermore, the US government has no authority to tell citizens which of these gods, if any, to worship.

Fundamentalists disregard the fact that the decalogue is not a useful ethical code. Nine of the commandments are stated as prohibitions against extreme behavior and don't tell us how to act ethically. The absence of anti-social behavior does not constitute good citizenship.

In addition to these difficulties, most fundamentalists don't know that violators of the first nine commandments must be executed. Are these pious proponents of public posting willing to advocate for the application of the death penalty as God's ordained punishment?

It is entirely reasonable to expect fundamentalist supporters of Ten Commandments displays to: (a) Reproduce the complete text exactly as God dictated it to Moses, (b) List the required penalty for violators with each commandment, and (c) Enforce the Commandments in a manner consistent with God's will. Any deviations from these stipulations constitute blasphemy, which requires and deserves punishment by execution.

Family Values

The foundational conceptual theme in the fundamentalists' pantheon of theopolitical positions is that of "family values." The oft-repeated central claim permeating the ubiquitous family values mantra is that God loves children. The biblical evidence summarized in this section demonstrates that the claim is thoroughly contradicted by God's behavior and is utterly false.

1. There are fourteen unspeakable scriptural slaughters in which all residents are killed, with infants and children specifically identified as targeted victims. Children are murdered as punishment for the disobedience of their parents or other adults in the community.
2. The vast majority of infants, babies, and children killed by God were victims in three biblical massacres, Noah's flood, Sodom and Gomorrah, and the Conquest of Canaan, and in eighteen major slaughters in which children are not specifically named. Of course, tens of millions of "unborn children" are also murdered in the above events and several others.
3. Six bible verses invoke the abhorrent godly tradition of killing infants and children by dashing them to the ground or dashing them to pieces or dashing them against the rocks.
4. Three gory stories in which innocent children were executed with their disobedient parents illustrate the despicable practice of collective punishment and document God's unfathomable cruelty.
5. An especially macabre technique that God employs to kill children and adults as punishment for disobedience is the use of wild animals, which is mentioned in the section on capital punishment.
6. Child sacrifice by parents is required by God in cases of false prophecy and thanksgiving for military success and in five horrific instances of parental cannibalism of their children.
7. Contrary to fundamentalists' claim, Jesus doesn't love the little children. In point of biblical fact, there are good reasons to conclude that Jesus is not particularly fond of children. For example, he adopted the barbaric language of dashing children to the ground in his horrifying prophecy for the total destruction of Jerusalem as punishment for the residents because they do not acknowledge him as God's emissary.

He coldly confirmed without regret or sorrow that everybody died by drowning—including infants, children, and "unborn children"—in Noah's flood by drowning and in the incineration of Sodom and Gomorrah. And he did not express any special concern for children or "unborn children" during the anticipated end times.

Jesus's anti-family values are expressed in four well-known statements that document his attitude of complete disregard for children: Anyone who does not hate parents, siblings, spouse, and children cannot be my disciple; anyone who leaves homes, parents, siblings, spouse, or children for my sake will receive eternal life; anyone who loves sons or daughters more than me is not worthy of me; and a person's worst enemies will be the members of his own family.

Jesus's Teachings

The basic premise of Christianity is that the sacrificial execution of the Son of God guarantees eternal life for those who acknowledge him as their Lord and Savior. In other words, Jesus's adherents are assured of immortality in the blissful world to come following this temporary earthly sojourn.

Believers are expected to conform their current lives to what fundamentalists refer to as "Christian values" and the "Christian worldview." While some of Jesus's teachings are commendable, e.g., love neighbors, reject violence, help the poor, and forgive sinners, many other declarations are not so easily obeyed and therefore are simply disregarded by fundamentalist biblists:

1. The vast majority of humankind faces an irrevocable eternity of horrific torture for failure to obey inviolable biblical commandments.
2. In order to achieve the highest calling in life, acolytes must permanently separate themselves from home and family.
3. Atonement for sinful thoughts and actions requires the physical mutilation of limbs and eyes, including emasculation to preserve godly purity.
4. Acceptable human relationships include communal ownership of property, subordinate status of women, involuntary servitude, and collective punishment.
5. Those who renounce worldly success, desert family and home, eschew personal needs, and devote one's mortal life to Jesus will be rewarded with everlasting existence.

These gospel principles are never proclaimed by fundamentalists as integral to the highly vaunted "Christ-centered life." And there are many other teachings attributed to Jesus that are studiously disregarded. For example, "To those who have much, more will be given. From those who have little, even that will be taken away." This dictum, which is repeated four times, would appear to contradict Jesus's portrayal as a dedicated advocate for the poor.

Another unsavory feature of Jesus's personality that is carefully avoided by fundamentalists is his obsession with hell. The gospel is dominated by Jesus's detailed, highly repetitive descriptions of this horrific realm of unending torture. According to Jesus, hell is:

1. A real place of terrible suffering, unbearable pain, unimaginable misery, excruciating agony, endless torment, and utter hopelessness.
2. A furnace of fire that is never extinguished, where the damned suffer from unquenchable thirst and they are infested with intestinal parasitic worms that never die, causing weeping and grinding of teeth, in the terror of absolute darkness.
3. An everlasting, eternal, unending expression of God's infinite wrath, revenge, and cruelty. The condemned never experience the relief of death.
4. An irrevocable judgment that can never be nullified or reversed. No reprieves are ever issued and nobody is ever pardoned.

Even though fundamentalists take great satisfaction in relating the terrible fate that unbelievers face, they are reluctant to acknowledge their savior's unique role in formulating the frightful features of hell. Four additional elements of Jesus's teachings are discussed in other sections. These are his thorough rejection of family values, his unquestioning acceptance of slavery, and his unequivocal condemnation of public prayer and sworn oaths.

Public Prayer

Fundamentalists not only consider prayer to be an essential component of the "Christ-centered life," they also want to be recognized by others as profoundly pious disciples of Jesus. The National Day of Prayer events and the ubiquitous mayoral prayer breakfasts are among the most grandiose examples of fundamentalists' public displays of holiness.

There is just one problem with their ostentatious behavior: Jesus said not to do it! In his unambiguous instruction in the Sermon on the Mount he cautioned: "When you pray, go into your room, close the door and pray to your Father, who is unseen. Then your Father, who sees what is done in secret, will reward you."

In plain language, prayer is a personal matter that should be carried out in private. Jesus was absolutely clear: Do not make a public spectacle of prayer. The baffling question is: Why do fundamentalists reject Jesus's teaching about prayer?

Same-Sex Marriage

Fundamentalists define God-ordained marriage exclusively as a biblically approved relationship between one natural man and one natural woman. In fact, Hebrew scripture provides many illustrations of another acceptable form of family alliance, polygyny, wherein one man has multiple wives or concubines, e.g., Lamech, Gideon, David, and Solomon. Three additional forms of bible-sanctioned unions are slave, captive, and levirate (a person marrying his brother's widow) marriages.

Moreover, scripture does not prohibit or condemn same-sex nuptials, because the topic is never mentioned. The reason for this omission is simple: Marriage is irrelevant for dead sinners and the bible mandates execution for homosexuals, including lesbians. Almighty God (Genesis 19:4–5, 24–25) and his chief spokesmen, Moses (Leviticus 20:13), Jesus (Matthew 5:17–18), and Paul (Romans 1:26, 27, 30) are absolutely clear about the death penalty for homosexuals.

Why don't anti-LGBTQ fundamentalists who oppose same-sex marriage so vehemently and claim that homosexuality is an abhorrent sin, just obey God's unequivocal command? Why don't they advocate execution of homosexuals just as scripture requires? They could encourage state legislatures to enact laws that would expand application of the death penalty to homosexuals and they could ask the federal courts to include the provision in the US criminal code.

It is apparent that the vast majority of fundamentalists do not have the courage to pursue a political program designed to implement biblical law in America, but they are perfectly willing to promote an agenda of hateful harassment directed at the LGBTQ community. Their standard demands include:

1. Reverse the US Supreme Court decision that legalized same-sex marriage.
2. Rescind public accommodation laws that supposedly require businesses to violate their Christian beliefs about homosexuality.
3. Do not allow placement of adoptive children with same-sex couples.
4. Require that bathroom use correspond to biological sex.
5. Ban educational curricula that teaches that homosexual and transgender lifestyles are normal.

The foundational postulate that motivates fundamentalists' hysteria about same-sex marriage encompasses the false belief that homosexuality is a chosen behavior that is contrary to God's plan for humanity. Rational critics of these bigots should ask them to explain the unconventional lifestyles of the two principal founders of Christianity—Jesus and Paul. In particular, what were their sexual proclivities?

Slavery Endorsement

The largest fundamentalist denomination in the United States, the Southern Baptist Convention, formed in 1845, because Baptists in nine Southern states justified slavery by pointing out that scripture sanctioned this institution. The issue has contemporary implications for the Confederate memorial controversies and the resurgence of white supremacy politics.

It is a fact that both the Hebrew and Christian Testaments are sympathetic to and supportive of slavery. For this reason, many Southern slave owners argued that Christian abolitionists were defying God's will by opposing slavery. Of special relevance for bibliolatrists is the strong authorization of slavery in the statements of the bible's three leading Christian figures: Jesus, Paul, and Peter.

Jesus's approval of slavery is readily apparent in his inclusion of servants and their masters in eight of his parables. Because he never criticized or condemned slavery, and he did not forbid people from owning slaves, he tacitly endorsed the practice. In one of these parables, he explicitly authorized the cruel master-slave relationship when he recommended whipping disobedient slaves.

Five of the eight slave parables are noted for their extreme violence through murder, killing, or maiming. The central figure of the master or the son is Jesus himself, and the consistent theme in these violent stories is that those who disobey Jesus or reject him as Messiah will be punished with unending torture in hell.

Jesus granted authority to slave owners to discipline their slaves, establishing the divine Christian mandate used to justify the beatings of black slaves in southern states. Jesus also approved of the rules for slave owners in chapter 21 of Exodus and two of his miracles involved slaves, the healing of the centurion's servant and the restoration of the ear of the slave boy Malchus.

In the Epistles, Paul decreed that slaves should obey their masters with respect and fear in everything, just as they would obey Jesus. And for their obedience they will be rewarded in the next life. The apostle Peter emphasized that slaves are obligated by Christian faith and fear of God to submit to their owners, no matter how brutal. He said that it is commendable when slaves endure unjust suffering that is willed by God.

Sworn Oaths

Prescribed oaths are promises by those giving testimony in courts of law or preparing to serve in government office, in which they provide assurance they will speak the truth or obligate themselves to perform specified duties. For fundamentalists, oaths are regarded as holy rituals in which God's name is invoked while holding the bible, as the guarantor of truth and ethical behavior.

As with public prayer, there is just one problem with swearing oaths: Jesus said don't do it! In clear language in the Sermon on the Mount, he warned: "But I tell you, do not swear an oath . . . All you need to say is simply 'yes' or 'no'; anything beyond this comes from the evil one."

Again, why do fundamentalists reject Jesus's clear teaching about sworn oaths? An episode from Williamson County, Texas (where I live), illustrates just how utterly meaningless sworn oaths are to fundamentalists. Three county commissioners swore on the bible to uphold the US Constitution. They were subsequently convicted in federal court of violating the constitutional rights of a resident. Did they acknowledge their illegal behavior? No. Did they apologize to their constituents? No. Did they resign from office? No. Were they removed from office? No. Their oaths sworn on the Holy Bible not only violated Jesus's edict, but they were obviously worthless as guarantors of anything.

Why Do Fundamentalists Lie?

To address this critical question it is necessary to explain what is meant by the allegation that fundamentalists lie about the bible. In general usage, a lie is a statement that is known by the speaker or writer to be untrue. In this analysis, a lie refers to the intentional misrepresentation or distortion of what scripture says about a major theopolitical issue.

In plain language, I am accusing Christian fundamentalists of biblical dishonesty. They assert that their positions on the ten issues summarized at the end of this chapter are supported by God's perfect word. It is abundantly evident that their claims are unequivocally false. In every case, they have disregarded the voluminous scriptural content that contradicts their political opinions.

It is impossible to avoid the conclusion that fundamentalists have willfully ignored those verses, passages, and episodes that disaffirm their positions. They talk endlessly about inerrancy of scripture as the foundation of their "Christian worldview" and they constantly quote the bible in defending their incomparable "Christian values." Hence, it is entirely reasonable to assume that they are fully knowledgeable about scripture.

With this premise, we can address an important question: How do the inerrantists delude themselves into believing that their theopolitical positions have biblical support? How do they reconcile the monumental disparities between scripture and their sociocultural views? By what mental contortions do they resolve the obvious contradictions? Based on their writings, we see that they invoke three primary strategies of scriptural interpretation that enable them to decide what God really means in his allegedly perfectly accurate decrees that are without error.

The first strategy, known as textual selectivity, entails identifying those verses and passages that support their previously adopted views, while simultaneously omitting unsupportive or contradictory material. The favorite verse of the fundamentalists is the barely relevant assertion,

"Before I formed you in the womb I knew you" (Jeremiah 1:5). But, the antiabortion zealots never mention the dozens of verses and events that completely negate their position.

The second strategy depends on the vague interpretive criterion of "proper exegesis" or "proper understanding," which means simply that believers can decide whether or not scripture is applicable to a given issue and, if so, how it applies. This broad-based concept provides what is essentially a universal screening tactic, an interpretive panacea. Of course, the operative term is "proper," with the fundamentalists deciding for themselves exactly what constitutes "proper" interpretation.

The third strategy maintains that principles and commandments from the Old Testament are only binding if New Testament teachings concur. This transparent rationalization for setting aside the brutal norms and standards of Mosaic Law fails, because Jesus endorsed every word of the Hebrew Testament. Furthermore, his unsympathetic attitude toward women, children, and slaves, and his rejection of "family values" are untouched by this disingenuous interpretive filter.

These three interrelated strategies of scriptural interpretation are remarkably ingenious excuses to bypass the sacrosanct postulate of biblical inerrancy. They enable believers to give their idiosyncratic renditions of passages and episodes extracted from scripture precedence over the literal reading of the text. These highly creative techniques should be seen as additional evidence of the fundamentalist propensity to prevaricate whenever necessary to salvage the claim of absolute truth of scripture.

To answer the difficult question of why fundamentalists lie about the bible requires extensive speculation, because they will not assist in the task. Despite overwhelming evidence, they won't even concede that their theopolitical positions are not supported by scripture. Of course, they can't acknowledge this well-documented truth, because to do so would force them to admit that their strong commitment to biblical inerrancy is untenable.

Another question that can be tentatively addressed concerns the origins of the ten thoroughly unbiblical political positions. When did they emerge in the fundamentalists' war against modernity? How were they derived and verified? Who pronounced them to be official doctrine? By what process was abortion declared to be murder and same-sex marriage asserted to be contrary to God's plan for humanity, and so forth? Careful analysis could locate the historical antecedents of these theopolitical opinions.

A reasonable guess is that the political viewpoints of fundamentalists developed over the past century from a variety of sources and influences, including early revivalist traditions, community tolerance, and popular acceptability. An excellent example of substantial secular determination is provided by the very recent development of the entirely unbiblical statement on animal welfare. One unchallengeable conclusion is that the ten fundamentalist political positions were formulated independently of scripture.

As a final question, we can ask why fundamentalists don't acknowledge some degree of disparity between their views and scripture as a basis for adjusting some of their positions so as to conform to biblical truth? To do so would require them to rehabilitate their "Christian worldview" and adopt some positions that they have condemned as contrary to God's word for as long as a century or more. This is probably not going to happen across the board, but it is the only reasonable course of action if they want to respect the doctrine of scriptural inerrancy without continuing with their ongoing program of public deceit.

There are at least two easy modifications that fundamentalists could implement. First, they could eschew sworn oaths, because Jesus commanded his followers to simply affirm or disaffirm. Second, they could stop fighting to place decalogue displays on public property and, instead, initiate a national effort to erect Ten Commandments monuments on the lawns of every Christian church in America.

Is there any possibility that fundamentalists will adjust, revise, modify, or even reverse their positions in the other areas of political commitment? Probably not, because they are so heavily invested emotionally in issues like "family values" and opposition to abortion and same-sex marriage. For this reason, it would be difficult for them to embrace the concepts of women's reproductive rights and marriage equality. Perhaps the greatest barrier to compromise is that they would have to admit that their allegedly scripture-based views were wrong—and this would be hard to do.

Conclusion

Because fundamentalists are irremediably committed to their predetermined theopolitical views, humanists have the opportunity and responsibility to exploit this tremendous vulnerability in the illogic of scriptural inerrancy. Humanists must relentlessly publicize fundamentalists' biblical dishonesty and political hypocrisy, pointing out on every appropriate occasion the monumental discrepancy between their beloved "Christian values" and God's perfect word. Humanists should aggressively report the well documented fact that the fundamentalist worldview is premised on biblical lies.

Summary of Fundamentalists' Biblical Lies

Abortion Rights

Fundamentalists never cite the dozens of verses, passages, and episodes in which God murdered tens of millions of mothers-to-be and their unborn fetuses, while advancing an allegedly bible-based agenda designed to end women's reproductive rights.

Animal Welfare

They never mention the extensive bible content describing barbaric animal sacrifice, which is required in godly worship, as well as wanton animal cruelty, while disingenuously endorsing the humane perspective on animal care.

Capital Punishment

They identify one crime, premeditated murder, and possibly a few others, for which they advocate the death penalty, while knowingly disregarding twenty other violations for which God mandates execution.

Decalogue Displays

They fanatically pursue placement of Ten Commandments monuments on public property, which display a severely edited and blasphemous version of the highly offensive and practically useless edicts.

Family Values

They maintain the scriptural fiction called family values, including the claim that God loves children, which is thoroughly contradicted by scores of gruesome bible stories, by simply omitting from consideration all of this disgusting material.

Jesus's Teachings
They focus their obsessive attachment to Jesus on the belief that he was sacrificed so that they can live forever, while rejecting his many horrific commandments, especially his anti-family values.

Public Prayer
They reject Jesus's unequivocal declaration that prayer is a personal activity which should be conducted in private, while continuing to make a public spectacle of their false piety.

Same-Sex Marriage
They disregard the unambiguous bible teachings that mandate execution of homosexuals and permit marriage arrangements other than monogamous heterosexual unions.

Slavery Endorsement
They ignore the scriptural truth that slavery is a Christian-approved human institution, with full support from Jesus, Paul, and Peter.

Sworn Oaths
They disregard Jesus's prohibition against sworn oaths, typically swearing obedience to secular authorities, while ostentatiously invoking God's approval.

THREE
Texas Fundamentalist Theocratic Obsessions

The Texas Republican Party's 2016 platform was a formulation that embodied complete disrespect for the rights of all Americans who do not share their theocratic values. This extreme fundamentalist worldview derived from a highly selective interpretation of the bible.

This ultraconservative theological conception of political doctrine contains fourteen references to God, including the God-given sanctity of life, God-ordained rejection of homosexuality, and God-given right to carry guns. Only the idolized "free market principles" are equal to God in the Republican pantheon of panaceas, also with fourteen citations.

The Texas Republican platform also renounced humanistic doctrine in any form. It asserted the right to publicly display the Ten Commandments and to engage in public prayer. Only Christian holidays should be recognized in public schools and by government. It was also committed to dispelling the "myth" of separation of church and state, contradicting Ronald Reagan's declaration that "church and state are, and must remain, separate."

Equally important to this platform was its desire to preserve the freedom it averred was given to Americans by God, which it would do by restraining government from supposedly intruding into the lives of free citizens. Specifically enumerated were the freedoms of conscience, worship, and prayer.

The five issues summarized below with bulleted items taken directly from the platform constituted the Texas Republicans' blueprint for implementing a fundamentalist theocracy in America.

Antiabortion Zealotry

- Protect sanctity of innocent human life, created in the image of God, from fertilization to natural death.
- Deny the US Supreme Court jurisdiction over abortion.
- Give authority over abortion to the states.
- Abolish abortion: stop "the murder of unborn children."
- Reverse the Supreme Court decision that legalized abortion.
- Refuse to enforce all laws that permit abortion.
- Eliminate public funding for elective abortion, fetal tissue research, and Planned Parenthood.
- Prohibit the manufacture and sale of abortifacients.
- Legally prosecute people who injure or kill the unborn.
- Grant total constitutional rights for "the unborn" as the final goal.

What is immediately apparent is that the obsession with personal liberty did not extend to women's freedom of choice in their own reproductive health care. Did God give women this freedom? According to this theology, he did not. In fact, the God of the Holy Bible is history's greatest abortionist, contrary to the platform's blatantly false assertions, such as the notions that God loves the unborn and that there is a God-given right to life. The US Supreme Court recently rebuked Texas legislators for their dishonest attempt to restrict Texas women's access to legal abortion.

Anti-Secular Intolerance

- America is a nation under God, founded on Judeo-Christian principles.

- Judeo-Christian principles form the basis of America's legal, political, and economic systems.
- Discussion of religion in our founding documents should be encouraged, including the bible as their basis.
- School curricula should emphasize US founding documents, including the Declaration, Constitution, and the founders' writings.
- Thanksgiving, Christmas, Easter, St. Valentine's Day, St. Patrick's Day, and Good Friday should be public holidays.
- US foreign policy toward Israel should be bible-based.
- "Original intent" is repeatedly invoked for interpreting law and the US founding documents.
- Dispel the "myth" of separation of church and state.

Four themes underlie this theocratic scheme: (a) The animosity directed at the secular foundations of America; (b) The blatant attempt to promote fundamentalist civil government; (c) The entirely false claims that the founding documents are based on the bible and that US law, politics, and economics are grounded in Judeo-Christian principles; and (d) the strategy shift from "America is a Christian nation" to "American history reflects our Judeo-Christian tradition," thus explicitly implicating Jews in their proposed theocracy, even though fundamentalists believe that Jews are going to hell for rejecting Jesus as Messiah.

LGBTQ Hatred

- God-ordained traditional marriage is between a natural man and a natural woman.
- Homosexuality is a chosen behavior contrary to God.
- The US Supreme Court ruling that legalized same-sex marriage must be reversed.
- All laws and regulations that require businesses to violate their religious beliefs must be opposed.
- Traditional Judeo-Christian family values must be supported.

- Placement of adoptive children with same-sex couples must be opposed.
- Bathroom use should correspond to biological sex.
- Teaching about homosexuality, transgender, and other nontraditional lifestyles as normal must be opposed.
- Unmarried persons should not have the legal rights of spouses.

There is already the constitutionally protected right to hate LGBTQ people, but the platform demanded the right to discriminate against this American minority group. This was restated five times in the platform, emphasizing that to be required to provide services to LGBTQ people would violate their consciences, beliefs, convictions, and commitment to traditional values guaranteed by the First Amendment. The platform demands exemption from public accommodation laws through the passage of so-called "religious liberty laws." Rev. Larry Bethune of the University Baptist Church in Austin argues that biblical principles fully support same-sex marriage. Fundamentalist Republicans should answer one question: What was Jesus's sexual orientation?

Antiscience Denialism

- The basic educational standards do not list general science, biology, physics, or chemistry, or even mention science as a curricular area.
- "Support objective teaching and equal treatment of all sides of scientific theories, which should be taught as challengeable with discussion of strengths and weaknesses of the theories."
- The State Board of Education (with its history of antiscience activism) should have coercive authority over local school districts' curricular decisions.
- "Climate change is a political agenda promoted to control every aspect of our lives."
- Abolish the Environmental Protection Agency and repeal the Endangered Species Act.
- Abolish the US Department of Education.

These positions reject not only the basic scientific disciplines but also the scientific method, which is the most effective strategy for the discovery of knowledge ever developed. While biology and evolution are not mentioned in the platform, the standard "stealth creationism" ploys are advocated. However, these have been repeatedly rejected by the courts because biblical creationism is not science. The bizarre allegation about climate change was clear evidence of the conspiratorial delusions and chronic paranoia that characterize the fundamentalist mindset. Also apparent was the deeply rooted anti-environmentalism reflected in Genesis dominionism.

Anti-Muslim Bigotry

- Support an aggressive war on terrorism, including radical Islamic terrorists.
- Prohibit implementation of foreign law, including Sharia law.
- American law for American courts, no foreign law.
- Suspend contact with the Council on American-Islamic Relations.

What about theocratic biblical law? Is it foreign law? Is the bible an American book? It was compiled in Palestine and surrounding territories two thousand years ago. The Texas Republican platform claimed the bible is the basis of the US founding documents and American law. Should the founding documents be declared invalid because they are based on foreign law? Where do their Judeo-Christian principles come from?

Conclusion

The dishonest exploitation of God, the bible, and Judeo-Christian principles by the writers of this platform suggests that they would not be satisfied until they transformed America into a theocracy incorporating their fundamentalist dogmas. Given the overwhelming negativity and hostility expressed in the platform, it is reasonable to ask: What does it mean to be a Christian? Jesus said love your neighbors, love your enemies, and treat others as you want to be treated.

There is no evidence of Christian love and charity in the worldview of this platform. The dominant features revealed were egocentricity, intolerance, and unmitigated anger. The real threat to American democracy is not socialists, humanists, or Muslims. It is the fundamentalist extremists who want to inflict their ungodly biblical falsehoods on everybody else.

Addendum: More Texas Fundamentalist Bigotry

The Texas Republican Party's 2018 platform propounds additional false ideas about scripture. Summarized below are four claims, each followed by a statement of truth.

- Socialism in any form should be rejected because it contradicts the biblical form of government.

  Truth: Early Christians practiced strict socialism in their community, with severe punishment for violators (Acts 1–5).

- Traditional Judeo-Christian family values, the strength of the nation, are under continued assault.

  Truth: Family values have been disparaged since the beginning of the Christian era, with Jesus being the initial dissenter.

- Public practice of religion including prayer should be encouraged.

  Truth: Jesus condemned public piety, charitable acts, and prayer as contrary to God's will.

- Public displays of the Ten Commandments and Confederate monuments should be protected by government.

  Truth: the Decalogue endorses collective punishment, chattel slavery, and subservience of women, while Confederate statues also commemorate slavery.

In conclusion, Texas Republican values are unbiblical, unchristian, unhistoric, unscientific, and unAmerican.

FOUR
Fundamentalism on Trial: Twelve False Claims

The eminent University of Chicago historian Daniel Boorstin identified American humanism as the defining characteristic of the nation, which is the legacy of Thomas Jefferson and the entirely secular US Constitution. The real menace to the United States, Boorstin contended, is the emphasis on our differences, including religious opinion and practice, rather than a focus on our shared values and common beliefs.

For the past 100 years, Christian fundamentalism has been dedicated to the goal of transforming the United States into a theocracy by implementing policies and laws that advance a so-called biblical worldview, while simultaneously limiting the freedoms and rights of other citizens who don't share it. This worldview consists of definitive positions on a series of major political and social issues that supposedly derive from the bible when, in fact, almost none do. Moreover, fundamentalist theocratic-political dogmas are antithetical to the cardinal values of American humanism: freedom, community, tolerance, science, reason, and democracy.

Fundamentalism begins with the foundational postulate of scriptural inerrancy or literal biblical truth, which is based on the hypothesis of verbal inspiration (in 2 Timothy 3:16, scripture is said to be "God-breathed"). The problem for fundamentalists occurs when scripture partially or completely contradicts their preconceived political views. To solve this difficulty they invoke a highly flexible criterion of biblical interpretation, maintaining through textual selectivity and textual omission that scripture must be "properly understood." These tactics are applied in concert to identify or cherry-pick verses that support predetermined fundamentalist positions, while rejecting passages that contravene favored views.

Obviously, this interpretive strategy violates the sacred fundamentalist axiom of scriptural inerrancy and thus constitutes blatant biblical dishonesty. This is the greatest fundamentalist vulnerability, and humanists must be prepared and willing to attack it, pointing out the egregious inconsistency between the assumption of absolute scriptural truth and the techniques of textual selectivity and omission.

What follows is a review of a dozen sociopolitical or cultural issues on which fundamentalists claim they have determined the biblically correct positions. Three critical questions are addressed in bringing them to trial: Do the fundamentalist positions derive from scripture? Are the positions consistent with historical or scientific fact? And, are the positions endorsed by a majority of Americans, or are they minority views?

The purpose of documenting fundamentalist or conservative Christian positions that are either unbiblical, historically incorrect, unscientific, or unconstitutional (or some combination thereof) is to expose the weakness and/or immorality in them. It isn't sufficient for humanists just to propose an alternative perspective. With President Donald J. Trump's embrace of the conservative Christian agenda, humanists must attack and expose Christian positions that impede the potential and well-being of any human being.

Christian fundamentalism emerged early in the twentieth century in a series of twelve booklets titled *The Fundamentals*. Scholars debate whether "evangelical" and "fundamentalist" are synonymous terms in Christianity, but most agree that fundamentalism is one form of evangelicalism, along with Pentecostalism, and other charismatic strains of Christianity. During the past fifty years in particular, fundamentalist Christians have become increasingly vocal and politically committed to the goal of imposing their theocratic, socially conservative views on all Americans, and thus are rightly characterized as members of the religious right.

The fundamentalist impulse is basically reactionary, almost always in opposition to social progress. Fundamentalists seek security in traditional modes of belief and behavior and proclaim the bible to be without error, completely accurate, and a source of stability and certitude to those who follow it to the letter.

The following summaries comprise a catalogue of fundamentalists' obsessions that are the anchor sites for their twenty-first century political theology. Listed in alphabetical order, each concludes with a verdict based on scripture, history, constitutionality, or science.

AntiAbortion

Fundamentalists say that outlawing all abortion in the United States is their highest priority. They assert the bible supports their position, a claim which is unequivocally false. Abortion opponents cite four verses that refer to the developing fetus in the womb, but in truth none condemns or prohibits abortion. Nor did God or his chief spokesmen, Moses, Jesus, or Paul. In fact, God is history's greatest abortionist. He has murdered hundreds of millions of unborn children beginning with the Noachian Deluge and continuing to the present day. In summary, there is no biblical justification for the fundamentalists' relentless assault on women's reproductive rights. Even though 70 percent of Americans identify as Christian, nevertheless people in this country support legal abortion by a margin of 70 percent to 25 percent.

Verdict
Biblically dishonest—because scripture refutes antiabortion zealotry.

Pro-Capital Punishment

Fundamentalists are strong proponents of capital punishment. They regularly invoke the dictum of an eye for eye, a tooth for tooth, and a life for a life. However, God's word expands the application of the death penalty to cover a total of sixty violations. Criminals deserving execution include adulterers, astrologers, blasphemers, false prophets, homosexuals, idolaters, mediums, parent cursers, perjurers, rebellious sons, Sabbath breakers, sorceresses, unbelievers, and unchaste daughters. Why don't the fundamentalist devotees of biblical truth demand that these sinners be executed, as scripture requires? This is just one more example of convenient dismissal of biblical mandates that are regarded as laughable by almost all Americans. Finally, it should be emphasized that both Jesus and Paul endorsed pro-capital punishment Old Testament law.

Verdict
Biblically dishonest—because scripture requires execution for sixty violations that are no longer enforced.

Pro-Christian Nation

For the past 200 years, Christian activists have been trying to promote the false idea that America was founded as a Christian nation whose laws are based on the bible. For example, in the 1860s, an organization of Christian ministers attempted to expand the preamble of the US Constitution to include "as the Divine Authority of the Holy Scriptures and Jesus, the Messiah, the Savior and Lord of all." The greatest success occurred in the 1950s, when a coalition of Christian businessmen collaborated with the Eisenhower Administration to have "In God We Trust" recognized as the national motto and "under God" inserted in the Pledge of Allegiance. The most recent efforts by pseudohistorian David Barton to recognize the United States as a Christian nation have failed.

Concerning the claim that our laws are grounded in scripture, it's ironic that fundamentalists want to ban Sharia law as "foreign law," but embrace the bible as a source of judicial precepts, even though it was compiled in Palestine and surrounding territories two thousand years ago. Clearly, biblical law is foreign law, too.

Verdict
Historically dishonest—because documentation and scholarship contradict the claims.

Pro-Creationism in Public Schools

Fundamentalists are unyielding proponents of biblical creationism as the scriptural alternative to ungodly evolution. They advocate disingenuous legislative strategies devised to infuse the bible story into public school science classes, such as equal treatment, academic freedom, and "theistic science." They cite efforts to teach sound science as anti-Christian bias and the promotion of atheism. While fundamentalists and other Christian conservatives are perfectly willing to misrepresent and distort science in their efforts to inculcate biblical nonsense, the facts remain. Although most Americans identify as Christian, they still massively oppose teaching creationism in public schools.

Verdict
Scientifically dishonest—all evidence refutes the Genesis story of creation—and unconstitutional.

Anti-Death with Dignity

Fundamentalists constantly proclaim their unbiblical belief that life begins at conception and ends with "natural death." Hence, they oppose all legislation that would put end-of-life decisions in the hands of patients, doctors, and their families. Previously called "voluntary euthanasia" or "physician-assisted suicide," current language is death with dignity, the right to die, or medical aid in dying. Fundamentalists are motivated by anxiety associated with impending demise, but promote the idea that suicide, or unnatural death, is against God's will. Regarding the commandment "Thou shalt not kill," the bible makes clear that murder is prohibited but allows for capital punishment and other forms of "lawful" killing. Even though seven in ten Americans identify as at least nominally Christian, the same proportion of the population thinks that the law should allow for end-of-life decisions to be made by individuals and their families, not by theocratic officials.

Verdict
Biblically dishonest—because there is no scriptural justification for "natural death."

Pro-Decalogue Displays on Public Property

Fundamentalists continue to fight to display their cherished Ten Commandments in public venues, especially classrooms, courthouses, and state capitols. This is a violation of the Establishment Clause; government has no business telling citizens which god to worship or imposing religious rules on them. But such public postings likely wouldn't pass muster with fundamentalists if they read the full text of the edicts. For example, children are to be punished for the transgressions of their parents, slavery is endorsed, and a man's wife is classified as property along with his livestock. Most importantly, violators of the first nine commandments must be executed, according to God's law.

Verdict
This is biblically dishonest—because the required punishments are never listed along with the full text of the commands. And it's unconstitutional—because the First Amendment prohibits the establishment of a religion.

Pro-Free Enterprise

Fundamentalists argue that society will function optimally if free enterprise principles are implemented and government regulations are minimized or eliminated. They enthusiastically advocate economic competition and the accumulation of personal wealth. In contrast, Jesus promulgated an austere doctrine of selflessness, eschewing material possessions and ignoring daily needs. He said that an absolute requirement for salvation is to give up all earthly attachments. Moreover, the first model Christian community was explicitly communistic in conception.

Verdict
Biblically dishonest—because Jesus's unambiguous teachings are disregarded.

Anti-Marriage Equality

No current sociopolitical issue angers conservative fundamentalists more than same-sex marriage. They condemn the concept of marriage equality that is embodied in the recent Supreme Court decision legalizing same-sex marriage, which they assert is unconstitutional. The fundamentalist claim that the bible prohibits homosexual marriage has been discredited, for example, by Rev. Larry Bethune of the University Baptist Church in Austin, Texas. Contrary to fundamentalist propaganda, Americans substantially support same-sex marriage, even though a majority identify as Christian.

Verdict
Biblically dishonest—although some ambiguity exists. (See below.)

Pro-Public Prayer

Fundamentalists emphasize their right and duty to promote and participate in public prayer activities. For example, they are enthusiastic supporters of government leaders holding prayer breakfasts and fully support the National Day of Prayer. These events clearly violate Jesus's command that his followers should not make a public spectacle of prayer. He stressed that prayer is a personal matter that should be conducted in private.

Verdict
Biblically dishonest—because Jesus's unequivocal teaching is rejected.

Pro-School Vouchers

Since the late 1970s, conservative Christians have been doggedly pursuing their goal of funneling money away from public education in the United States. Currently, 90 percent of K–12 children attend public schools, with the others enrolled in Catholic schools, Christian academies, elite prep schools, military academies, and other denominational schools. Some are also homeschooled. Numerous schemes have been implemented to foster "school choice" that gives taxpayer money in the form of vouchers to parents of children who want to send them to private institutions, often religious. These voucher programs have no basis in scripture and have been rejected by voters in more than two-dozen initiatives and referenda in a country that's majority Christian.

Verdict
Unconstitutional—because the basic principle of separation of church and state is violated.

Anti-LGBTQ

Fundamentalists vehemently condemn the "gay lifestyle," which they assert is a choice. They don't want LGBTQ people to adopt children, teach in the public schools, serve in the military, occupy sensitive government positions, or be legally protected from discrimination. However, they disregard the bible verses that mandate execution for homosexuals, including lesbians. Also, fundamentalists demand exemption from public accommodation laws through passage of what they label religious liberty or freedom of conscience legislation, which would allow them to discriminate against LGBTQ citizens and anyone else they regard as sinners. Of course, Jesus said his adherents should love neighbors and enemies alike and he never denounced homosexuality.

Verdict
Biblically dishonest—because scripture requires execution of homosexuals.

Pro-Sworn Oaths

Fundamentalists are committed to participation in political ceremonies that involve swearing on the bible to fulfill the duties of public office, always concluding with "so help me God." These ostentatious events violate Jesus's specific prohibition against swearing: "But I say unto you, swear not at all; neither by heaven; for it is God's throne."

Verdict
Biblically dishonest—because Jesus's clear teaching is rejected.

Not included in this roster of unbiblical positions are traditional fundamentalist concerns, such as imbibing alcohol or drugs, gambling, and pornography. This is because the twelve positions summarized above have taken precedence in the fundamentalist theopolitical agenda. On the truly bizarre front, previous proposals to ban Halloween, Harry Potter, Pokémon, Teletubbies, and Transcendental Meditation are no longer advanced.

A majority of the political positions summarized above are legitimately described as unbiblical because they disregard scriptural mandates, including most prominently Jesus's unequivocal teachings. However, the evaluation of marriage equality isn't definitive, because scripture is ambivalent on this topic. Three fundamentalist positions are contradicted by historical evidence or constitutional principle, and one is refuted by science, yet firmly based in scripture. Finally, the majority of Americans reject most fundamentalist viewpoints.

Data from a 2016 NARAL Pro-Choice America report, for example, indicate that more than half of US senators, representatives, and governors oppose abortion rights, while about one-third are supporters. This is just the reverse of the opinions of the American people, who support legal abortion by almost three to one and have done so for the past decade. State legislatures are even more extremely antiabortion, as indicated by their enactment of hundreds of extreme measures in recent years.

The dishonesty of fundamentalists concerning abortion is predicated on their untruthful claims. They make medically false assertions that abortion causes sterility, cancer, and mental illness, and propound the biblically false declaration that scripture prohibits abortion and that God loves fetuses and children. These deceitful claims are promoted in Jesus's name to achieve the political goal of outlawing and criminalizing abortion in the United States.

In addition to limiting access to abortion and contraception, fundamentalists have also achieved disproportionate legislative influence on same-sex marriage and LGBTQ discrimination, taxpayer funding for private schools, and biblical creationism. They have manipulated the US political system by deceiving their fellow Americans.

The behavior of fundamentalists reveals a disregard for God's word: the Holy Bible. Fundamentalist truth is not biblical truth or Christian truth, and it is certainly not American truth. Biblical dishonesty is the Achilles' heel of fundamentalism. Humanists have a responsibility to expose and actively oppose fundamentalists to prevent them from imposing their unscientific, unconstitutional, and unpopular doctrines on everybody else. The fact is that Christian fundamentalism is a continuing threat to the civil liberties of all Americans.

FIVE
A Fundamentalist Centennial in America

Few Christians know that the year 2010 initiated the centennial celebration of a uniquely American theological perspective. Summarized below are the landmark historical events and current positions associated with the religious orientation known as fundamentalism.

Beginning in the last decades of the nineteenth century, fundamentalism emerged from respectable traditions of revivalism and evangelicalism and acquired a thoroughly independent identity. Specifically, fundamentalism was a reaction to liberal Protestant theology, which was attempting to accommodate Christianity to scientific, intellectual, and theological developments occurring at the time.

The doctrinal foundation of fundamentalism was expounded in a series of twelve paperback booklets published between 1910 and 1915. Titled *The Fundamentals*, the tracts covered a range of topics, including a defense of inerrancy, an attack on biblical scholarship, and polemics against Mormonism, Catholicism, and Christian Science. A fundamentalist is someone who accepts the propositions detailed in the pamphlets.

The central dogma of fundamentalist theology is the absolute inerrancy of scripture. Subsidiary postulates include the deity of Jesus, the virgin conception, the substitutional atonement for sin, the authenticity of miracles, the reality of bodily resurrection, and the imminent Second Coming. Fundamentalism expanded into an all-encompassing life stance, which included disapproval of drinking, dancing, gambling, card playing, attending movies, and other unsuitable activities.

Fundamentalists fought and ultimately lost two major battles in the 1920s that permanently shaped the public image of fundamentalism. The first was the long-cherished goal of making the manufacture and sale of liquor illegal in the United States, and the second was the struggle to outlaw the teaching of Darwinian evolution in the public schools. In addition to these conflicts, fundamentalists were involved in three other damaging disputes: They opposed the Social Gospel movement; they allied with the Ku Klux Klan in the South; and they refused to support a presidential nominee because he was a Catholic.

At this point, fundamentalists had become completely alienated from mainline Protestantism and isolated from mainstream American culture. Fundamentalism receded from the public consciousness for the next two decades, due in part to the Great Depression and World War II.

In the 1950s, fundamentalism was reanimated in conjunction with McCarthy-era paranoia, when two expressions of religious patriotism were instituted: The phrase "under God" was inserted in the originally secular Pledge of Allegiance, and "In God We Trust" was placed on all currency and made the national motto by Congress, replacing *E pluribus unum*, which was crafted to celebrate America's ethnic and cultural diversity.

The fundamentalist strategy of Christianizing America through mandatory bible reading and prayer in the public schools received an unanticipated setback in the 1960s when the US Supreme Court ruled that these activities were unconstitutional. Concurrently, the fundamentalist political agenda was substantially strengthened with the establishment of the Chalcedon Foundation, which promotes Christian Reconstructionist theonomy (a government based on biblical principles).

In the 1970s, the US Supreme Court legalized abortion, thereby recognizing that women possess constitutionally guaranteed rights in the sphere of reproductive health and choice. On another front, fundamentalists instigated an unrelenting assault on secular humanism, which they alleged was a dangerous philosophy that was destroying America.

In a monumental ecclesiastical victory, fundamentalists assumed control of the Southern Baptist Convention in the 1980s, resulting in the de-emphasis of traditional principles that had defined the denomination for generations. Simultaneously, fundamentalists failed in several attempts to impose "creation science" on the biology curriculum in public schools, with the US Supreme Court rendering the final decision. A magazine called the *Fundamentalist Journal* was published.

In the 1990s, the fundamentalist political doctrine that falsely asserts that the country's founding documents established a Christian nation received renewed attention. A declaration that redefined the role of women in church and society was approved by the Southern Baptist Convention, which also sponsored a well-publicized confrontation with the Mormon Church.

The first decade of the twenty-first century witnessed yet another attempt by fundamentalists to force into public school science classes the erroneous claim that humankind was divinely created 6,000 years ago, which was ruled unconstitutional again. Following the September 11 attacks, fundamentalists launched a concerted assault on Islam and continued their criticism of several other world religions, as well as various US Christian denominations.

Although several new issues have emerged, the broader social and political themes encompassed by fundamentalism have remained remarkably consistent over the past century.

The major contemporary positions endorsed by fundamentalists are American exceptionalism, a biblical worldview, capital punishment, Christian nationalism, conservative values, fetal personhood, free enterprise, militarism, public prayer, Republican politics, school vouchers, and Zionism. Concepts that fundamentalists vehemently reject include animal rights, ecumenism, environmentalism, euthanasia, feminism, gay rights, gun control, modern science, multiculturalism, reproductive rights, sexuality education, and socialism.

Because extreme theologies never fail to polarize committed religionists, it is not surprising that many believers consider fundamentalists to be the last defenders of biblical truth while others regard them as reactionary zealots who dishonor holy scripture.

SIX

Living in a Fundamentalist Enclave

Williamson County, Texas, may be the most politically and religiously conservative governmental entity in the United States. Only Republicans are elected to public office and they often tout their alleged Christian credentials.

For example, a district attorney once compared herself to Jesus, explaining that "Christ's example shows us that doing what's right often comes at a price" (she spent a weekend in jail for disobeying a judge's order), while vilifying her opponent in full-page advertisements as an ally of dangerous criminals.

With a population of 50,000 and more than 70 Christian churches, Georgetown (where I live) is the county seat. A historic courthouse dominates the downtown square. Sprawling Williamson County, with a population approaching half a million, is governed by a judge and four commissioners. They are paid about $100,000 a year.

Three very different newspapers are available in Georgetown. The *Williamson County Sun* is a moderately conservative, semiweekly newspaper that reports local news. The *Georgetown Advocate* is published biweekly and promotes an incendiary blend of Tea Party politics and fundamentalist zealotry that featured virulent anti-Obama tirades during his presidency. The *Good News Journal* is a bimonthly "Judeo-Christian newspaper that delivers a message of hope, inspiration, and patriotism."

The following examples illustrate how fundamentalist extremism can thoroughly infuse, infect and distort community values.

Constitutional Corruption

A Williamson County constable resigned from his position in midterm a few years ago. The county commissioners decided that they would handle the replacement process. After inviting applications, they interviewed the top five candidates.

The county judge and three of four commissioners interrogated the nominees, asking a series of questions about religious affiliation and participation and views on abortion and same-sex marriage. Three of the rejected candidates filed a federal lawsuit against the judge and commissioners. Two subsequently settled for monetary damages, and one continued to court. Most every high-school student knows that the US Constitution prohibits religious tests for public office. Not only did the county judge and the commissioners demonstrate contempt for a basic constitutional principle, they actually rationalized their behavior by stating that voters in the next election would ask the same questions!

The total cost to the taxpayers was well over a million dollars for this official governmental bigotry. One remarkable irony is that the recalcitrant commissioners were represented in court by Rudy Giuliani's law firm, given that at the time he was a supposed advocate of women's reproductive rights and marriage equality!

This scenario would be unbelievable anywhere except in Williamson County, Texas.

Christian Nationalism

Speaking at the groundbreaking for a fundamentalist megachurch in Georgetown, the local state senator said, "Our nation was built on the cornerstones of Christ, the church, the family and the community." The Georgetown mayor proclaimed "Georgetown Vacation Liberty School Week" at a council meeting. The Vacation Liberty School merges traditional summer bible school with Christian nation propaganda: "Our goal is to teach students to understand that no matter what they might have heard, America is a Judeo-Christian-based culture."

The editor of the *Advocate* suggested in a signed editorial that the public schools are not teaching that the United States is a Christian nation in order to be "progressive" or politically correct. His opinion supports the distrustful attitude toward public schools expressed in the goal statement of the Vacation Liberty School.

After the *Good News Journal* published an article titled, "Prayer That Birthed a Nation," which claimed that delegates to the Constitutional Convention began each session with "prayer for God's guidance and wisdom," I wrote to the managing editor and publisher explaining that Benjamin Franklin's motion to begin each session with prayer was not adopted.

No correction or apology to readers was ever issued. Interestingly, the publisher had previously written in a brief editorial statement that, "Truth is hidden in scandals, bad media and lies." Remember, this is a self-described Judeo-Christian newspaper!

Abortion Opposition

I wrote to a reporter asking that the *Sun* give more attention to the American majority viewpoint than to a small minority of antiabortion extremists. That informal note was published as a letter to the editor, and then a personal attack on me was published in response.

The author of the reply said that I write articles about atheism and spew an anti-God secular agenda. He wondered why people like me choose to live in Georgetown, where God, family, and country still have deep roots.

My reply, which summarized what the bible actually says (and doesn't say) about abortion, was finally published six weeks later after I pressed an argument based on journalistic ethical responsibility.

Within a month of publication of my letter, the editorial assistant who initiated the episode lost his position and one month after that the managing editor left the *Sun*. A cause-and-effect inference would not be unreasonable because the cautious publisher carefully avoids the abortion controversy.

I also wrote a letter to the editor of the *Advocate* responding to the false assertion that the bible prohibits abortion. The confused author based her claim entirely on the pronouncement that "God knew us when we were still in our mother's womb." Like several other passages that refer to "the womb," this verse does not condemn or prohibit abortion. My letter, which explained that there is no biblical basis for the assault on women's reproductive rights, was not published. The *Advocate* does not tolerate any opinions that contradict fundamentalist Christian dogma.

The Georgetown Life Chain conducts an annual streetside demonstration where 100 activists hold signs such as "Abortion kills children" (which is not true) and "Pray for the End of Abortion." Some people driving by honk their support. From this evidence, the local organizer concluded: "Georgetown is pro-life."

An antiabortion operation called the Heidi Group, with the demonstrably false motto "God Loves the Unborn," alleged that comprehensive sexuality education programs in the schools encourage teen sexual activity, illustrating the confused ideas that permeate the antiabortion movement.

Finally, six antiabortion protesters demonstrated outside the local Bank of America branch, with a display saying that the "Bank of Abortion donates to Planned Parenthood." Actually, the bank matches employees' contributions to all approved charitable organizations.

Blasphemy Punishment

Christian football legend Tim Tebow visited a Georgetown evangelical megachurch for Easter Sunday service. He gave his popular testimony in a twenty-minute interview conducted by the pastor.

Reflecting the size of this resurrection celebration, 15,000 attendees were transported to the church by 110 chartered school buses. The big trouble began the following Wednesday when the *Sun* published a front-page story with numerous photographs under the banner headline, "Tim Tebow Has Risen, Indeed."

The reaction to the headline was immediate and vociferous. Letter writers called it offensive to Christians and disrespectful to their lord and savior Jesus Christ. In a groveling apology, the editor declared that he was "deeply sorry" and assured readers that he was a devout, lifelong Christian. He concluded by calling Jesus "the most important figure in history."

The fundamentalist blitzkrieg not only brought the editor to his knees, he became increasingly defensive and belligerent in responding to reader criticism. Few people in the community were surprised when the editor announced his resignation and moved to Colorado at the end of the year. Ironically, he had received an award from the Texas Press Association for excellence in headline writing a few months earlier!

Conclusion

Despite the radical political and religious views and the occasional unconstitutional activities, Georgetown is generally a good community in which to live. The government operates efficiently, and there are few major problems. The residents are friendly and helpful, and controversies are always resolved peaceably.

The real problem for nonbelievers in predominantly Christian communities is the relentless effort of the radical fundamentalist minority who want to impose their extreme ideas on everyone else. Mainstream Christians and members of smaller sects are reluctant to engage in combat with the self-righteous zealots out of fear of being labeled un-Christian or worse.

Nonreligious Americans have legitimate reasons to be concerned about fanatical fundamentalist activism. Texas is one of the seven states that still have prohibitions against unbelievers holding public office or serving on juries. Moreover, the neofundamentalist agenda would not permit atheists or agnostics to teach school, adopt children or even to vote.

Finally, while the River Rock Bible Church held two Christmas Eve services in the historic courthouse and Bethlehem Village was a prominent feature of the Christmas extravaganza on the square, there was one positive note: The Georgetown Utilities System wished all residents "Happy Holidays."

Postscript: More Fundamentalist Hypocrisy!

Three commissioners were convicted in federal court of violating the US Constitution by illegally interrogating the constable candidate about his religious opinions. All three commissioners claim to be devout Christians and uncompromising opponents of abortion and same-sex marriage. The three sanctimonious commissioners did not resign from office, nor did they reimburse taxpayers for the one million dollars they expended defending their fundamentalist Christian bigotry.

The state senator who promotes family values and is the legislature's foremost opponent of women's reproductive rights, was investigated for alleged sexual harassment of a female graduate student. After he refused to cooperate with the university's inquiry, claiming that a third party he knew but would not identify actually communicated the vulgar image, the antiabortion zealot thanked god for giving him the strength to persevere. The professional consensus is that the senator (who is an orthopedic surgeon) is a present-day Dr. Jekyll and Mr. Hyde and that there was no third party.

II. The Hateful Biblical God

SEVEN
God Hates Fetuses

Along quite a few roadways in America is a billboard that says, "Before I formed you in the womb I knew you, and before you were born I consecrated you." This quote, from Jeremiah 1:5, is attributed to "God." Next to the quote is a depiction of a human fetus. In the verse, antiabortion zealots find their justification for doing everything possible to eviscerate women's reproductive rights by outlawing abortion. The message is also available on a bumper sticker, often adorning vehicles driven by people with "In God We Trust" on their license plates.

The other bible passage popular with antiabortion activists is Psalm 139:13–16, which says, "For you created my inmost being; you knit me together in my mother's womb. I praise you because I am fearfully and wonderfully made; your works are wonderful, I know that full well. My frame was not hidden from you when I was made in the secret place, when I was woven together in the depths of the earth. Your eyes saw my unformed body; all the days ordained for me were written in your book before one of them came to be." It should be emphasized that abortion is not prohibited or condemned in this lengthy extract.

These two citations contain the strongest biblical support fundamentalists have to argue that life is a gift from God, that God loves the unborn, and that aborting a fetus is murder. Defenders of women's reproductive rights should know what the bible actually says about abortion and, by extension, related issues, including contraception, the morning-after pill, in vitro fertilization, and fetal tissue research. In fact, God is history's greatest abortionist.

Scriptural Truths

Summarized here are twelve biblical episodes and prophecies that provide an unequivocal expression of God's attitude toward human life, especially the ontological status of "unborn children" and their pregnant mothers-to-be.

- A pregnant woman who is injured and aborts the fetus warrants financial compensation only, suggesting that the fetus is property, not a person (Exodus 21:22–25).
- God promised the Israelites that if they worshipped him alone, he would not cause their women to miscarry (Exodus 23:24–26).
- The gruesome priestly purity test to which a wife accused of adultery must submit will cause her to abort the fetus if she is guilty, indicating that the fetus does not possess a right to life (Numbers 5:11–31).
- God enumerated his punishments for disobedience, including "cursed shall be the fruit of your womb" and "you will eat the fruit of your womb," directly contradicting sanctity of life claims (Deuteronomy 28:18, 53).
- Elisha's prophecy for soon-to-be King Hazael was that he would attack the Israelites, burn their cities, crush the heads of their babies, and rip open their pregnant women (2 Kings 8:12).
- King Menahem of Israel destroyed Tiphsah (also called Tappuah) and the surrounding towns, killing all residents and ripping open pregnant women with swords (2 Kings 15:16).
- The dead are happier than the living, but more fortunate than both are those who have never been born, indicating that life is not sacred (Ecclesiastes 4:2–3).

- Isaiah prophesied doom for Babylon, including the murder of unborn children: "They will have no pity on the fruit of the womb" (Isaiah 13:18).
- For worshipping idols, God declared that not one of his people would live, not a man, woman, or child, not even babies in arms, again confuting assertions about the sanctity of life (Jeremiah 44:7–8).
- God will punish the Israelites by destroying their unborn children, who will die at birth, or perish in the womb, or never even be conceived (Hosea 9:10–16).
- For rebelling against God, Samaria's people will be killed, their babies will be dashed to death against the ground, and their pregnant women will be ripped open with a sword (Hosea 13:16).
- Jesus did not express any special concern for unborn children during the anticipated end times: "Woe to pregnant women and those who are nursing" (Matthew 24:19).

These twelve incidents and declarations document God's complete rejection of the antiabortion crusaders' claims about the sanctity of life and a divine right to life. There is clearly no biblical justification for the radical theology they espouse.

Biblical Atrocities

This section summarizes God's monumental history of murderous behavior as recorded in holy writ. We know that God killed millions of unborn children and their pregnant mothers-to-be in Noah's flood (Genesis 6, 7, 8), the Conquest of Canaan (Joshua 6, 8, 10, 11, 12), the incineration of Sodom and Gomorrah (Genesis 18, 19), and in twenty major slaughters described in the bible (e.g., Judges 1:25, 21:10–14; 1 Samuel 15:1–8; 1 Kings 16:11; 2 Chronicles 36:17–20). The critical feature of these horrific events is that all people were exterminated (Luke 17:26–29). Whenever entire communities were massacred, we can be sure that pregnant mothers-to-be and their unborn children were among the victims, along with infants, babies, and children. Moreover, there are no stated exemptions for this specific segment of the population.

This ghastly program of human annihilation makes the God of the bible the greatest mass murderer in history, an entity who does not care about unborn children or living children or living adults. If God really opposes abortion, why didn't he just say so? Why didn't he authorize one of his trusted spokesmen, Moses, Jesus, or Paul, to issue a definitive statement on the subject? Why didn't he include "Thou shalt not abort a fetus" in the Ten Commandments?

It is also noteworthy that while the bible requires the death penalty for sixty specified criminal violations, abortion is not among them. When all relevant documentation in the bible is examined, it is obvious that God does not love the unborn, and he certainly does not disapprove of abortion.

Theological Questions

Antiabortion zealots assert that life begins at the moment of conception and, therefore, the destruction of a fertilized egg is murder. This is the basis for the concept of "personhood," which has been defeated in five statewide initiatives since 2010, but has recently gained traction in some states.

The bible declares that God breathed into man's body the breath of life, and man then became a living person (Genesis 2:7). At least a dozen additional verses indicate that breath is synonymous with life (e.g., Job 33:4; Psalm 104:29; Isaiah 42:5; Acts 17:25). Therefore, because fetuses don't breathe, this scriptural "truth" completely contradicts the personhood dogma.

More importantly, if the fertilized ovum is a person, as antiabortion extremists claim, then God's record as the greatest murderer of unborn children is expanded further. This is because most fertilized eggs either fail to implant in the uterine wall and pass out of the body or, if they do implant, they begin to develop but then are spontaneously aborted. Fewer than one-third of fertilized ova survive to be born nine months later.

Why does God murder untold millions of these "persons" every year in the United States alone? Why did God, who allegedly loves the unborn and hates abortion, kill so many unborn children, infants, babies, children, adolescents, and adults throughout biblical history? Why do fundamentalists pursue a political agenda that is thoroughly refuted by God's word?

Inapplicable Verses

Abortion opponents believe that eight verses referring to the development of the fetus establish the continuity of human existence from conception to life following birth (Psalms 22:10, 127:3, 139:13; Ecclesiastes 11:5; Isaiah 49:5; Jeremiah 1:4–5; Hosea 12:3; Luke 1:41). These verses contain undeniably poetic and sometimes literal truth. But while they illustrate why abortion may be an emotional and controversial issue, they do not provide an explicit prohibition against it.

Four additional verses referring indirectly to abortion or miscarriage that are sometimes cited by antiabortion extremists are Leviticus 26:22, Isaiah 47:8–9, Jeremiah 15:7, and Ezekiel 5:17. In none of these cases is the practice of abortion prohibited or condemned, and it is often described as God's ordained punishment.

Antiabortion Antilogies

Among those who deny women's reproductive rights, numerous contradictory positions exist. For example, some prominent politicians who want to overturn *Roe v. Wade* would allow exceptions for rape, incest, severe fetal abnormality, and/or life of the pregnant woman. These abortion exceptions necessarily require destroying the fetus, which is the very action they condemn. In other words, the murder of "unborn children" is acceptable when antiabortion politicians approve.

A disgusting contradiction exists between the antiabortion activists' preferred label "pro-life" and their horrific record of godly violence. In the forty years since *Roe v. Wade* was decided, twelve abortion providers have been murdered and seventeen have been maimed or seriously injured. More than 6,000 acts of violence have been perpetrated, including fire bombings, arsons, kidnappings, assaults and death threats. These agents of godly violence are accurately labeled "radical Christian terrorists."

The political activists who want to make abortion illegal in the United States invariably call themselves "Christian conservatives," stating that they want to reduce government intrusion into the lives of Americans and eliminate burdensome regulations that limit personal liberty. They say they want to get government off our backs and out of our lives—except, of course, when they want to use the coercive power of government to inflict their theological beliefs on everybody else, especially in matters of reproduction and sexuality.

After forty years of at least one million elective abortions performed annually, opponents still refuse to endorse programs that are proven to reduce the number of abortions, such as family planning that stresses contraception and comprehensive sexuality education in the schools. Instead, they promote ignorance with their abstinence-only curricula. If they would focus their efforts on preventing unwanted pregnancies, they would stop many more abortions than their politically coercive and sometime violent tactics have. Ironically, the antiabortion crusaders help to cause the abortions they denounce!

Antiabortion dogmatists condemn what they call the "holocaust" of fifty-six million abortions since *Roe v. Wade* became the law of the land. At the same time, they spend tens of billions of dollars annually building and operating their grandiose megachurches, Christian academies, and other programs that promote fundamentalist Christian doctrines. If they really want to prevent the murder of "unborn children," why don't they just use some of their vast wealth to pay women cash stipends not to have abortions?

The most egregious contradiction occurs whenever the antiabortion religionists invoke a biblical justification for their sanctimonious stance, because the Judeo-Christian god of the Holy Bible simply does not care about the lives of pregnant mothers-to-be and their "unborn children."

Summary

The bible is an unending compilation of atrocities illustrating God's penchant for feticide, infanticide, and the wholesale slaughter of adults. There is no biblical basis for the alleged principle of respect for the sanctity of life, the assertion that life is a gift from God, or the claim that fetuses possess a God-given right to life. God does not love the unborn or their pregnant mothers-to-be or living children or adults. He is the greatest murderer of fetuses and the preeminent mass murderer of living people in human history, according to the bible itself.

The bible does not support today's fundamentalist Christian assault on women's reproductive rights. This crusade is a political campaign that is thoroughly refuted by God's holy word. God causes all abortions, spontaneous and elective, as well as the destruction of fertilized ova or "persons," because he is omnipotent and therefore is the cause of everything.

The bible demonstrates conclusively that God is pro-abortion.

EIGHT
God Hates Children

The oft-repeated assertion that God loves children permeates Christian propaganda and is utterly false. God himself murdered infants, babies, and children, and he commanded the murder of guiltless offspring. In clear contrast, children were highly valued by the early Israelites and were regarded as gifts from God, according to Old Testament scholars like Gerald Larue and Robert Wilson. Large families were considered to be a divine blessing, while barrenness was seen as a curse or godly punishment. Sons were preferred over daughters, and children generally enjoyed few rights.

So while children were prized in early Hebrew communities, the biblical God their parents worshipped displayed a cruel disposition that was manifested in murderous behavior. It will be helpful to divide this summary of scriptural documentation into two parts, a longer one for the father (Yahweh) and a shorter one for the son (Jesus). The third member of the Trinity (the holy ghost) will not be considered, with the ardent hope that this omission will not be construed as blasphemy against the royal personage, which is, of course, the unpardonable sin.

The content of this chapter should be useful to writers of op-ed pieces and letters to the editor, and even useful to Sunday school teachers. Six categories of God's horrors are enumerated.

Horrific Slaughters of Innocent Children

We begin this review with those unspeakable biblical slaughters in which all residents were killed, with infants and children specifically identified as targeted victims. Children were murdered as punishment for the disobedience of their parents or other adults in the community—in other words, children were truly innocent victims.

- "At midnight God struck down all the firstborn sons in Egypt . . . there was not a house without someone dead" (Exodus 12:29–30). God repeatedly reminds us of this slaughter of children in Psalms 78:51, 135:8, 136:10.
- God's vengeance on the Midianites included killing all men, boys, and married women, while the young girls were kept as captives by the Israelites (Numbers 31:7–18).
- God slaughtered all the subjects of King Sihon and King Og, including men, women and children—there were no survivors (Deuteronomy 2:32–34, 3:3–6).
- "In the street the sword will make them childless; in their homes terror will reign. The young men and young women will perish, the infants and those with gray hair." These are lyrics from *The Song of Moses*, which was composed by God (Deuteronomy 32:25).
- The Israelites killed all residents of Jabesh-Gilead, including the women and children, with the exception of 400 unmarried young women, who were given to the surviving swordsmen (Judges 21:10–14).
- God ordered Saul to totally destroy the Amalekites, including men, women, children, infants, and all animals (1 Samuel 15:3).
- Saul commanded Doeg the Edomite to kill the priests of Nob, along with the men, women, children, infants, and animals (1 Samuel 22:19).

- God killed David's son as punishment for David's sins (2 Samuel 12:13–18).
- God killed Jeroboam's son because Jeroboam worshipped idols (1 Kings 14:12–17).
- God collaborated with Satan to test Job's faith by killing his sons and daughters in addition to numerous other cruelties inflicted on this good man (Job 1:18–19).
- God destroyed the men, women, children, and infants of Judah as punishment for their idolatry (Jeremiah 44:7–14).
- God ordered the slaughter of the unrepentant men, women, mothers, and children of Jerusalem as his judgment for their detestable idolatry (Ezekiel 9:6).
- God commanded the destruction of Jerusalem, including the murder of sons and daughters, as punishment for the sin of idolatry (Ezekiel 23:46–49).
- God will punish the idolatrous Israelites by causing barrenness and miscarriage, and by murdering those children that are born (Hosea 9:11–16).

The vast majority of infants, babies, and children murdered by Yahweh were victims in three biblical massacres, Noah's flood (Genesis 6–8), Sodom and Gomorrah (Genesis 18–19), and the Conquest of Canaan (Numbers 21, 31, 33; Deuteronomy 2, 3, 7, 20; Joshua 6, 8, 10–12), and in eighteen major slaughters in which children were not specifically named (Judges 1:17, 25, 4:23–24, 9:45, 11:32–33, 18:27, 20:48, 1 Samuel 27:8–9, 30:17, 31:1–6, 1 Kings 15:29, 16:12, 2 Kings 15:16, 17:19–20, 21:16, 24:2–4; 2 Chronicles 36:17–20; Lamentations 2:20–22).

Of course, tens of millions of "unborn children" were also murdered by Yahweh in the above events and several others.

Infanticide by Severe Physical Trauma

Six bible verses invoke the abhorrent Yahwehean tradition of killing infants and children by dashing them to the ground or dashing them to pieces or dashing them against the rocks:

- Elisha's prophecy for soon-to-be King Hazael was that he would attack the Israelites, burn their cities, kill their young men with the sword, dash their little children to the ground, and rip open their pregnant women (2 Kings 8:12).
- "Happy is the one who seizes your infants and dashes them against the rocks" (Psalm 137:9).
- God will punish the people of Babylon by dashing their infants to pieces before their eyes; their enemies will have no mercy on their infants and children (Isaiah 13:16, 18).
- Hosea's prophecy of devastation for the people of Bethel for their great wickedness includes mothers and their children being dashed to death against the rocks (Hosea 10:14–15).
- For rebelling against God, Samaria's people will be killed, their babies will be dashed to death against the ground, and their pregnant women will be ripped open with a sword (Hosea 13:16).
- God tells the people of Nineveh that they will be punished like he punished Thebes, whose infants were dashed in pieces (Nahum 3:10).

Innocent Children Murdered with Their Parents

Three gory stories in which innocent children were executed with their disobedient parents illustrate the despicable practice of collective punishment and document the unfathomable cruelty inherent in Yahweh's diseased character. The faultless children were buried alive, stoned to death, or eaten alive by lions.

- God caused the earth to open and swallow three disobedient men—Korah, Dathan, and Abiram—as well as their wives and children. They went down alive into the realm of the dead as their cries frightened the other Israelites (Numbers 16:27–33).
- God decreed that for stealing booty, Achan, with his sons and daughters and livestock, would be stoned to death and their bodies burned (Joshua 7:13–26).
- The men who had falsely accused Daniel were thrown, along with their wives and children, into the lions' den where they were eaten

alive (Daniel 6:24). Why did God refuse to protect the innocent children like he had protected Daniel?

Three crimes for which God mandated the death penalty are for children who attack (or kill) their parents (Exodus 21:15), curse their parents (Exodus 21:17, Leviticus 20:9), or will not obey their parents (Deuteronomy 21:18–21). In the episode from Deuteronomy, parents are instructed to take their rebellious son (daughters apparently don't engage in this behavior) to the local officials where he will be stoned to death.

An unresolved biblical issue concerns the punishment of children for the sins of their parents. In a dozen statements on the subject, God endorsed patrilineal guilt only half of the time (Exodus 20:5; 2 Samuel 12:13–18; 1 Kings 13:34, 14:10, 21:25–29; 2 Kings 25:7; Isaiah 14:20–21). He rejected this appalling idea the other half of the time (Deuteronomy 24:16; 2 Kings 14:5–6; 2 Chronicles 25:4; Jeremiah 31:29–30; Ezekiel 18:2–4). Either God is thoroughly conflicted or completely confused, or possibly he just doesn't care about the blatantly unfair treatment of children.

Children Killed by Wild Animals

An especially macabre technique that God regularly employed to kill children and adults as punishment for disobedience was the use of wild animals.

- God made general statements invoking the ferocity of lions, leopards, and bears in dismembering their prey to express his fierce anger (Hosea 5:14–15, 13: 4–8). Even though he also issued a specific threat to the Israelites that wild animals would eat their children (Leviticus 26:22), some apologists say that his language is just metaphorical; however, the incidents summarized below suggest otherwise.
- God actually did enlist bears and lions to kill children in two grisly episodes. After he was teased by some boys for having a bald head, the prophet Elisha asked God to punish them; two bears then ripped forty-two boys to pieces (2 Kings 2:23–24). And just for emphasis, let's recall the previously mentioned children of Daniel's false accusers, who were eaten alive by lions while God did not intervene to prevent the carnage (Daniel 6:24).
- God sent venomous snakes to punish the complaining Israelites

(Numbers 21:6), and he sent lions to punish Assyrian settlers in Samaria who refused to worship him (2 Kings 17:24–25). In both events, many people died. However, God did not exempt infants and children from either attack, so we can reasonably assume that they were also victims of his wrath.

Child Sacrifice by Parents

There is no question that during certain periods of early Hebrew history, children were routinely sacrificed to Yahweh or (more often) competing gods or idols (e.g., 1 Kings 16:34; 2 Kings 16:3–4, 17:17, 21:6, 23:10). These ritual murders are confirmed by Psalm 106:37–39. The requirement to sacrifice firstborn sons in Israel is unquestionable (Exodus 13:1–2, 12, 22:29). Furthermore, the rationale is also beyond dispute; firstborn male children are dedicated to Yahweh because he protected them from slaughter in Egypt (Exodus 13:14–15).

An especially sadistic commandment issued by God illustrates his extreme jealousy directed at unauthorized prophets who (he alleges) are controlled by evil spirits and speak lies in his name. He decreed that these false prophets must be executed by their own parents—by stabbing to death with a sword (Zechariah 13:2–3).

What is not entirely clear is whether the firstborn sons *must* be redeemed by the parents (Exodus 13:13,15) or if the sons cannot be redeemed (Leviticus 27:28–29). Some scholars say that Leviticus is referring to "devoted things," which are irredeemably dedicated to Yahweh, and not to sacrificial victims. It appears that Yahweh himself may have had doubts about the advisability of child sacrifice. This is evident early when he spared Isaac from becoming the burnt offering that he originally demanded from Abraham (Genesis 22:1–12). His concerns were expressed later through both Jeremiah (7:31) and Ezekiel (16:20–22, 20:30–31, 23:37–39). Or was Yahweh only condemning child sacrifice to other gods and idols?

There is one unambiguous episode that makes Yahweh's position perfectly clear. Jephthah was a mighty warrior who destroyed twenty Ammonite towns after he vowed to God that in exchange for military success he would sacrifice as a burnt offering the first creature to emerge from his house upon his triumphal return from battle. Much to his dismay, his only daughter came out to meet him, dancing to the sound of timbrels.

After Jephthah explained his unbreakable promise to her, she accepted her fate, but requested a two-month stay of execution, after which Jephthah sacrificed her as a burnt offering to God, just as he had vowed to do (Judges 11:29–39). Why did God refuse to spare Jephthah's innocent daughter as he had done with Isaac? We know that frail humans should never question God's omniscience, because to do so constitutes willful disobedience.

Now, if you think that God's barbaric punishments could not get any worse than child sacrifice, or killing children with wild animals, or beating infants to death, then consider cannibalism! Parents eating their own children is the ultimate penalty in God's seemingly unlimited arsenal of retribution inflicted on disobedient Israelites.

- "You will eat the flesh of your sons and daughters" (Leviticus 26:29).
- "You will eat the fruit of the womb, the flesh of your sons and daughters" (Deuteronomy 28:53).
- "I will make them eat the flesh of their sons and daughters" (Jeremiah 19:9).
- "Women have cooked their own children who became their food" (Lamentations 4:10).
- "Parents will eat their children and children will eat their parents" (Ezekiel 5:9–10).

Jesus Doesn't Love the Little Children

The Sunday school hymn that begins "Jesus loves me this I know, for the bible tells me so" probably derives from the brief episode where he embraced the little ones and declared that adults who do not possess the simple faith (i.e., intellectual immaturity) of children will not be saved (Mark 10:13–16, Luke 18:15–17). In fact, there are good reasons to conclude that Jesus was not particularly fond of children. He generally approved of the death penalty for Old Testament violations (Matthew 5:17), and he specifically endorsed capital punishment for children who curse their parents (Matthew 15:4; Mark 7:10). It should be noted that "cursing" does not mean "swearing at," but rather asking God to cause tragedy or misfortune for another person.

Jesus adopted the barbaric language of dashing children to the ground from Hebrew history in his horrifying prophecy for the total destruction of Jerusalem as punishment for the residents because they did not acknowledge him as God's emissary: "The days will come when your enemies will dash you to the ground, you and the children within your walls because you did not recognize the time of God's coming to you" (Luke 19:43–44). Jesus coldly confirmed without regret or sorrow that everybody died—obviously including infants, children, and "unborn children"—in Noah's flood by drowning and in the incineration of Sodom and Gomorrah (Luke 17:26–29). Moreover, he did not express any special concern for children or "unborn children" during the anticipated end times: "Woe to pregnant women and those who are nursing" (Matthew 24:19).

Jesus's anti-family values are expressed in four quotes that document his attitude of complete disregard for children.

- "Anyone who comes to me and does not hate parents, siblings, spouse, and children—and even himself—cannot be my disciple" (Luke 14:26).
- "Everyone who has left homes, parents, siblings, spouse, or children for my sake will be rewarded in this life and will inherit eternal life" (Matthew 19:29; Mark 10:29–30; Luke 18:29).
- "Anyone who loves father or mother more than me is not worthy of me; anyone who loves sons or daughters more than me is not worthy of me" (Matthew 10:37).
- "I have not come to bring peace to the earth. Rather, I have come to divide—father against son, mother against daughter—a person's worst enemies will be the members of his own family" (Matthew 10:34–36 ; Luke 12:51–53).

Deserting one's family for Jesus's sake is an essential requirement for attaining eternal life, so we can reasonably conclude that Jesus was an egomaniac, just like his father.

Two uses of the word "children" in connection with the Jesus mythology in the Gospel actually refer to descendants: the infamous blood libel,

"His blood be on us and on our children" (Matthew 27:25) and "You are children of your father, the Devil" (John 8:44, [NLT]). However, Jesus did deliver some frightful prophecies about parents and children at the long hoped for and still excitedly awaited end times (Matthew 10:21; Mark 13:12; Luke 21:16).

Jesus revealed his vengeful, unforgiving disposition toward all people in three gruesome stories where all who disobey him will be executed using blood-curdling methods and then sent to hell to be tortured forever.

- "He will cut him to pieces and assign him to a place where there will be weeping and gnashing of teeth" (Matthew 24:51).
- "He will cut him to pieces and assign a place with the unbelievers" (Luke 12:46).
- "But those enemies who did not want me to be king over them—bring them here and kill them in front of me" (Luke 19:27).
- "Everyone who falls on that stone will be broken to pieces; anyone on whom it falls will be crushed" (Luke 20:18).

Jesus used the popular technique of speaking in parables to disguise his aberrant predilection for severely punishing anyone who rejected him or disagreed with him. He was not a pleasant person.

Conclusion

It is appropriate to conclude this truly unpleasant review of biblical truth by returning to one of the dominant themes, that of parents sacrificing their children to gods or idols. Devout Christians believe that Yahweh's greatest deed of selfless devotion to humankind was the blood sacrifice of his only begotten son, the "lamb of God" as atonement for our sins. In fact, Yahweh's decision is the cornerstone of nauseating death-obsessed Christian theology, which encompasses human creation, the fall, and endless cycles of disobedience and severe punishment culminating in the monumental sacrifice of Jesus and his subsequent restoration to life and ascension to heaven.

Believers are still awaiting the repeatedly promised and long-overdue return of the Messiah, at which time they will be raptured into the hereafter to live forever with loving Yahweh and his son, while the vast majority of humanity faces unending torture inflicted in the most terrifying ways imaginable, as lovingly described by Jesus himself. God not only hates children and "unborn children," he despises everybody except his three selves (father/son/holy ghost) and his/their sycophants.

NINE
God Hates Women

Hillary Rodham Clinton was the first woman to become a major party candidate for the office of President of the United States. While it may not be surprising that a majority of men voted for Donald Trump, it was stunning that 53 percent of white women actually refused to support the first female presidential candidate who had a good chance of winning.

The outcome of any election is determined by many interacting factors, but there is some evidence that patriarchal religious indoctrination assumed a primary role in the 2016 presidential race. A slight majority of Catholic voters (60 percent) favored Trump, while an overwhelming majority of fundamentalist Protestants (81 percent) preferred the bellicose billionaire.

The justification for patriarchal domination as a God-given mandate is, of course, Holy Scripture. Because so many Americans accept the myth of Judeo-Christian nationalism, it is entirely appropriate to look to the bible as the source for this severely oppressive, anti-woman theme in fundamentalist Christianity.

The content of the bible was recorded, transmitted, and compiled over a span of almost two millennia in male-dominated, agrarian, Middle-Eastern societies. Therefore, the treatment of women in the bible reflects the cultural context in which these chauvinistic rules and beliefs developed. Because these misogynistic edicts, decrees, and mandates were codified in the Judeo-Christian scriptures, they became part of a vast compendium of commandments that devotees today believe to be God's perfect word.

Origins of Patriarchalism

In the second most-cited version of creation, it was only after God created animals and birds, which Adam then named, that God fashioned woman as Adam's helper from his spare rib (Genesis 2:22). The woman, Eve, caused the fall of humankind, at which time death entered the world. She ate the forbidden fruit and gave some to her husband, and he ate it as well (Genesis 3:6, 12). Eve's punishment was painful labor in childbearing and total submission to her husband (Genesis 3:16). In 1 Timothy 2:13–14, Paul provided the Christian rendition of this fictitious event when he said that because Eve was the one who was deceived, it was she, and not Adam, who became the sinner.

Obedience and subjugation of women are dominant themes throughout the bible. For example, God approved of multiple wives and concubines for men (Genesis 4:19, 16:1–4; Judges 8:30; 2 Samuel 5:13; and 1 Kings 11:3), but he did not endorse multiple husbands for women. Moreover, a woman's pledges, vows, or obligations could be subject to patriarchal nullification (Numbers 30).

Unjust Punishments

God generally considers women to be less valuable than men (Leviticus 27:1–7), an attitude reflected in several degrading biblical regulations and judgments, such as the classification of a man's wife as one of his possessions along with his slaves and livestock (Exodus 20:17). In a frightening illustration of cruel injustice, God ordered the rape of David's wives to punish *his* disobedience (2 Samuel 12:11–12). In another instance of grisly punishment that should mortify "pro-life" zealots, God caused a woman to abort her fetus because she committed adultery (Numbers 5:21, 27).

Equally horrible is the command that an unbetrothed virgin must marry her rapist (Deuteronomy 22:28–29). Some Muslim countries like Jordan and Morocco, which share the Abrahamic traditions, have similar laws on their books and are currently changing or revoking them.

Some Capital Crimes

In additional heinous decrees and actions, God requires that women be killed for violations that are not viewed as crimes in contemporary Western societies. For example, an evil enchantress must be executed (Exodus 22:18), and unchaste brides must be stoned to death (Deuteronomy 22:21). Lot's wife was instantly destroyed for disobeying the Lord's command to not look back when her family was fleeing Sodom (Genesis 19:26). Arguably the most abhorrent event in the bible is Jephthah's sacrifice of his daughter, whom he unknowingly promised to God as a burnt offering (Judges 11:29–39). Why did God not spare Jephthah's innocent daughter as he had done previously with Abraham's innocent son, Isaac (Genesis 22:1–18)?

Disgusting Attitude

Several gruesome episodes with a common theme illustrate another feature of God's disgusting disregard for the lives of women. In one of them, Lot offered the men of Sodom his betrothed daughters in lieu of his male guests because handing over the guests would have violated the accepted standards of hospitality. But the men of Sodom rejected the young girls (Genesis 19:4–10). In another episode, a Levite offered his concubine to a group of men in a similar circumstance; she died as a result of the ensuing gang rape (Judges 19:20–30). He cut the deceased concubine into twelve pieces and distributed them to the tribes of Israel, precipitating a murderous war with the Benjamites (Judges 20, 21).

There are an additional four ghastly events in which the bellies of pregnant women were ripped open with swords, killing them and their fetuses (2 Kings 8:12, 15:16; Hosea 13:16; Amos 1:13).

Treacherous Women

There are many bible stories about treacherous, dangerous, dishonest, manipulative, untrustworthy women. Three are notable for their savage behavior. Jael was clever, fierce, and violent. She killed General Sisera by hammering a tent peg through his skull into the ground while he was asleep (Judges 4:17–22). Delilah betrayed Samson to the Philistines for a monetary reward. The Philistines subsequently gouged out his eyes and imprisoned him (Judges 16:4–21).

Evil Jezebel was most certainly the worst of all scriptural shrews. She arranged for Naboth to be falsely accused of blasphemy and then stoned to death so that her husband could take possession of Naboth's vineyard (1 Kings 21:7–16). She was so diabolical that the prophet Elijah fled because he was afraid of her (1 Kings 19:1–9). She suffered a brutal death herself (2 Kings 9:30–37). Many centuries later, Jesus criticized the church in Thyatira for tolerating a false prophetess, also named Jezebel (Revelation 2:18–23).

The depiction of women as untrustworthy even extends to political symbolism, as when Israel's lack of fidelity to God is represented as the adultery of a faithless wife in Hosea 1–3. In fairness, it should be noted that there were heroines among the Hebrew women, including Ruth, Rahab, and Rachel.

Christian Womanhood

Along with slaves and children, wives are commanded to be under the jurisdiction of their husbands. Paul is the preeminent New Testament spokesman concerning Christian marital relationships. He said repeatedly that wives should submit to their husbands in everything because the husband is the head of the wife, just as Christ is head of the church (Ephesians 5:21–23, Colossians 3:18–25). He did, however, stress that husbands should love their wives and not be harsh with them.

Peter reiterated this advice concerning spousal submission and declared that wives should exhibit purity and reverence in their lives. He referred to wives as the "weaker partner" (1 Peter 3:1–7).

In addition to marriage, Paul provided specific admonitions for women in the church. They should dress modestly, with decency and propriety, adorning themselves only with good deeds. Women should learn in quietness and full submission, and they cannot teach or have authority over men (1 Timothy 2:8–15). Moreover, it is disgraceful for women to speak in church (1 Corinthians 14:34–35). Although Jesus did not specifically address women's status in his ministry, it is clear that men were preferred. All twelve apostles were men, and the Last Supper was a stag affair, while women were typically portrayed as committed helpers or servants.

The Christian Testament's description of women's roles is consistent with the definition in Proverbs 31 of the "wife of noble character" as capable, dutiful, dedicated to family, and fearing the Lord. The restrictions, limitations, and standards detailed above are enforced in many fundamentalist Christian churches today, even after two thousand years have elapsed. Does this testify to the enduring truth of traditional scriptural views of women or to the obstinacy of the dominant ecclesiastical patriarchy?

TEN
God Hates Homosexuals

Fundamentalist Christians continue to express their hysterical reactions to the new reality of marriage equality in contemporary America. For example, religious right lawyer Matt Staver declared that same-sex marriage is "the beginning of the end of Western civilization." Senator Rand Paul echoed this apocalyptic appraisal, saying that same-sex marriage constitutes a "moral crisis" in the United States. An avalanche of similar doomsday prophesies was unleashed by overwrought fundamentalist leaders, suggesting that God's wrath would punish a nation awash in sin.

Illustrating the extreme response to the legalization of same-sex marriage, the Texas Republican Party has incorporated the fundamentalist perspective into its platform, asserting that "homosexuality is a chosen behavior contrary to God" and calling for reversal of the US Supreme Court decision that legalized same-sex marriage. The Texas Republican manifesto repeatedly condemns public accommodation laws that "require business people to compromise their Christian convictions," emphasizing that to be forced to serve LGBTQ customers violates their constitutional rights. They demand exemption from allegedly unjust regulations through the passage of so-called "religious liberty laws."

The undisputed empirical fact is that fundamentalists have lost their battle against same-sex marriage. The US public strongly favors marriage equality, with 60 percent supporting and 35 percent opposed. Approval among young adults is even higher at 75 percent. All major segments of the religious spectrum have moved toward greater acceptance of same-sex marriage during the past twenty years.

While change has been slow, a number of mainline Protestant denominations now routinely ordain gay ministers and marry gay couples, based on the theological argument that Jesus was an advocate of inclusion. Even in fundamentalist churches, there has been an active minority movement toward tolerance, acceptance, and recognition of LGBTQ Christians, with some congregations and denominations becoming openly "gay affirming." Organizations like Evangelicals for Marriage Equality, the Gay Christian Network, and the Reformation Project are reaching out to major fundamentalist organizations and denominations for dialogue.

What Caused the Shift?

Several factors have helped to bring about one of the most dramatic shifts ever observed in modern American attitudes. First, the role of parents of gay children has been substantial, especially through organizations like Parents and Friends of Lesbians and Gays (PFLAG). Most Americans can empathize with parents caught in the agonizing dilemma of family commitment versus faith conviction. Prominent political parents like Dick Cheney, Rob Portman, and Ileana Ros-Lehtinen have put a human face on this difficult issue.

Second, the welcoming acceptance of LGBTQ students by their peers at all educational levels, especially in the middle and high schools, has certainly been influential. Third, the persuasive argument for the majority of religious believers is the oft-repeated dictum that LGBTQ people are also God's children and deserve the same rights and respect as everyone else.

In this chapter, I review and summarize what the bible actually says about marriage and homosexuality. This documentation establishes a basis for exposing and persuasively arguing against fundamentalist Christians' dishonest theopolitical agenda directed at same-sex marriage and LGBTQ Americans. Fundamentalists hope to accomplish their goal of denying equality under the law to gay people through promotion of misnamed religious freedom legislation.

One Man and One Woman?

Fundamentalists define marriage exclusively as a biblically approved relationship between one man and one woman, with no other permissible arrangements. For example, Texas Republicans assert that God-ordained traditional marriage is between "a natural man and a natural woman." This definition is affirmed by numerous scriptural verses (e.g., Genesis 2:24; Exodus 21:22; Deuteronomy 24:5; Proverbs 5:18–23; 1 Peter 3:1–7). Jesus also endorsed the conventional view of marriage (Matthew 19:4–9; Mark 10:6–9).

However, it is important to recognize that Hebrew history provides many illustrations of another apparently acceptable form of family alliance, known as polygyny. This term refers to a circumstance in which one man has multiple wives and concubines (e.g., Genesis 4:19, 16:1–4, 29:15–30). Three prominent Old Testament patriarchs who enjoyed this type of union were Gideon (Judges 8:30), David (2 Samuel 3:2–5, 5:13–16), and Solomon (1 Kings 11:1–3). Three other forms of marriage sanctioned in the bible are slave (Exodus 21:1–11), captive (Deuteronomy 21:10–14), and levirate, in which a man is strong-armed into marrying his brother's widow (Deuteronomy 25:5–7). It appears that the fundamentalist definition of marriage is not the only God-ordained marital configuration.

Scripture also provides ample evidence of another type of nontraditional affiliation: homosexuality. Male shrine prostitutes (referred to as homosexuals, sodomites, or dogs) participated in worship rites at some temples in ancient Israel. The practice was routinely condemned (Deuteronomy 23:17–18; 1 Kings 14:23–24) and two kings attempted to terminate the activity (1 Kings 15:12; 2 Kings 23:7). Four verses are suggestive of homosexual orgies (Isaiah 57:8; Habakkuk 2:15–16; 2 Peter 2:7–14; Jude 7–13).

Execution of Homosexuals Mandated?

This section renders all earlier discussion and scriptural conclusions moot, because marriage is irrelevant for dead sinners, and this is why the bible doesn't prohibit or even mention same-sex marriage. As the verses quoted in this segment conclusively demonstrate, God and his chief spokesmen (Moses, Jesus, and Paul) made unequivocal statements about mandatory capital punishment for homosexuals, including lesbians.

First, God's definitive action in the gruesome tale of Sodom and Gomorrah is summarized.

> All the men from every part of the city of Sodom called out to Lot, "Where are the men who came to you tonight? Bring them out to us so that we can have sex with them." Then the Lord rained down burning sulfur on Sodom and Gomorrah and the entire plain, destroying all those living in the cities (Genesis 19:4–5, 24–25).

This horrific story makes absolutely clear God's abhorrence of homosexuality and the appropriate punishment warranted: burning alive. The episode also illustrates God's preference for collective punishment: In addition to the homosexual men of Sodom, all other residents were also incinerated, including women and children we reasonably assume, plus all innocent citizens of Gomorrah and the other two major cities of the plain, Admah and Zeboiim (only the little city of Zoar was spared).

Second, Moses's statement as part of the legal code revealed to him by God is unambiguous and impossible to misconstrue: If a man has sexual relations with a man as one does with a woman, both of them have done what is detestable. They are to be put to death (Leviticus 20:13).

Third, Jesus endorsed every word and action contained in the Hebrew Covenant. Of course, the Son would fully support the Father's commands:

> Do not think that I have come to abolish the Law or the Prophets; I have not come to abolish them but to fulfill them. For truly I tell you, until heaven and earth disappear, not the smallest letter, not the least stroke of a pen, will by any means disappear from the Law until everything is accomplished (Matthew 5:17–18). (Note that Luke 16:17 repeats Matthew 5:18.)

Jesus also invoked the terrible fate of the residents of Sodom and Gomorrah in condemning those who rejected him and his revolutionary message (Matthew 10:15, 11:23–24; Luke 10:12). Jesus was knowledgeable about the Sodom and Gomorrah story and we assume that he understood the justification for God's fiery judgment on all residents (Luke 17:29), thus endorsing his Father's penchant for collective punishment.

Fourth, Paul clearly approved of execution for homosexuals, including lesbians and other perverts.

> Even their women exchanged natural sexual relations for unnatural ones. In the same way the men also abandoned natural relations with women and were inflamed with lust for one another. Men committed shameful acts with other men, and received in themselves the due penalty for their error. Although they know God's righteous decree that those who do such things deserve death, they not only continue to do these very things but also approve of those who practice them (Romans 1:26, 27, 32).

The entire passage from Romans describes homosexuals as degenerate criminals comparable to those who commit every type of illegal and immoral behavior. It is important to emphasize that Paul extends Moses's definition of homosexuality to include women. Three other passages in Paul's epistles contain additional condemnation of homosexuals (1 Corinthians 6:9–10; Colossians 3:5–6; 1 Timothy 1:8–11). See Romans 9:29, 2 Peter 2:6, and Jude 7 for more references to Sodom and Gomorrah.

Religious Discrimination Protection?

"Religious liberty laws" have their genesis in the federal Religious Freedom Restoration Act that dates back to 1993. Interestingly, it was then-Governor Mike Pence's signature on Indiana's RFRA in 2015 that initially propelled him to heroic status and subsequently to infamy among fundamentalist voters for championing "religious freedom" from public accommodation laws and then collapsing when business leaders told him to rescind the Indiana RFRA or else—which he quickly did.

More than twenty state legislatures across the country have considered various types of so-called "religious liberty laws" that would allow fundamentalist Christians to refuse to provide services to LGBTQ people, thereby expressing their merciless imprecation of homosexuality. Most of these efforts have failed, due primarily to criticism from the business community, including large corporations like Walmart, sports organizations like the NCAA and NBA, and the US Chamber of Commerce. When legislators have been obstinate, as in North Carolina, the financial punishment has been severe.

Religious liberty legislation was conceived of and promoted by fundamentalists to demonstrate their outrage at what they claim is the defilement of God's sacred institution of holy matrimony. Underlying this manifest anger is their bible-based revulsion directed at homosexuality, which they call an abomination and sin against God. While same-sex marriage is the ostensible target of their wrath, the emotional fuel for this extreme reaction is generated by less than 4 percent of Americans who identify as LGBTQ and whose very existence fundamentalists find to be so upsetting.

The obvious question is: Why don't these anti-gay, scripture-citing fundamentalist zealots who oppose same-sex marriage so vehemently and assert that homosexuality is an abhorrent sin, just obey God's clear command? Why don't they advocate execution of homosexuals just as God authorizes? Why do Bryan Fischer, Mike Huckabee, Sarah Palin, Mike Pence, Tony Perkins, Matt Staver, Phil Robertson, and other fundamentalist spokespersons refuse to invoke God's unequivocal mandate to kill homosexuals?

The answer to this question is simple: They do not possess the courage of their claimed Christian convictions. They know that the bible requires execution of homosexuals, because anti-LGBTQ activist Pastor Kevin Swanson reminded them of this scriptural decree at an annual National Religious Liberties conference just a few years ago. If they really respected God's perfect Word, they would initiate a national movement to encourage state legislatures to enact laws that would expand application of the death penalty to homosexuals. Surely, they could ask the federal courts to include this provision in the US criminal code, a request that follows logically from their (bogus) claim that the US Constitution is based on the bible.

Of course, this will not happen because the disingenuous fundamentalists know that their reputation as a national laughing stock would be exacerbated by these bible-based proposals. In other words, they are cowards for Christ. By refusing to endorse execution for homosexuals, fundamentalists again demonstrate that they are willing to adopt theopolitical positions, like advocacy for "religious liberty laws," that avoid the public ridicule associated with invoking God's unambiguous command. This is just one more example of their biblical dishonesty.

What Should Humanists Do?

Fundamentalists have recently escalated their assault on the LGBTQ community with the development of "Project Blitz." This infamous ecclesiastical action plan expands Christian Nation ideology to include a focus on what these extremists deem to be acceptable sexual expression. Specifically, they demand that lawful sexual behavior be restricted to relations between heterosexual, married couples and that discrimination against LGBTQ people be legalized by approving religious exemptions to civil rights legislation.

To thwart this hateful agenda, it's necessary to directly confront fundamentalist Christians about their blatant biblical hypocrisy. Their claim that God only endorses marriage between one man and one woman is false. Their unwillingness to discuss Jesus's sexual orientation is simply denial of an embarrassing possibility. Their refusal to acknowledge that God requires execution of homosexuals is outright dishonesty. Rather than addressing the issue truthfully they use the deceitful subterfuge of attacking same-sex marriage by demanding exemption from public accommodation laws that they allege violate their constitutionally guaranteed religious freedom.

Fundamentalists assert that people who support same-sex marriage are rejecting biblical authority, when in actuality it is the fundamentalists themselves who disregard God's clear commandments on this subject and numerous others. US fundamentalists falsely accuse their fellow Americans of persecuting them because of their avowed sincere commitment to obeying God's Word, a charge that is not true. Everyone recognizes that fundamentalists do have the constitutional right to hate and condemn LGBTQ citizens; however, they do not have the legal right to discriminate against this small minority or anyone else.

Humanists should take appropriate action to expose the dishonest fundamentalist jihad against the gay community. It is not enough to defend the rights and dignity of LGBTQ people. It is essential that Humanists publicly expose the false assertions, biblically dishonest claims, and devious legislative strategies of the fundamentalists. There are many opportunities and venues for disseminating the biblical truth about homosexuality and same-sex marriage, including letters to the editor, op-eds, call-in radio programs, community forums, public demonstrations, and legislative hearings. Humanists should make clear that their targets are false claims and unbiblical actions, and not the fundamentalists themselves. As they say, hate the sin but love the sinner.

What Was Jesus's Orientation?

This is a controversial topic that has generated much conjecture and debate among scholars. This section provides gospel references for interested readers.

- The beloved disciple: John 13:23-35, 19:26-27, 20:2-4, 21:7, 20, 24.
- The jealous disciple: Matthew 26:49-50, 27:3-5; Mark 14:44–46.
- The foot-washing ritual: John 13:2–15.
- The activities at Gethsemane: Matthew 26:36-45; Mark 14:32–42; Luke 22:43–44.
- The naked youth fleeing: Mark 14:51–52.
- Also, Paul and Onesimus: Philemon 1:10-20; Romans 7:18–25.

ELEVEN
God Hates Animals

We share our lives with 150 million dogs and cats, and ten million birds, fish, reptiles, and small mammals. More than one billion farm animals are raised and slaughtered for food in the United States each year. We coexist with untold billions of wild animals. However, we still tolerate the horrific killing of hundreds of millions of sentient creatures for sport, the fashion industry, traditional medicine, and by motor vehicles.

Possibly after considering similar information and sobering facts about animals in America, Barrett Duke of the Southern Baptist Convention, working with several other religious leaders, drafted an "Evangelical Statement on Responsible Animal Care." Christine Gutleben of the Humane Society praised the statement, saying that it is the result of wise and thoughtful reflection and has the potential to create enormous good. Her effusive endorsement is unjustified.

To establish a foundation for principles of compassionate care and responsible rule over animals, the statement's authors outlined three requirements. First, they declared that their thinking must come from scripture, with the goal of identifying key bible passages. Second, they specified that the emergent guidelines must be based not only in scripture, but also in God's unchanging character. Third, they asserted that humans are expected to show the same respect for animals that God does.

Although the authors refer to themselves as evangelicals, they are, in fact, fundamentalists, i.e., they believe the bible to be literally true. The belief that bible stories actually happened—that biblical events really occurred—is the hallmark of fundamentalism. The necessary implication of this theological commitment is that all of scripture is relevant to discussion of any issue, not just carefully selected verses and passages.

Contradictions

After establishing the theological foundation for their principles of animal care, the authors proceed to completely contradict their premise of absolute scriptural truth. They do this by deploying the fundamentalist exegetical strategies of textual selectivity (cherry-picking) and textual omission (disregarding or rejecting). In other words, they identify and cite verses and passages that are supportive of their preconceived perspective, while ignoring unpalatable material that tells a very different story.

The authors assert that "God uniquely created humans in his own image and likeness, in contrast to animals, who are created after their own kind." Because of this unique creation, they say, "Humans have greater worth than every animal and were appointed by God to rule over animals." They declare further that, "Scripture is clear on humanity's greater value, uniqueness, and rule, and sole status as God's image bearers."

These statements express unequivocally the fundamentalist doctrine of special creation of humankind, which is thoroughly contradicted by the overwhelming evidence for evolution. The false claim of human separateness from and superiority over all other animals is the basis for the dogmatic assertion of human exceptionalism and the pernicious doctrine of dominionism.

Credit Where Due

It is important to give the statement's authors credit where it is warranted. They assert that God commands humans to give animals the respect they deserve, because all animals have inherent God-given value. They declare that cruelty toward animals is sinful and an affront to God. Furthermore, they say that humans are obligated to work for the protection and preservation of all of God's animals.

This highly commendable and appropriate condemnation of animal cruelty and endorsement of humane treatment of animals is weakened considerably by the authors' final phrase: "while prioritizing human needs." Another qualifying condition obliquely cautions that "any attempt to idolize or divinize animals should be rejected." What exactly do these statements mean?

Another series of three declarations that focus on God's character further clarifies the fundamentalist view of the relationships between humans and animals: (a) "All animals ultimately belong to God and exist to bring him praise and reveal his character," (b) "Humans' responsible rule over and compassionate care for animals is rooted in the unchanging character of God," and (c) "After the flood, God caused all animals to fear humankind and gave them to humans for food."

In other words, animals are God's possessions, and, therefore, he can do whatever he chooses to do with them. This includes using animals as innocent sacrificial victims. Is this the respect for animals that humans are expected to show?

Now we come to the greatest failure of the "Statement on Animal Care." Even though Barrett Duke said that everything in the statement is based in scripture, it is the omission of many of God's edicts and actions concerning animals that stand out. The strong condemnation of animal cruelty is mitigated substantially by God's horrific penchant for animal sacrifice and his many other immoral uses of animals.

Animal Sacrifice

Animal sacrifice is a major requirement in God's theology of worship. Twenty chapters of the Hebrew Testament books are dedicated to specifying in precise detail how animals are to be sacrificed. In addition to lengthy discourses on ritual methods, three dozen gory descriptions of sacrificial episodes are reported.

The sacrificial animals are killed and their blood is sprinkled or smeared on the altar. Then the carcasses are burned. While the typical ritual sacrifice involves a few dozen animals, there are some that are especially repugnant for their huge numbers alone. Four horrific episodes entail the slaughter of tens of thousands of oxen, sheep, and goats as worshipful tributes to a bloodthirsty God.

Illustrating how important animal sacrifice is to God, he stopped a plague that had already killed 70,000 men only after a proper sacrifice was completed. He also threatened to kill Aaron if he entered the Holy Place without proper preparation involving an elaborate animal sacrifice.

Considering God's proclivity for animal sacrifice, an observer would expect the fundamentalists to leap to the defense of Santerian priests who routinely make offerings of domestic animals in their services and Hmong shamans who sometimes kill dogs as part of their healing rituals. Most Americans regard these inhumane practices with disgust and horror. Yet, a federal court struck down a Hialeah, Florida, ordinance banning animal sacrifice, ruling that it was aimed at religion. Likewise, the bible clearly approves of animal sacrifice.

The writers of the statement may have anticipated the introduction of the gruesome subject of animal sacrifice by unfriendly critics, because they invoked a standard fundamentalist exegetical technique for no apparent reason. They state that any ethical norms derived from the Old Testament must be applied today "in light of the New Testament." In other words, Hebrew Testament principles may not be applicable today if an excuse can be located in the Christian Covenant.

This exegetical ploy will not work for three reasons. First, God instigated the blood sacrifice of his only begotten son, who is often referred to as the "Lamb of God." Second, Jesus's parents conducted a sacrifice upon his birth as required by God's law. Third, Jesus himself endorsed animal and human sacrifice.

Innocent animals were routinely killed in the hundreds of massacres and slaughters that dominate Hebrew Bible history. Some especially detestable instances of animal cruelty were portrayed in Joshua's intentional crippling of horses, Samson's abuse of 300 foxes, Balaam's beating of his donkey, and the stoning and burning of Achan's livestock, along with him and his family, because he stole some "devoted things" from God.

Americans have a profound appreciation and admiration for our best friend, the dog. Especially praiseworthy are the canine traits of steadfast loyalty and constant companionship. How ironic that none of the bible's

40 references to dogs are positive. Dogs are typically viewed with disgust and are often described as scavengers. For example, Jezebel's corpse was eaten by dogs, with the exception of her skull, feet, and hands. Dog is also a derogatory label for homosexuals. Jesus referred to those he disrespected as dogs, as well as calling them swine and vipers.

Meat Industry

The statement's authors present a vigorous defense of the God-given human right to kill animals for food. This carnivorous plea occurs on seven different pages of the 10-page document. Particularly noteworthy are the assertions that eating meat is affirmed in the New Testament, that the bible does not mandate a vegetarian or vegan diet, and that God provided animals as food for humans beginning with Noah and continuing with Jesus and Paul, since it is alleged both ate meat. The writers are diligent lobbyists for the meat industry and they clearly reject any modern doctrine of "animal rights."

The Humane Society Legislative Fund periodically evaluates all 535 US senators and representatives on their support for animal welfare issues, such as animal cruelty, horse slaughter, endangered species, cosmetics testing and wildlife trafficking. Conservative politicians typically receive low scores on a scale of zero to 100. Prominent conservatives with scores of zero have included: Ted Cruz, Louie Gohmert, Trey Gowdy, Charles Grassley, Steve King, Rand Paul, Marco Rubio, and Jeff Sessions. For these lawmakers, their zero scores are seemingly a badge of honor, reflecting complete disdain for the welfare of animals.

Conclusion

The "Evangelical Statement on Responsible Animal Care" asserts that God commands humans to show respect and compassion for animals, including the praiseworthy condemnation of animal cruelty and the exhortation to work for the protection and preservation of all of God's animals.

Unfortunately, God's extensive and abhorrent abuse of animals for his own selfish purposes is entirely inconsistent with the statement's call for respect and compassion for animals. Specifically, God's horrific obsession with animal sacrifice thoroughly contradicts the statement's condemnation of wanton cruelty to animals. This is most certainly why the authors disregarded this gruesome content.

It is exceedingly difficult for readers to have any confidence in the statement's conclusions because they do not accurately reflect God's character and behavior as recorded in the bible. Much of the content of scripture is unacceptable to most Christians and virtually all Americans. Of course, the vast majority don't know how terrible it really is—for the simple reason that few people read the bible.

Top Ten Biblical Animal Sacrifices

- 252 bulls, oxen, goats, lambs, rams (Numbers 7:84–88).
- 294 bulls, rams (Numbers 23:1–30).
- 712 bulls, rams, lambs, goats (Ezra 6:16–18).
- 1,000 animals (I Kings 3:3–4)
- 3,000 bulls, rams, lambs (1 Chronicles 29:21).
- 3,970 sheep, goats, bulls, rams, lambs (2 Chronicles 29:32–33).
- 7,700 sheep, goats, oxen (2 Chronicles 15:10–11).
- 19,000 sheep, goats, bulls (2 Chronicles 30:23–24).
- 41,400 sheep, goats, bulls, oxen (2 Chronicles 35:7–14).
- 142,000 sheep, goats, oxen (1 Kings 8:62–63; 2 Chronicles 7:5).
- Sheep and cattle could not be counted (1 Kings 8:5; 2 Chronicles 5:6).

For additional analyses see "Animal Welfare: A Quantitative Study of Fundamentalist Biblical Dishonesty," Free Inquiry, April/May 2020 (pp. 44–49).

TWELVE

God is a Slave Owner's Best Friend

Among the Confederate monument controversies that have made national news over the past few years is one in Williamson County, Texas. I live in the county seat of Georgetown, where the majority of residents hold conservative religious, political, and social views. One expression of their respect for tradition is the twenty-foot Confederate soldier statue in front of the courthouse. Nearby are a half-dozen additional statues and historical markers recognizing prominent figures. Three years ago, a liberal religious advocacy group called Courageous Conversations began a controversial campaign to add a small marker to acknowledge African Americans' role in the Confederacy.

Like almost everywhere else, the issue at the center of this local controversy is whether the statue insults black citizens by honoring the institution of slavery. Some assert that the Civil War was really about states' rights or northern aggression, but the 1861 Texas Ordinance of Secession is clear:

"We hold as undeniable truths that the governments of the states and the confederacy were established exclusively by the white race for themselves and their posterity, and the African race was rightfully held and regarded as an inferior race, and in that condition only could their existence be beneficial or tolerable."

Because the 1861 Constitution of Confederate States of America called on the "favor and guidance of Almighty God," it is entirely appropriate to ask if the God of Judeo-Christian scripture sanctions the institution of chattel slavery.

A Brief History of Slavery

The origins of slavery date back to the ancient tribes of our early ancestors who, after fighting and killing each other for many millennia, came to the realization that it would be more advantageous for the conquerors to enslave rather than kill their adversaries. The economic benefits of a system of forced labor in which one person owns another person became immediately apparent, and the concept was quickly extended to the acquisition of personal servants. For this reason, the institution of slavery is found among both primitive and advanced peoples.

Slavery was common and accepted in classical Greek and Roman civilizations. In Athens, about 50 percent of its half-million inhabitants were slaves who were essential laborers in the heralded democracy. Prominent citizens like Plato and Aristotle owned household slaves.

The early Christian church tolerated slavery mainly because it was an unavoidable economic necessity. The first influential Christian to condemn slavery was Bishop Gregory of Nyssa in the fourth century C.E. Although he argued that slavery is morally wrong, he did not unambiguously advocate abolition of the practice.

Following the colonization of the Americas and the opportunity to extract the wealth from the land, Africa became an unwilling labor pool from which millions of people were captured and transported to the new colonies. In the seventeenth and eighteenth centuries, England maintained a monopoly on the slave trade due to its dominance of the seas.

The first cargo of slaves arrived at Jamestown, Virginia, in 1619, coincidentally the same year that a democratic government was instituted in the colony. Although they acknowledged the injustice, several eminent US founders, including George Washington and Thomas Jefferson, owned slaves, as did most wealthy landowners, to carry out the extensive labor required on plantations. By 1850, out of a total population of nine million people in the South, about three million were slaves, most of whom worked on just a few thousand large plantations where cotton was a major crop.

The movement to abolish slavery began in the seventeenth century, and the practice was outlawed in the British Empire in 1833. The abolitionist movement in the United States gathered steam in the 1820s, demanding immediate freedom for slaves. Scripture unequivocally sanctions slavery. In fact, many Southerners argued that abolitionists were defying God's will by opposing slavery.

President Abraham Lincoln issued the Emancipation Proclamation on January 1, 1863, freeing all slaves in the Southern states. In December 1865, slavery was abolished by the ratification of the US Constitution's Thirteenth Amendment, followed by the Fourteenth and Fifteenth Amendments, which granted former slaves full citizenship and (if they were male) the right to vote.

There can be no doubt that slavery was an accepted societal institution throughout history up to the early nineteenth century. Only then did Western nations become sensitive to the moral questions raised by the ownership of humans as acquired property by other people.

Slavery in the Bible

Ethical concerns about slavery were not a consideration for the compilers of the Hebrew Testament, which contains more than eight hundred references to slaves and servants (these two terms are used interchangeably throughout scripture). The Genesis stories about Abram, Hagar, Jacob, and Joseph established the framework for the biblical view of slavery. Additional verses in other Pentateuch books outline the rules that govern the relationship between master and servant. These are exemplified in the sagas about David and Solomon and their slave laborers in the Histories. It is undeniable that scripture teaches that servants are the property of their owners.

The much shorter New Testament includes about 150 references to slaves and servants.

Obviously, it would not be feasible to review every mention here. It's also not necessary because there is never any condemnation of the institution of slavery, and Christians today are primarily concerned with the declarations about slavery issued by Jesus, Paul, and Peter. Therefore, only a few major slavery episodes in the Old Testament are cited.

God's mythical rescue of the ancient Israelites from enslavement in Egypt is the foundational event in early Hebrew history, creating the basis for the covenant between God and his chosen people. The Exodus story concludes with the delivery of the Ten Commandments by Moses at Mount Sinai, along with detailed guidelines to instruct the Israelites, who were once slaves themselves, on how to be masters to their own slaves (see the Ten Commandments for Slave Masters at the end of this chapter). With this unequivocal background, there can be no doubt that God the Father approved of the institution of slavery, and his son and spokesmen continued the tradition.

Jesus's approval of slavery is readily apparent in his inclusion of servants and their masters in eight of his parables (see also at the end of this chapter). Because he never criticized nor condemned slavery, and he did not forbid people from owning slaves, he tacitly endorsed the practice. In one of these parables, he explicitly authorized the cruel master-slave relationship when he recommended whipping disobedient slaves:

> The servant who knows the master's will and does not get ready or does not do what the master wants will be beaten with many blows. But the one who does not know and does things deserving punishment will be beaten with few blows. From everyone who has been given much, much will be demanded; and from the one who has been entrusted with much, much more will be asked (Luke 12:47–48).

Five of the eight slave parables are notable for their extreme violence through murder, killing, or maiming, with phraseology including:

- delivered him to the torturers
- cut him in two, grind him to powder
- cast him into outer darkness
- weeping and gnashing of teeth
- beaten with many stripes, and
- slay them before me.

Interspersed with this very disturbing language are several standard expressions of Christian imagery:

- kingdom of heaven
- my heavenly Father
- kingdom of God, and
- beloved son.

The central figure of the master or the son is Jesus himself, and the consistent theme in these five violent stories is that those who disobey Jesus or reject him as Messiah will be punished with unending torture in hell.

This is the dark side of Jesus, the "Prince of Peace," who condemned interpersonal violence, even in self-defense, while granting authority to slave owners to discipline their slaves. This is the divine mandate used to justify the beatings of black slaves in Southern states. Jesus also endorsed the rules in the book of Exodus for slave owners, and two of his miracles involved slaves: the healing of the centurion's slave (Luke 7:1–10) and the restoration of the slaveboy Malchus's ear (Luke 22:50–51 and John 18:10).

In the Epistles, Paul decreed that slaves should obey their masters with respect and fear in everything, just as they would obey Jesus. And for their obedience, they will be rewarded in the next life:

> Slaves, obey your earthly masters with respect and fear, and with sincerity of heart, just as you would obey Christ. Obey them not only to win their favor when their eye is on you, but as slaves of Christ, doing the will of God from your heart. Serve wholeheartedly, as if you were serving the Lord, not people, because you know that the Lord will reward each one for whatever good they do, whether they are slave or free. And masters, treat your slaves in the same way. Do not threaten them, since you know that he who is both their Master and yours is in heaven, and there is no favoritism with him (Ephesians 6:5–9).

> Slaves, obey your earthly masters in everything; and do it, not only when their eye is on you and to curry their favor, but with sincerity of heart and reverence for the Lord. Whatever you do, work at it with all your heart, as working for the Lord, not

> for human masters, since you know that you will receive an inheritance from the Lord as a reward. It is the Lord Christ you are serving. Anyone who does wrong will be repaid for their wrongs, and there is no favoritism (Colossians 3:22–25).

> All who are under the yoke of slavery should consider their masters worthy of full respect, so that God's name and our teaching may not be slandered. Those who have believing masters should not show them disrespect just because they are fellow believers. Instead, they should serve them even better because their masters are dear to them as fellow believers and are devoted to the welfare of their slaves. These are the things you are to teach and insist on. If anyone teaches otherwise and does not agree to the sound instruction of our Lord Jesus Christ and to godly teaching, they are conceited and understand nothing (1 Timothy 6:1–4).

> Teach slaves to be subject to their masters in everything, to try to please them, not to talk back to them, and not to steal from them, but to show that they can be fully trusted, so that in every way they will make the teaching about God our Savior attractive (Titus 2:9–10).

The apostle Peter emphasized that slaves are obligated by Christian faith and fear of God to submit to their owners, no matter how brutal. He said that it is commendable when slaves endure unjust suffering that is willed by God:

> Slaves, in reverent fear of God submit yourselves to your masters, not only to those who are good and considerate, but also to those who are harsh. For it is commendable if someone bears up under the pain of unjust suffering because they are conscious of God. But how is it to your credit if you receive a beating for doing wrong and endure it? But if you suffer for doing good and you endure it, this is commendable before God. To this you were called, because Christ suffered for you, leaving you an example, that you should follow in his steps (1 Peter 2:18–21).

The bible's three leading Christian figures testify in unequivocal language to the legitimacy of the institution of slavery, yet Christians today abhor the concept as much as anyone. There is no better example of selective disregard of scriptural mandates.

From the founding of the nation in the 1770s to the beginning of the Civil War, the issue of slavery fractured Protestant denominations, including Baptists, Methodists, Presbyterians, and Episcopalians. John Wesley called American slavery "the vilest that ever saw the sun."

It should not be surprising, then, that Christian clergy in the South at the time that abolition was gaining strength found justification for slavery in scripture. For example, in 1845, a South Carolina preacher named Richard Fuller declared, "God sanctioned slavery in the bible, and therefore it cannot be wrong." It should also be noted that surveys indicate that most Americans today believe that slavery was the worst moral evil to ever afflict American society.

Implications

What does this definitive scriptural documentation mean for humanists, civil libertarians, and social progressives who view Civil War monuments as tributes to an embarrassing and shameful aspect of American history? What are the implications of biblical truth for activists who generally reject all forms of religious mythology?

First, the irrefutable conclusion that emerges from this focused review is that the God of Judeo-Christian scripture sanctioned slavery as an honorable human relationship. He is the slave owner's best friend, and his perfect word, the Holy Bible, is the slave owner's instruction manual and rule book. Furthermore, God's designated spokesmen—Moses, Jesus, Paul, and Peter—amplified and extended his pro-slavery mandate for the Judeo-Christian community.

Second, it should be made perfectly clear that Confederate statues and historical markers are primarily symbols of slavery. Although some defenders of Confederate honor deny that this was the major issue, others argue that their ancestors sincerely believed that slavery was a God-ordained practice. Both the ancestors and descendants are, in fact, correct. The bible that condoned slavery back then is the same bible used today.

Third, we should channel our energy to correcting the present-day inequalities, oppression, and unfairness that minorities of *all* races, ethnicities, and orientations experience in America.

After Courageous Conversations' effort of three years to add a small marker to Georgetown's Confederate soldier statue, the conservative county commissioners summarily voted down the proposal on November 14, 2017.

This chapter is dedicated to the memory of the late bible scholar A.J. Mattill Jr., who called the bible "the slave owner's best friend."

The Ten Commandments for Slave Owners

from Exodus 21:2–32 (with specific verses in parentheses)

1. If you buy a Hebrew slave, he is to serve you for six years. But in the seventh year, he shall go free, without paying anything (2).
2. If he is bought alone, he is to go free alone. But if he has a wife when he's bought, she is to go with him (3).
3. If his master gives him a wife and she bears him sons or daughters, the woman and her children shall belong to her master, and only the man shall go free (4).
4. But if the servant declares, "I love my master and my wife and children and do not want to go free" then his master must take him before the judges. He shall take him to the door or the doorpost and pierce his ear with an awl. Then he will be his servant for life (5–6).
5. If a man sells his daughter as a slave, she is not to go free as male slaves do. If she does not please the master who has selected her for himself, he must let her be redeemed. He has no right to sell her to foreigners, because he has broken faith with her (7–8).
6. If he selects her to be his son's wife, he must grant her the rights of a daughter (9).
7. If the son takes on another wife, he must not deprive the first one of her food, clothing, or marital rights. If he does not provide her with these three things, she is to go free, without any payment of money (10–11).

8. Anyone who beats their male or female slave with a rod must be punished if the slave dies as a direct result, but they are not to be punished if the slave recovers after a day or two, since the slave is their property (20–21).
9. A slave who goes blind in one eye from being punched by their master is to be freed as compensation for the eye. The same goes for an owner who knocks out a tooth, and this applies to male and female slaves (26–27).
10. If a slave (male or female) is gored by a bull, the bull's owner must pay the slave's owner thirty shekels, and the bull must be stoned to death (32).

Jesus's Eight Slave Parables

1. Unmerciful Servant

Matthew 18:23–35
Those who do not forgive others will not be forgiven by God and will be tortured forever.

2. Wicked Tenants

Matthew 21:33–46, Mark 12:1–12, Luke 20:9–19
Those who do not recognize Jesus as Messiah will not enter eternal life.

3. Wedding Banquet

Matthew 22:2–14
Those who reject God's generous offer of salvation through his son will be thrown into hell.

4. Unfaithful Servant

Matthew 24:45–51, Luke 12:42–48
Those who are not prepared to receive the kingdom of God will be sent to hell.

5. Talents/Minas

Matthew 25:14–30, Luke 19:11–27
Those who do not use God's bountiful resources productively will endure everlasting suffering.

6. Watchful Servants
Mark 13:32–37, Luke 12:35–40
Be ready for Jesus's return, because only God knows when he is coming.

7. Great Banquet
Luke 14:15–24
Those who are too busy to accept God's invitation will not enter the kingdom of Heaven.

8. Master and His Servant
Luke 17:7–10
Don't expect to be rewarded for only doing what is required of you.

III. The Murderous Biblical God

THIRTEEN

Is Yahweh a Loving God? The Pentateuch

The assertion that the bible is the most-often purchased and least-read book in America has been well documented. Christian bookstores sell scores of translations, editions, and versions of the alleged Good Book, along with an endless line of study materials. Copies are typically given to young people at milestone life events and distributed widely by organizations such as the Gideons. It is doubtful that these volumes receive much use.

Almost all Christians believe that the bible is the divinely inspired word of God. The fundamentalist Protestant denominations subscribe to the dogma of scriptural inerrancy, i.e., that the bible is absolutely accurate in every statement. The larger segment of the Christian community—Catholics and mainline Protestants—does not accept the proposition that the bible is literally true but instead depends on skillful interpretation by experts to identify the essential core of biblical truth.

Of course, both perspectives are demonstrably wrong. Many biblical claims, such as a worldwide flood and the restoration of life to corpses, cannot be literally true. On the other hand, those who insist on interpreting God's word are contradicting the basic premise of their theology, i.e., God is an omnipotent being. If God is the perfect authority, then his word must be perfectly true and therefore does not require or permit interpretation.

Moreover, it is not possible to address through rational analysis the assertion that the bible (or any other sacred text or "holy" book) is God's word, because the answer ultimately comes down to the issue of faith. However, it is entirely reasonable to address more directly answerable questions such as: Is the bible a good book? Is the bible a compendium of useful advice for successful living? Is the god portrayed in the bible a benevolent deity?

While the answers to these and similar questions involve subjective judgment and personal opinion, they can be based at least in part on a careful analysis of the content of the book. This chapter documents three conclusions about the god of the Hebrew Bible known as Yahweh:

1. The dominant and unifying theme in the bible, both Hebrew and Christian Testaments, is *punishment for disobedience.*
2. The greatest sin in the Hebrew Testament is *worshipping other gods,* which means worshipping or sacrificing to gods other than Yahweh.
3. The preferred mode of punishment for those who disobey Yahweh's commandments, especially worshipping other gods, is *killing the violators.*

While punishment for disobedience is the central moral principle in both major divisions of Scripture, there is an important distinction between the types of punishment that are either administered or promised. Yahweh the father administers or threatens to inflict his terrible punishments on his chosen people and their enemies *during their lifetimes.* In contrast, Jesus the son promises an even more horrific punishment for those who disobey his commandments: torture forever in the imagined afterlife.

Because Yahweh's chief attribute is omnipotence, he is by definition the *universal cause* of everything. He is the architect of history. All occurrences are the product of his master plan for humankind. All punishments, regardless of agent or instrument of application, e.g., foreign enemies, disease, famine, hailstorm, and wild animals, are the direct result of Yahweh's jealousy and anger and an expression of his divine will. All events are preordained by Yahweh and therefore are properly called "acts of God."

The Greatest Sin: Worshipping Other Gods

In Yahweh's egocentric theological scheme, the worst sin that his chosen people can commit is to worship other gods or idols, which includes sacrificing animals or children to heathen gods or idols, worshipping the sun, moon, or stars, and consulting fortunetellers, sorcerers, astrologers, witches or magicians. These interrelated offenses constitute rebellion against Yahweh and result in severe punishment.

The prohibition against worshipping other gods or idols is first propounded in Exodus 20 and repeated 332 times throughout much of the Hebrew Testament. Subsidiary aspects of the generic sin of worshipping other gods or idols co-occur with the following frequencies: sacrificing animals or children (thirty-nine); worshipping the sun, moon, or stars (ten); and consulting mediums, sorcerers, or astrologers (twenty-one).

Condemnation of various expressions of the transgressions that constitute worshipping other gods occurs 332 times in 176 chapters of twenty-four Hebrew books. The distribution of chapters that mention these violations by categories is Pentateuch (twenty-seven), Histories (forty-five), Wisdom (zero), Major Prophets (seventy-nine), and Minor Prophets (twenty-five). These figures serve to document Yahweh's obsessive jealousy directed at competing gods, idols, rituals, and occult practitioners (referred to hereafter as "worshipping other gods").

It is especially noteworthy that the writers of fifteen books of the Hebrew Testament do not even mention this prominent feature of Yahweh's personality, which is his uncompromising requirement of absolute loyalty and exclusive devotion. Specification of this worst sin is disproportionately concentrated in three major prophets, Deuteronomy, four histories, and one minor prophet. While other violations are occasionally discussed, such as murder, adultery, usury, and blasphemy, Yahweh's overwhelming concern is with his self-proclaimed status as the only god worthy of worship. As he often stated, he is a very jealous god (e.g., Exodus 20:5), and his never-ending punishment of the chosen people and their enemies for this ubiquitous violation confirms this characterization of himself.

Yahweh's favored punishment for those who violate his prohibition against worshipping other gods is the death penalty. This is communicated through explicit decree (Pentateuch), murderous action (Histories), or threatened elimination (Prophets) more than eighty times. When Yahweh did not kill those who violated his First Commandment, he severely punished his people by allowing them to be conquered and enslaved by their enemies, thus destroying their communities.

What is truly remarkable is how the data document the degree to which Hebrew Testament events reflect Yahweh's single-minded obsession with one type of misbehavior. Violations of the prohibition against worshipping other gods provoke Yahweh's fury, anger, and rage directed at miscreants. Because Yahweh's severe punishments are inflicted tirelessly on his incorrigible children, it can be reasonably concluded that Hebrew history developed to a great extent around violations of the commandment *Thou Shalt Have No Other Gods Before Me.*

Yahweh's Severe Punishments

The bible states with monotonous regularity that the sin of disobeying Yahweh's directives, especially worshipping other gods and idols, makes Yahweh extremely angry with his chosen people and causes him to punish them by having their enemies invade, conquer, and destroy them. Those not killed are either reduced to poverty or enslaved in foreign countries, often for several generations. But when the Israelites behave as Yahweh demands, he rewards them by allowing them to annihilate their enemies.

This chapter and the next present an organized catalogue and analysis of the massacres, slaughters, and killings that Yahweh administered to his people and their enemies in the Pentateuch and Histories.

An issue that required an early decision was placement of the Conquest of Canaan. This major biblical event was located with the Pentateuch stories because the Conquest actually began with Moses's military victories in the Transjordan, when he captured the territories of Sihon and Og (see Numbers 21, 31, 33 and Deuteronomy 2, 3, 7, 20). Furthermore, this rearrangement is consistent with the Hexateuchal narrative, which articulates the concept of Israel as the people chosen to live in the Promised Land.

To illustrate Yahweh's unmitigated propensity for murderous violence when administering punishment to his disobedient children or their enemies, the top twelve episodes within each of six categories of punishment were selected for presentation in capsule summaries. These selected events emphasize the ruthless, unforgiving, bloodthirsty nature of Yahweh's personality, and this is why few of the seventy-two gruesome stories appear in Sunday school curricula for children.

Massacres in the Pentateuch and Joshua

For the inventory of massacres, slaughters, and murders in the Pentateuch and Joshua, a total of eighteen events were identified. Most of these events were caused by Yahweh's direct intervention, not by enemies or individuals under his influence.

- Yahweh destroyed by drowning all life on Earth, except Noah, his family, and the ark full of animals (Genesis 6–8). This horrific annihilation of almost all living people, including men, women, babies, infants, and mothers-to-be and their unborn children, was carried out as punishment for human wickedness and depravity, including human women crossbreeding with evil spirit beings, which produced mutant offspring called "Nephilim" (giants). Yahweh's preoccupation with giants continues with a dozen references in four subsequent books.
- Yahweh engineered the Conquest of Canaan (and the Transjordan), which involved the eradication of all inhabitants of the cities ruled by thirty-three kings and the soldiers in the combined armies of seventeen kings, an undertaking that required many years to complete (Numbers 21, 31, 33; Deuteronomy 2, 3, 7, 20; Joshua 6, 8, 10, 11, 12). The total number of military and civilian casualties may be estimated to be between fourteen and twenty million at a minimum, based on Deuteronomy 7:1–2. This monumental massacre fulfilled Yahweh's promise to Abraham.
- Yahweh destroyed Sodom and Gomorrah and nearby cities and villages (except Zoar) because the people were utterly evil. All living

things, including people, plants, and animals (except Lot and his daughters), were incinerated with fire and flaming tar from heaven. As many as nine godly residents of Sodom may have been "collateral damage" (Genesis 18, 19).

- Yahweh decreed that Achan and his family be stoned to death and their bodies burned with all their personal possessions because Achan kept some loot from the slaughter of Jericho. This episode again illustrates Yahweh's proclivity for collective punishment (Joshua 7:13–26).
- Yahweh rewarded Phinehas by making him and his descendants priests forever (the Phinehas priesthood) after he thrust a spear through an Israelite man (Zimri) and a Midianite girl (Cozbi) who were copulating in his tent, thereby stopping a plague that had already killed 24,000 people (Numbers 25:1–18).
- Yahweh drowned 600 of Pharaoh's charioteers and their horses so that he could achieve great honor and glory; the Egyptians washed up dead on the seashore (Exodus 14:21–31).
- Yahweh commanded the Levites to kill about 3,000 of their sons, brothers, friends, and neighbors because they were fornicating and were worshipping an idol: Aaron's golden calf (Exodus 32:27–29).
- Yahweh killed Nadab and Abihu by burning them alive because they placed "unholy fire" in their censors (Leviticus 10:1–7).
- Yahweh commanded the people to stone to death an Israelite man who was caught gathering firewood on the Sabbath day (Numbers 15:32–36).
- Yahweh killed many of his complaining people with venomous snakebites (Numbers 21:6).
- Yahweh caused the Earth to open up and swallow three rebellious men and their families. Then he burned up 250 men who were offering incense (Numbers 16:31–35).
- Yahweh sent plagues that killed 14,700 people because unauthorized individuals burned incense (Numbers 16:48–50) and killed 24,000 Israelites for worshipping Baal (Numbers 25:9).

Other episodes involving punishment in this section that are not described in capsule summaries occur in: Genesis 34: 24–29; Exodus 9:12–26, 12:29–30; Leviticus 24:10–23; and Numbers 11:33–34. It should be noted that the Yahwehean slaughters recounted in Numbers 31 and Deuteronomy 2 and 3 were subsumed in the conquest of Canaan.

The eighteen massacres, slaughters, and murders summarized or listed above established the foundation for Yahweh's horrific theology of punishment. Integral to his strategy is the practice of collective punishment, in which innocent children and families are killed along with the guilty parties, who are typically described as evil, wicked, and depraved. Is this godly justice?

FOURTEEN

Is Yahweh a Loving God? The Histories

The basic requirement that defines a violent punishing event here is that human death must be the result; affliction with leprosy for life (2 Kings 15:4–5) or banishment or enslavement did not qualify for inclusion. Legendary exploits are not included, e.g., Jashobeam killing 300 men with his spear (1 Chronicles 11:11). And when Yahweh or one of his agents ordered or commanded that a killing take place, it is assumed that the murder actually occurred, such as David ordering Rechab and Baanah killed (2 Samuel 4:12) or Yahweh promising to destroy Ahab's descendants after his death (1 Kings 21:29). Episodes that are repeated in successive books are included only once, e.g., numerous events in 1 Chronicles are reported earlier in 2 Samuel 6, 8, 10, 21, 24, and 31, such as the well-known murder of Uzzah by an angry Yahweh and Saul's grisly death. Applying these criteria resulted in a total of 134 punishing episodes.

When all types of punishing events, including monumental massacres, smaller slaughters, and various killings, are considered together, the History books are ranked as follows in descending order: Judges (thirty),

2 Kings (twenty-eight), 2 Samuel (twenty-two), 1 Samuel (eighteen), 2 Chronicles (fifteen), 1 Kings (thirteen), 1 Chronicles (five), and Esther (three). The books of Ruth, Ezra, and Nehemiah record no capital punishments. The substantial variation in severe punishments inflicted by Yahweh across the eleven History books indicates that the Yahwehean temperament is conceptualized very differently by the various writers/compilers of the Hebrew Histories.

A preliminary review of the 134 qualifying events representing Yahweh's murderous rampages and senseless killings reveals that there's a meaningful typology with relatively clear boundaries. First, there are the truly monumental massacres. Within this classification, there are those for which numerical body counts are given (between 3,000 and one million) versus those characterized by general descriptions of the scope of destruction, typically stating that "all persons were killed." Second, within the classification of smaller slaughters and killings there are those for which Yahweh takes personal credit versus those that are attributed to his agents. Finally, of those atrocities committed by Yahweh's agents there are the gory murders of individuals versus slaughters of groups ranging in size from just two people to 1,000 victims.

The results can be broken down into five categories:

1. Monumental massacres with body counts
2. Monumental massacres with general descriptions
3. Smaller slaughters and killings by Yahweh
4. Smaller slaughters by Yahweh's agents
5. Murders by Yahweh's agents

It must be emphasized that *all* the horrific massacres, slaughters, and killings are authorized and carried out under the celestial dictatorship of Almighty Yahweh. It cannot be otherwise, because everything that ever happens is an integral and necessary component of omnipotent Yahweh's perfect master plan for humankind.

Of the twenty-three massacres with body counts given, twenty involved military personnel only, while three probably included some civilians. In contrast, only two of the twenty-six massacres without body counts were military battles; the rest involved civilian populations. Most of the body counts are exaggerated estimates, which is obvious from the impossibly large round numbers. Also, the implements of warfare available at the time would not have enabled the magnitude of human killing reported. Lastly, in the three categories of smaller slaughters and killings all but four of the eighty-five punishing episodes involved civilian victims.

Although it can be reasonably assumed that casualties in military battles were adult men, it is equally obvious that the massacres and slaughters of civilian populations included substantial numbers of children, babies, and pregnant women. Sometimes the victims are specifically identified, but when all people were killed or the entire population was wiped out, the murder of innocent babies, infants, and "unborn children" was guaranteed. The scores of diabolical massacres and slaughters carried out under the malevolent authority of Yahweh demonstrate that claims by antiabortion zealots that "God loves children" and "God loves the unborn" are simply false. The evidence shows that Yahweh does not love either unborn or living children. His supreme obsession is with punishing his chosen people for disobeying him.

The final five sections of this presentation consist of capsule summaries of the Top Twelve punishing events in each category followed by listings of the episodes not summarized.

The first of the five compilations organizes the massacres in descending order of numbers of victims. The other four lists place the massacres, slaughters, and killings in chronological order from the books. It is important to stress that these are just capsule summaries; to fully appreciate the ghastly horror of the episodes, it is necessary to read the entire stories.

1. Monumental Massacres with Body Counts

- One million troops of General Zerah's Ethiopian army were wiped out by King Asa's Judean army—not one man remained alive (2 Chronicles 14:8–15).
- 500,000 elite troops of Israel were slaughtered in one day by King Abijah's army (2 Chronicles 13:15–17).
- 185,000 Assyrian troops were killed by the angel of the Lord and their dead bodies littered the landscape the next morning (2 Kings 19:35).

- 127,000 Syrian infantrymen were killed by the Israelites on the first day or died the next day when a wall fell on them (1 Kings 20:29–30).
- 120,000 soldiers of King Ahaz's army were killed in a single day by King Pekah's troops (2 Chronicles 28:5–8).
- 120,000 troops of the allied armies of Midian, Amalek, and other eastern nations were killed by Gideon's small army (Judges 8:10).
- 75,810 enemies (Gentiles) of the Jews were slaughtered throughout King Ahasuerus's provinces (Esther 9:5–19).
- 70,000 Israelite men were killed by a plague sent by the Lord (2 Samuel 24:15).
- 42,000 people of Ephraim were killed by Jephthah's troops (Judges 12:6).
- 40,700 Syrian charioteers and cavalrymen, including General Shobach, were killed by David's army (2 Samuel 10:18).
- 40,000 Israelite soldiers were slaughtered on two consecutive days by the Benjaminites (Judges 20:21, 25).
- 30,000 Israelite soldiers were killed by the Philistine army (1 Samuel 4:10).

Punishing episodes in this section that are not described in capsule summaries above are: Judges 20:35–39; 2 Samuel 8:5; 2 Chronicles 25:11–12; 2 Samuel 8:13, 18:6–8; Judges 1:4–6, 3:29; 2 Kings 14:7; 1 Samuel 4:2; Judges 16:25–30; 2 Chronicles 25:13.

2. Monumental Massacres with General Descriptions

- The entire population of Bethel was slaughtered (Judges 1:25).
- Gideon killed the entire male population of Penuel (Judges 8:17).
- Jephthah slaughtered Ammonites in twenty cities (Judges 11:2–23).
- The Israelite army slaughtered the entire tribe of Benjamin—men, women, and children (Judges 20:48).
- David and his men attacked the Geshurites, Girzites, and Amalekites, killing every person in the villages (1 Samuel 27:8–9).

- Saul had all the mediums and fortunetellers executed (1 Samuel 28:9).
- The Philistines slaughtered the Israelites on Mount Gilboa, including Saul and his three sons (1 Samuel 31:1–6).
- Jehu killed all Ahab's family and friends (2 Kings 10:11).
- King Menahem killed the entire population of Tiphsah (Tappuah) and the surrounding area and ripped open the pregnant women (2 Kings 15:16).
- King Manasseh murdered great numbers of innocent people—Jerusalem was filled with the bodies of his victims (2 Kings 21:16).
- The Reubenites killed a great number of Hagrites in battle and took 100,000 captives (1 Chronicles 5:18–22).
- The Syrian army killed all the leaders of Judah as punishment for forsaking the Lord (2 Chronicles 24:23–24).

Punishing episodes in this section that are not described in capsule summaries above are: Judges 1:17, 19, 4:16, 23–24, 9:45, 18:27, 21:10–14; 1 Samuel 11:11, 14:31, 23:5, 30:17; 1 Kings 15:29, 16:11, 20:21.

3. Smaller Slaughters and Killings by Yahweh

- Yahweh killed seventy men of Beth-Shemesh because they looked in the Ark (1 Samuel 6:19).
- Yahweh commanded Saul to destroy the entire Amalek nation completely—men, women, children, and babies—and he did so (1 Samuel 15:1–8).
- Yahweh killed Uzzah because he touched the Ark, breaking the taboo against handling sacred objects (2 Samuel 6:3–8).
- Yahweh killed David's baby for David's sin (2 Samuel 12:15–18).
- Yahweh sent two female bears that mauled forty-two children who had mocked Elisha because of his bald head (2 Kings 2:23–24).
- Yahweh destroyed his people for worshipping other gods and idols and consulting fortunetellers (2 Kings 17:19–20).
- Yahweh sent lions to kill some of the Assyrian colonists because

they did not worship him (2 Kings 17:24–25).

- Yahweh sent armies of enemies against Judah to destroy the nation because of the many sins of King Manasseh (2 Kings 24:2–4).
- Yahweh killed Saul because he was disobedient and consulted a medium (1 Chronicles 10:13–14).
- Yahweh killed Jehoram, who died with terrible suffering because he required idol worship (2 Chronicles 21:13–19).
- Yahweh promised not to destroy his people for worshipping heathen gods until *after* the death of King Josiah (2 Chronicles 34:24–33).
- Yahweh sent Nebuchadnezzar to kill his people in Jerusalem and burn down the Temple, because they worshipped heathen idols (2 Chronicles 36:14–20).

Punishing episodes in this section that are not described in capsule summaries above are: 1 Samuel 5:6, 25:35–42; 1 Kings 13:24, 21:25–29; 2 Kings 1:10–12, 16–17; 1 Chronicles 2:3, 14:11–16; 2 Chronicles 12:1–12, 20:21–26, 32:21.

4. Smaller Slaughters and Killings by Yahweh's Agents

- Gideon killed seventy-seven leaders of Succoth by scraping them to death with wild thorns and briars (Judges 8:16).
- Gideon's seventy sons (except Jotham) were slaughtered by Abimelech's henchmen (Judges 9:5).
- Samson killed 1,000 Philistines with a donkey's jawbone (Judges 15:15).
- David and his men killed 200 Philistines and presented their foreskins to King Saul (1 Samuel 18:27).
- Saul ordered Doeg the Edomite to kill eighty-five priests and their families—men, women, children, babies—and all the livestock (1 Samuel 22:18–19).
- Jeroboam's family was killed because of his idolatry (1 Kings 13:34).
- Elijah killed 450 prophets of Baal (1 Kings 18:40).

- King Ahab's seventy sons were murdered and their heads were packed in baskets and presented to Jehu (2 Kings 10:6–8).
- Athaliah killed all the children of her dead son, except for Joash who was rescued by his aunt (2 Kings 11:1–3).
- King Josiah executed the heathen priests and exterminated the mediums and wizards (2 Kings 23:20–24).
- King Zedekiah's sons were killed before him, then his eyes were put out (2 Kings 25:7).
- Two men were impaled alive for plotting to assassinate King Ahasuerus (Esther 2:21–23).

Punishing episodes in this section that are not described in capsule summaries above are: Judges 7:25, 8:21, 9:49, 14:19, 15:6–8; 1 Samuel 19:8; 2 Samuel 2:14–16, 30–31, 4:12, 8:2, 21:5–9, 15–22; 2 Kings 10:14, 24–28, 25:19–21; 2 Chronicles 21:4.

5. Murders by Yahweh's Agents

- Ehud murdered King Eglon by plunging a dagger into his belly (Judges 3:12–25).
- Jael killed General Sisera by hammering a tent peg through his head (Judges 4:17–22).
- Jephthah sacrificed his only child as a burnt offering to Yahweh because he had vowed to do it (Judges 11:29–40).
- Samuel chopped King Agag in pieces before the Lord at Gilgal (1 Samuel 15:32–33).
- David killed Goliath and cut off his head (1 Samuel 17:50–51, 57).
- Rechab and Baanah murdered King Ish-bosheth and cut off his head (2 Samuel 4:5–8).
- Joab plunged three daggers into Absalom's heart as he dangled alive from an oak tree (2 Samuel 18:14–17).
- Joab stabbed Amasa and his bowels gushed out (2 Samuel 20:8–10).
- Sheba's head was cut off and thrown to Joab (2 Samuel 20:20–22).

- Jezebel arranged for Naboth to be falsely accused of cursing Yahweh and stoned to death (1 Kings 21:8–13).
- Jezebel was killed and eaten by dogs (2 Kings 9:32–37).
- King Manasseh sacrificed one of his sons as a burnt offering on a heathen altar (2 Kings 21:6).

Punishing episodes in this section that are not described in capsule summaries above are: 2 Samuel 1:15, 2:23, 3:27, 11:14–17, 13:28–30; 1 Kings 2:9, 25, 46, 16:10; 2 Kings 3:27, 8:15, 9:24, 11:16, 14:19, 16:3, 19:36–37; 1 Chronicles 10:9–10; 2 Chronicles 24:21, 25; Esther 7:9–10.

Summary

The transcendent theme in the bible is punishment for disobedience, documented by the analysis of 152 massacres, slaughters, and killings described in the Pentateuch and Histories. The greatest sin in the Hebrew Testament is worshipping gods other than an insanely jealous Yahweh, which is specified on 332 separate occasions. Yahweh's standard punishment for those who disobey his commandments is the death penalty, which he applies indiscriminately. Based on this careful review of punishing events in seventeen bible books, it is entirely fair and reasonable to conclude that Yahweh is most certainly not a loving god.

FIFTEEN
Is Yahweh a Loving God? The Prophets

The Hebrew Testament of the Holy Bible reports the handiwork of an angry, jealous, egocentric, insecure, malevolent, murderous godly dictator known as Yahweh. The greatest sin of worshipping gods other than himself is reiterated a total of 332 times in twenty-four books and predominates in twelve of them. In the Pentateuch and Histories, 152 punishing episodes that result in death for as many as hundreds of millions of victims who violate Yahweh's rules prove that punishment for disobedience is the central organizing theme in Hebrew history.

The Hebrew Testament is a horrific collection of homicidal rampages, malicious threats, and gruesome stories. It follows, then, that the Hebrew god, Yahweh, who is the architect of human history and Jesus's father, cannot be a benevolent deity. We can compile four categories of Yahweh's condemnable behavior.

Yahweh's Abhorrent Penchant for Animal Sacrifice

Animal sacrifice is a major requirement in Yahweh's theology. He distinguishes four categories of sacrifice: sin offering, guilt offering, peace offering, and burnt offering. The animals to be sacrificed are oxen, sheep, goats, turtledoves, and pigeons. They must be free of blemishes and defects—this is repeated dozens of times and restated in summary form in Malachi 1, where Yahweh rebukes his people for offering "imperfect sacrifices."

Twenty chapters of the Hebrew Testament books, nineteen in the Pentateuch and one in Prophets, are dedicated to specifying in exacting detail how animals are to be sacrificed, i.e., how many of what kind on which days by which procedures by whom. These chapters are distributed in the following books: twelve in Leviticus, five in Numbers, two in Exodus, and one in Ezekiel. In addition to the lengthy discourses on ritual methods, three dozen brief descriptions of sacrificial episodes are reported, mostly in the History books.

The sacrificial animals are killed and their blood is sprinkled or smeared on the altar, then the carcasses are burned. While the typical ritual sacrifice involves a few dozen animals, there are some that are especially repugnant for their huge numbers alone, e.g., 22,000 oxen and 120,000 sheep and goats (1 Kings 8:62–63); 700 oxen and 7,000 sheep (2 Chronicles 15:10–11); 2,000 young bulls and 17,000 sheep (2 Chronicles 30:23–24); and 3,000 young bulls, 800 oxen, and 37,600 sheep and goats (2 Chronicles 35:7–14). It should be emphasized that Yahweh derives great pleasure and enjoyment from these barbaric sacrifices of innocent animals, a point that is repeated many times.

The first sacrifice was carried out by Noah after the Ark landed, using animals and birds designated for that purpose (Genesis 8:20). The second sacrifice involved three animals and two birds (Genesis 15:9–11). The third sacrifice was the memorable substitution of a ram for Isaac by his father, Abraham (Genesis 22:13).

Next, Yahweh established the Passover sacrifice of the lambs (Exodus 12) and outlined procedures for the ritual dedication of priests (Exodus 29). In twelve chapters of Leviticus (1–10, 14, 16) and five chapters of Numbers (15, 18, 19, 28, 29), Yahweh provides precise instructions for carrying out ritual sacrifices and dedications.

Illustrating how important animal sacrifice is to Yahweh, he stopped a plague he had started as punishment that had already killed 70,000 men only after a proper sacrifice was completed (2 Samuel 24:25). He also threatened to kill Aaron if he entered the Holy Place without proper preparation involving an elaborate animal sacrifice (Leviticus 16:1–34). Disgusting animal cruelty was also portrayed in the intentional crippling of horses (Joshua 11:1–12), Samson's abuse of 300 foxes (Judges 15:4–5), and Balaam's beating of his donkey (Numbers 22:21–34).

What can be concluded about Yahweh's personality from this brief summary? Of course, there is no rational explanation for his insatiable appetite for the blood sacrifice of innocent animals. But Yahweh displayed the same brutal attitude toward humans, killing millions of his chosen people and their enemies, not to mention the blood sacrifice of his only son (John 3:16), who is often referred to as the "Lamb of God" (e.g., John 1:29). It should be noted that Jesus also endorsed animal and human sacrifice (e.g., Matthew 5:23–24, Mark 10:45, and Luke 5:12–14).

Yahweh's Threatened Future Punishment: The Prophets

The focus of the Hebrew prophets is on elaborating the punishment that Yahweh's recalcitrant and ever-disobedient chosen people will receive if they do not stop sinning. As in the Pentateuch and Histories, the intolerable violation is that of worshipping other gods or idols or consulting sorcerers and astrologers. Consistent with the concept of prophecy, the threatened punishments involving horrible suffering and death are framed in the future tense.

Yahweh was especially angry with the people of Jerusalem for their wicked sinfulness, and thus they were the foremost target of his vengeance, although traditional enemies referred to as "the nations" (or non-Israelite peoples) were also objects of his wrath. In order to document Yahweh's continuing jealous obsession with punishing his children for not worshipping him exclusively, selected verses are quoted or summarized from The Living Bible for a few of the major and minor prophets. It should be recognized that Yahweh's threatened punishments channeled through his prophets are essentially the same ones enunciated earlier in the Pentateuch, i.e., defeat by enemies, supernatural disasters, perpetual plagues, famine, parents eating their children, and dead bodies scavenged by wild animals. (See Leviticus 26 and Deuteronomy 28 for lengthy descriptions.)

Isaiah

"The day of the Lord is coming, the terrible day of his wrath and fierce anger. . . . Few will live when I have finished my work . . . the armies of Babylon that don't flee will be butchered. Their little children will be dashed to death against the pavement . . . their wives raped by the attacking hordes . . . no mercy will be shown for young people, babies, or children . . . Babylon will be as utterly destroyed as Sodom and Gomorrah" (13:9–19).

"The sword of the Lord is sated with blood and gorged with flesh . . . a mighty slaughter will occur in Edom . . . the land will be soaked with blood . . . the streams will be filled with burning pitch" (34:6–9).

Horrific punishments are described in gory detail for Babylon, Moab, Damascus, Egypt, Edom, Jerusalem, and Tyre in chapters 13 through 34.

Jeremiah

"I will wipe Jerusalem off the Earth . . . trapped residents will eat their own children . . . the slaughter will be so great that Jerusalem will be filled with dead bodies" (19:8–12).

"I will send massacre and famine and disease among them until they are destroyed from the land of Israel." (24:10)

"I will butcher you . . . I will give you to your enemies and they shall kill you . . . I will feed your dead bodies to the vultures . . . I will see to it that the cities of Judah are completely destroyed and left desolate without a living soul" (34:18–22).

"Not one of you shall live . . . not a man, woman, or child, not even the babies in arms . . . you are rousing my anger with the idols you have made and worshipped . . . causing me to destroy you completely" (44:7–8).

Yahweh's messages to the nations, including the Egyptians, Philistines, Moabites, Ammonites, Edomites, Damascus, Elam, and Babylon, are a litany of murderous destruction ("left without a living soul" is a common phrase) described in chapters 46 through 50.

Lamentations

This is a funeral song, written for the fallen city of Jerusalem and a declaration of the wrath of Yahweh. "The Lord without mercy has destroyed every home in Israel . . . you have killed them, Lord, in your anger, none escaped or remained . . . You have engulfed us in your anger, Lord, and slain us without mercy . . . tenderhearted women have cooked and eaten their own children, thus they survived the siege" (chapters 1 through 4).

Ezekiel

"Because of your terrible sins, I will punish you terribly . . . fathers will eat their own sons, and sons will eat their fathers" (5:9–10).

"You will be slaughtered all the way to the borders of Israel, and you will know that I am the Lord" (11:10).

"I will unsheath my sword and destroy your people, good and bad alike . . . I will not spare even the righteous (21:3–4).

"A sword is being sharpened and polished for terrible slaughter. . . . It is ready now to hand to the executioner . . . that sword shall slay my people and all their leaders. All alike shall die" (21:9–12).

"For their enemies will stone them and kill them with swords; they will butcher their sons and daughters and burn their homes. . . . My judgment will be a lesson against idolatry for all to see. . . . You will suffer the full penalty and you will know that I alone am God" (23:47–49).

Yahweh's threats of gruesome punishments for Israel's enemies, Ammon, Tyre, Egypt, Edom, and "enemies from the North" are detailed in chapters 25 through 39.

Hosea

"I will tear Ephraim and Judah as a lion rips apart its prey" (5:14).

"The glory of Israel flies away like a bird, for your children will die at birth, or perish in the womb, or never be conceived. And if your children grow, I will take them away from you; all are doomed" (9:11–12).

"Even mothers and children were dashed to death there. That will be your fate, too, you people of Israel, because of your great wickedness" (10:14–15).

"I alone am God, your Lord . . . You have no god but me, for there is no other Savior . . . I will come upon you like a lion, or a leopard . . . I will rip you to pieces like a bear . . . and like a lion I will devour you" (13:4–8).

"Samaria must bear her guilt, for she rebelled against her God. Her people will be killed by the invading army, her babies dashed to death against the ground, her pregnant women ripped open with a sword" (13:16). Contradicting himself, Yahweh condemned the Ammonites for ripping open the pregnant women of Gilead with their swords in Amos 1:13.

Joel and Amos

Yahweh's brutal vengeance (the day of judgment) on almost everybody, Judah and Israel and their enemies, is summarized: All will be killed.

Zephaniah

"I will destroy Judah. Mankind and all the idols that he worships will vanish. . . . I will destroy every remnant of those who worship Baal. I will destroy the idolatrous priests who bow to the sun, moon and stars" (1:3–6).

"I will gather together the kingdoms of earth, and pour out my fiercest anger and wrath upon them. All the earth shall be devoured with the fire of my jealousy" (3:8). (The earliest of Yahweh's declarations of universal jihad against all infidels was explicitly framed in Deuteronomy 13.)

Two episodes related by two other prophets give further confirmation of the portrait of Yahweh as a sadistic monster. After he had protected Daniel from being eaten by the lions, he took no action to save the innocent children of the misbehaving fathers from being torn to shreds by the same lions (Daniel 6:24). Then in a statement about the role of parents in meting out justice to their children, Yahweh declared that false prophets (who tell lies in the name of the Lord) should be executed by their own fathers and mothers (Zechariah 13:3).

Yahweh's Immoral Thoughts: The Wisdom Books

The Wisdom books do not once mention the most serious sin that can be committed against Yahweh (worshipping other gods), do not include a single massacre or slaughter carried out by Yahweh or his agents, and do not publicize Yahweh's animal sacrifice fetish. Yet, as indicated in the short summaries below, three of the five wisdom books are just as bad as other books of the Hebrew Testament, albeit for different reasons.

Job

The story of Job is another example of Yahweh's wanton cruelty. Yahweh allowed Satan to inflict terrible, undeserved suffering on Job, who is characterized by Yahweh as "the finest man on Earth." He did so because Satan challenged him to test Job's faith. After a prolonged theological discussion among three of Job's friends concerning the meaning of life and suffering, Yahweh restored Job's wealth and gave him a replacement family.

The Book of Job is traditionally regarded as an exploration of the meaning of undeserved suffering. In fact, the story of Job is a disgusting example of Yahweh's willingness to inflict pain and suffering on an innocent man with absolutely no justification—an expression of Yahweh's complete absence of humanity.

Psalms

This collection of 150 prayers or songs spans several hundred years, apparently all composed or recorded after the Babylonian exile, which dates to the sixth century BCE. The highly repetitious entreaties consist of endless whining and complaining, crying and begging, and egocentric pleas that alternately praise Yahweh for blessings and blame him for misfortune.

Nineteen of the 150 statements are called cursing or imprecatory psalms, which ask Yahweh to severely punish the enemies of the writers. The best-known of these is Psalm 109: "Let his years be few and brief. . . . May his children become fatherless and his wife a widow. May his fatherless children die. Punish his father and mother too."

Proverbs

This popular book is touted as a compendium of practical advice for successful living. In actuality, it contains more than 550 maxims in chapters 10 through 29 that are mostly truisms, tautologies, and highly redundant aphorisms. Three topics are emphasized, with all of them mentioned at least a dozen times: "trust and reverence for the Lord," dangers associated with prostitutes, and "common sense" as the key to wise decisions.

Yahweh's Unspeakably Evil Motivation

It is abundantly clear from the summaries above that the driving issue that thoroughly saturates the Hebrew Testament is Yahweh's incomprehensibly evil motivation. While this can certainly be inferred from the numerous gruesome massacres and slaughters he instigated and the punishments he threatened to carry out, his motives are described in unequivocal terms throughout the Hebrew scriptures. A few prominent examples are given here.

In the greatest slaughter for which body counts can be roughly estimated—the conquest of Canaan—we are told that Yahweh *caused* the enemy kings to fight the Hebrew invaders instead of asking for peace (Joshua 11:20). What God deserving of the label would prefer to see millions of people—including children, babies, and infants, as well as pregnant women and their "unborn children"—killed if this could be avoided? An omnipotent being such as Yahweh could have prevented this extended bloodbath, which claimed at least fourteen million lives. An omnibenevolent deity would certainly have handled the matter peaceably.

Another illustration of Yahweh's perverse motivation is detailed in the story of the Hebrew exodus from Egypt (an event preceded by Yahweh's killing of the first-born sons of every Egyptian family), which culminated in the drowning of Pharaoh's charioteers and their horses in the Red Sea. According to the account, Yahweh *caused* Pharaoh to pursue the fleeing Hebrews so that he could crush Egypt with a final major disaster, perform more miracles demonstrating his power, and convince Egypt to recognize him as Lord (Exodus 4–14).

After reviewing the misery he inflicted or threatened to inflict on the people of Israel and Judah for the sin of idol worship, Yahweh announced that he would put a desire in their hearts to worship him forever (Jeremiah 32:40). Why didn't this god of loving kindness put a desire to worship him in his people's hearts from the beginning? What purpose was served by their prolonged and thoroughly unnecessary suffering? Obviously, Yahweh derives tremendous satisfaction from inflicting pain on his disobedient children.

After ordering the annihilation of seven nations that occupied the Promised Land (Deuteronomy 7:1–2), Yahweh instructed the Israelite soldiers to kill every male in the distant cities while keeping as loot all the women, children, and personal property. But for cities within the Promised Land, insanely jealous Yahweh commanded the army to destroy every living thing and save no one, to prevent these people from luring the Israelites into idol worship (Deuteronomy 20:10–18).

In a battle in which the Philistines slaughtered the Israelite army, Saul was mortally wounded. The Philistines cut off Saul's head and nailed it to the wall of Dagon's Temple. But it was Yahweh who actually killed Saul because he was disobedient and had consulted a medium (1 Chronicles 10:1–13). Yahweh's action was ironic, considering that Saul had previously expressed his contempt for mediums and fortunetellers by ordering them executed (1 Samuel 28:9).

Here is another instance of Yahweh's apparent inability to resist Satan's provocation. Yahweh sent a plague upon Israel that killed 70,000 men (2 Samuel 24:15). Why? Because Satan made David conduct a census (1 Chronicles 21:1). Yahweh stopped the plague only after David sacrificed oxen upon an altar he built for the Lord (2 Samuel 24:25). In other words, one expression of Yahweh's cruelty was ended by satisfying another one of Yahweh's barbaric predilections.

A key to understanding Yahweh's pathological motivation is contained in his endless self-aggrandizement: "I am the greatest, I alone am God, there is no other God, I am the Lord, there is no other Savior, I am God, no one can oppose what I do" (Isaiah 43:10–13). Isaiah 44, 45, 46, and 48 boast about this further. These megalomaniacal proclamations betray an insecurity that characterizes a severely impaired character formation.

Further evidence of Yahweh's egocentric meanness is given in the following proverb: "The Lord has made everything for his purposes—even the wicked for punishment" (Proverbs 16:4). Why would an omnibenevolent deity ever create wickedness, when this is the very antithesis of godliness? The answer is that Yahweh is a bloodthirsty fiend who derives great pleasure from punishing the wicked people he created as well as the righteous (Ezekiel 21:1–5).

A final conundrum wraps up this review of Yahweh's evil motivation. In testing Abraham's obedience, Yahweh commands him to sacrifice his only son, Isaac, as a burnt offering. At the last moment Yahweh intervenes and provides a ram as a substitute for Isaac, because Abraham had already demonstrated his willingness to obey Yahweh (Genesis 22:1–13).

Why doesn't Yahweh display similar compassion for Jephthah after he had unknowingly vowed to sacrifice his only daughter as a burnt offering? Yahweh had two months to intervene before Jephthah killed his only child (Judges 11:29–40).

Summary

In twenty chapters of the Hebrew Testament, Yahweh specifies in grisly detail how animals are to be sacrificed for his great pleasure and enjoyment. The prophets explain with gruesome precision the punishments that Yahweh will impose on Jerusalem and the nations if they don't worship him exclusively. Three Wisdom books portray Yahweh as a cruel tyrant who derives immense satisfaction from his role as cosmic disciplinarian. Yahweh's incomprehensively evil motivation for inflicting pain and suffering on his chosen people and their enemies is described throughout the Hebrew Scriptures. It can be reasonably concluded that Yahweh is a sadistic monster unworthy of respect or worship by civilized people.

SIXTEEN

One Universal God—Or Many Territorial Deities

Why would a universal God tell some believers that abortion is murder (such as Southern Baptists) and others that women have the right to choose in reproductive matters (such as United Methodists)? Why would an infinite God reveal his approval of capital punishment to one church (Jehovah's Witnesses) and express his resolute opposition to another (Roman Catholics)?

These are just two examples of contradictory positions on contentious political issues existing among American religious denominations that claim to worship the same Judeo-Christian God who inspired the Holy Bible. The more general question that bedevils religious philosophers and laypersons alike is whether one almighty God unifies the multiplicity of domestic deities glorified across cultures and throughout history, or if the local gods exist independently and operate autonomously. We know that the parochial gods engage in unending competition with one another because they disagree on so many issues in the theological and political realms.

Of course, this divine dissension extends to the chief acolytes of the territorial gods, who routinely express their disdain for followers of other deities. For example, the esteemed Reverend Pat Robertson intoned, "Some say we should be nice to the Episcopalians, Presbyterians, and Methodists—I don't have to be nice to the spirit of the Antichrist." Referring to his Holiness the Pope, fundamentalist indoctrinator extraordinaire Bob Jones Jr. famously declared that he "would rather speak to the Devil himself." Obviously, these acclaimed evangelical gurus don't obey revelations from one universal God.

The Rationale for Territorial Gods

We begin with a simple question: Are the gods of the bible (Yahweh) and the Koran (Allah) the same god or different deities? Rephrased, are Yahweh and Allah just alternate names for the same god? Prominent religious leaders have stated diametrically opposing views. For example, the renowned Reverends Franklin Graham, Richard Cizik, Albert Mohler, and Ted Haggard assert that Allah is not Jehovah (Yahweh) and that Christians and Muslims do not worship the same god. In direct contradiction, the late Pope John Paul II, former President George W. Bush, Rabbi Jack Moline, and current Pope Francis claim that followers of the Abrahamic religions actually do worship the same God.

This difference of opinion may be expanded to encompass all two thousand gods that have been named and venerated throughout human history. Reiterating the question posed in the introduction: Is there one universal God that is unknowingly exalted by all religious and cultural traditions worldwide? The possibility is clearly assumed in the United States, with reference to a single ceremonial deity in the patriotic expressions "God Bless America," "In God We Trust," and "One Nation Under God."

In fact, scores if not hundreds of Christian gods are worshipped in America alone. How can this be true? The answer is straightforward: All gods are created by the theological creeds, doctrines, dogmas, and principles that are formulated by denominations, sects, cults, and churches. In addition to the endless subtle theological quibbles, ecclesiastical communities at all levels also enunciate positions on major political issues, such as abortion, capital punishment, contraception, ecumenism, evolution, gun access, marriage equality, right to die, and tax policy. Because our conception of gods entails absolute perfection, it follows logically that no deity could ever issue contradictory commands. Hence, every single theological or political distinction must establish yet one more unique god.

Would a Just God Tolerate Wanton Cruelty?

It appears that President Obama accepted the argument against a universal God. After Muslim extremists carried out a televised beheading of an American journalist, he declared, "No just god would stand for what ISIS did." He also said, "No god condones this terror." While almost everyone agrees that it was a horrific act, the then-president's response provides some insight into typically confused religious thinking.

First, Obama demonstrated by his remarks that he was not acquainted with a similar action taken by the Judeo-Christian God in whom he has professed his personal faith. According to the gospel accounts, King Herod ordered the beheading of John the Baptist, who was characterized by Herod himself as "a righteous and honest man," at the request of his wife Herodias as delivered through her daughter, exotic dancer Salome (Matthew 14:3–12; Mark 6:14–29; Luke 3:19–20, 9:7–9). Based on President Obama's assertion, should we conclude that the Judeo-Christian God is unjust? Many other episodes confirm this unflattering but accurate conclusion, for example, Achan's family, Jepthah's daughter, and Daniel's accusers' families.

Second, we should ask Obama if a just god would condone the massacre of innocent civilians in Iraq, Afghanistan, Yemen, and Somalia by American troops. Would a just god stand for the murder of Palestinian children by the Israeli army? All gods not only tolerate violence and cruelty carried out by devout believers, they encourage and approve of inhumane behavior if done in their sacred names. This is necessarily so because adherents create gods in their image and not vice versa. Moreover, the Judeo-Christian God of the Holy Bible ranks among the worst, judging by the actions of his followers throughout history.

Are There Confirmed Christian Heresies?

Each one of the hundreds of Christian denominations, sects, cults, and churches represented in the United States believes that they alone have identified "the truth" and have achieved "doctrinal purity." Fundamentalists not only know that they are absolutely correct, they have arrogated to themselves the authority to condemn all others, declaring that dissenting views constitute Christian heresies. Two targets of their judgmental propensity are summarized.

First, there is the Christian sect that reveres holy texts in addition to the bible, recognizes their human founder as the Lord's prophet, believes that God is corporeal and has a celestial wife, conducts posthumous baptisms of the dead, maintains that good works are necessary for salvation, and believes that men and women can become gods and goddesses.

Second, there is the large Christian denomination that encompasses numerous unusual practices, including veneration of angels, monasticism, confession, relic worship, use of the rosary (beads), celibacy of the priesthood, and prayers for the dead, and promulgates the doctrines of transubstantiation, baptism by desire, immaculate conception, and apostolic succession.

Fundamentalists deem these Mormon and Catholic beliefs, practices, and dogmas to be heresies because (they say) there is no scriptural justification for them. A major problem with this accusation is that the fundamentalists cannot even agree among themselves about what constitutes orthodox Christianity.

Take the Baptist denomination, which dates back almost 400 years in the United States. There are numerous divisions within the faith that reflect critical differences in theological and political emphases, for example, American, Cooperative, Free Will, Missionary, National, Northern, Orthodox, Seventh Day, and Southern. The very fact that this popular Protestant denomination cannot develop a unified Baptist theology and political perspective undermines all their criticisms of Mormonism, Catholicism, and other Christian viewpoints.

More generally the question can be posed: Why have all efforts at Christian ecumenism (or interfaith rapprochement) failed? Because all denominations, sects, and churches are absolutely convinced that they alone have identified ultimate truth in their creeds, doctrines, and practices. Obviously, they cannot all be right when they proclaim contradictory "truths." Moreover, the Jehovah's Witnesses assert that the bible condemns all Christian interfaith reconciliation.

Of course, the targets of fundamentalist bigotry contribute their share to the problem of interfaith animosity. For example, the Catholic Church issued a declaration on salvation that stated, "There exists a single church of Christ, which subsists in the Catholic Church, governed by the successor of Peter and by the bishops in communion with him." Retired Pope Benedict XVI further aggravated the situation when he asserted, "Only in the Catholic Church is there eternal salvation."

No wonder the Southern Baptist Convention discontinued ecumenical discussions with the US Catholic bishops after thirty years of meetings. It should be noted with disappointment that they still collaborate in attempting to thwart death with dignity or right-to-die legislation in states across America. In other words, they are still willing to cooperate to inflict their fears and superstitions on nonbelieving citizens.

Territorial Gods Are Also Rejected

The argument advanced in the previous sections, rejecting the claim that a universal God or ultimate first cause underlies and accounts for the thousands of territorial gods worshipped by faithful adherents, is itself contradicted by the theological postulates that define the very concept of God. Theologians and religious philosophers concur on four essential endowments of a supreme being: omnipotence (all-powerful), omniscience (all-knowing), omnipresence (all-encompassing), and omnibenevolence (all-good).

The preeminent attribute of God is omnipotence, which unequivocally translates to the universal cause of everything. It is impossible to conceive of a deity that does not possess this requisite quality. To fail to be the cause of everything would negate the very essence of an all-powerful supreme being. We now ask a critical question: Can more than one god be the cause of everything? Can multiple gods be the causes of everything? Careful examination of the language involved tells us that the answer to this question is manifestly no. There can exist only one omnipotent universal God that causes everything.

After reviewing the claims and counterclaims, contradictions and conundrums, and conjectures and conclusions of exegetical experts and pious preachers, we realize that the only verdict warranted is that the gods conceptualized by the theologians and philosophers do not possess independent existence in objective reality. With some regret, we must decree that the postulated universal God, as well as the thousands of idolized territorial deities, exist only in the fevered imaginations of terrified devotees.

IV. The Mythical Biblical Savior God

SEVENTEEN

Ten Questions about Jesus for Fundamentalists

Christian fundamentalists have in recent years fabricated the so-called "War on Christmas," which they have blamed on secularists and enemies of Christianity.

Conservative commentator Bill O'Reilly teamed up with Jerry Falwell some years ago to incite religious extremists with untrue incidents. They asserted that "Jesus is the reason for the season." The Catholic League threatened to boycott stores and businesses that proclaimed "Happy Holidays" or "Season's Greetings," rather than the preferred "Merry Christmas." Fundamentalist activists transformed a season of peace and goodwill into a campaign of dissension and enmity in Jesus's name. These zealots are hellbent on inflicting their superstitions on everybody. Below are gospel facts to refute this stream of fundamentalist propaganda.

Was Jesus Born on Christmas?

Neither does the word Christmas appear in the bible nor is Jesus's birthday specified. Consequently, there is no injunction to celebrate his birthday. This is why many Christian churches do not celebrate Christmas, including Jehovah's Witnesses, Worldwide Church of God, and Christian Science. The reason early Christians selected December 25 as Jesus's birthday is because this was the traditional birth date of prominent pagan savior gods, such as Adonis, Horus, and Mithra. Folklorists call December 25 the "birthday of the gods." For ancient people, it became apparent three days after the winter solstice that the sun was again rising against the horizon. The annual rebirth of the source of life was a cause for rejoicing. Based on the historical events and astronomical phenomena cited in the gospel accounts, scholars have concluded that Jesus, if he existed, would have been born on April 17, 6 BCE.

Was Jesus the Lamb of God?

Christianity is premised on a truly barbaric image of torture, suffering, and death, as gruesomely portrayed in Mel Gibson's *The Passion of the Christ*. The key component is the blood sacrifice, referred to in twenty New Testament citations, such as "redemption through his blood," "washed us from our sins in his blood," and "redeemed with the precious blood of Christ." Of course, this primitive idea derives from the ritual blood sacrifice of animals, which is prominent in the Hebrew Testament. What activity guarantees salvation? The sacrament called holy communion, which is really just vicarious cannibalism: "Whosoever eateth my flesh and drinketh my blood hath eternal life, and I will raise him up at the last day" (John 6:54).

Was Jesus Obsessed with Hell?

Jesus's major contribution to theology was his emphasis on the ubiquity of hell. No character in the bible spoke more often of hell than Jesus. His dozen direct references include: hell, hellfire, everlasting fire, everlasting punishment, and damnation. In addition, he made numerous indirect references to hell, such as condemnation, loss of the soul, absence of forgiveness, and consequences of Judgment Day. Surveys indicate that while 70 percent of Americans believe in the existence of hell, less than 10 percent think they might go there. This conviction contrasts sharply with Jesus's statements that the vast majority of humankind will go to hell (Matthew 7:14; 22:13–14). Jesus provided a graphic description of hell in the story of the rich man and Lazarus (Luke 16:19–31). Is eternal punishment consistent with the portrayal of a loving, forgiving god?

Is Jesus the Only Way to Heaven?

When George W. Bush was governor of Texas, he said that Jesus was the only way to achieve salvation. He subsequently apologized to the Anti-Defamation League for his insensitive remark. Former televangelist Jimmy Swaggart did not waste words: "It's Jesus or it's hell." Jesus himself framed the exclusivity principle directly: "He who believes and is baptized will be saved, but he who does not believe will be condemned" (Mark 16:16). Similar statements are found in John 14:6, Acts 4:12, and 1 Timothy 2:5. Yet, several mainline Christian denominations reject exclusivity. For example, the Catholic Church maintains that sincere believers of all religious faiths will be saved, under the doctrine of "baptism by desire."

What was Jesus's Sexual Orientation?

Christian fundamentalists vilify what they call the "gay lifestyle." They do not want homosexuals to adopt or teach children, serve in the military or occupy sensitive government positions. Before disparaging members of the gay community, the censors should examine Jesus's life circumstances. First, he was not married, he did not father any children, and he chose only men to be his twelve apostles. Second, John is repeatedly referred to as "the disciple whom Jesus loved" and the disciple "lying on Jesus's breast at the last supper" (e.g., John 13:25; 19:26; 21:20).

What Did Jesus Really Teach?

Jerry Falwell says that "the bible is God's infallible, inerrantly inspired word. There are no mistakes in the bible." In contrast to mainline Protestant denominations and the Catholic Church, which believe that scripture is subject to skillful interpretation, fundamentalists maintain that the bible is literally true as recorded. Consistent with the latter view, the following commandments have been extracted from the gospel accounts of Jesus's life and teachings:

1. You must obey Jesus's teachings—if not, you will suffer everlasting punishment (John 14:21; 15:6; Mark 8:38).

2. You must hate your life in this world for Jesus's sake to achieve eternal life (John 12:25; Matthew 16:24–25).
3. You must give away all your possessions for Jesus's sake to inherit everlasting life (Mark 10:21; Luke 14:33; Matthew 6:19–21).
4. You must leave your family for Jesus's sake to achieve eternal life (Matthew 19:29; Luke 18:29–30; 21:16).
5. You must reject all violence—even actions taken in self-defense—and dedicate yourself to the cause of peace (Matthew 5:44, 48; 26:52; 5:9).
6. You must always forgive others—if not, you will suffer everlasting punishment (Matthew 6:14–15; 18:21–22; Luke 6:37).
7. You must help people in need—if not, you will be punished in the everlasting fire (Matthew 25:31–46).
8. You must not pray in public—say your prayers in private (Matthew 6:6).
9. You must not swear an oath—only give an affirmation of truth (Matthew 5:34–37).
10. You must mutilate yourself to avoid hell (Mark 9:43–48).
11. You must consider castration for the kingdom of heaven (Matthew 19:11–12).
12. You must handle venomous snakes and drink poison as demonstrations of faith (Mark 16:14–18).

Did Jesus Advocate Family Values?

Christian fundamentalists promote a theology of so-called "family values." These include support for the death penalty, military intervention, gun ownership, public prayer, and unrestrained capitalism, and opposition to abortion, contraception, sex education, animal rights, and environmental protection. But the key construct is the "traditional family," consisting of God-fearing father, subservient mother, and obedient children. Hence, it is fair to inquire about Jesus's statements and personal example concerning family life. First, Jesus was conceived while his teenaged mother was betrothed to an older man (Matthew 1:18); Thomas Jefferson commented that Jesus's parentage was obscure. Second, Jesus refused to acknowledge his mother and brothers when they came to visit him (Mark 3:31–35). Third, Jesus stated in unequivocal terms that his goal was to destroy the family unit (Matthew 10:35–37). Fourth, Jesus said that a requirement to be his disciple was to hate one's parents, spouse, siblings, and children (Luke 14:26). Fifth, Jesus promised that those who desert their families will inherit everlasting life (Matthew 19:29). If Christians actually obeyed Jesus's teachings, the nuclear family would be abolished.

When Will Jesus Return?

Predictions of Jesus's imminent "second coming" are routinely announced and always prove to be false. For example, the Mission for the Coming Days predicted Jesus would return in October 1992 and human history would end in 1999. At the other extreme, the Reverend Sun Myung Moon claimed that he was the true Messiah! Christian Zionists believe that Jesus will return soon to the unholy land and some have urged that the Palestinian people be forcibly removed to Sudan. In all three synoptic gospels, Jesus said that he would descend from heaven in his glorious return and that some of his original disciples would live to see his second coming (Matthew 16:28; Mark 9:1; Luke 9:27). In Revelation, he stressed that he would return quickly.

Was Jesus a Living Person?

Christian fundamentalists believe that Jesus was unique in human history. The simple fact is that every item of the gospel account is taken from the biographies of earlier savior-gods (such as Apollonius and Zoroaster), e.g., conceived by a virgin, born on December 25, had twelve disciples, walked on water, cured diseases, raised the dead, was crucified between two thieves, was resurrected and ascended to heaven. There are numerous additional reasons to doubt the Jesus story. First, Roman and Jewish historians of the period did not even mention Jesus. Occasional brief references are interpolations. Second, purported physical evidence, such as the Shroud of Turin and the James Ossuary, have been demonstrated to be hoaxes or frauds. Third, the four canonical gospels are anonymous and contradictory compilations that are not based on eyewitness accounts. Fourth, Paul mentions only Jesus's death and the Last Supper and never quotes his sayings or cites his teachings. Fifth, the trial of Jesus by Pontius Pilate is entirely inconsistent with Roman law of the time and is not recorded in the Roman archives. Sixth, the elements of Jesus's crucifixion are thoroughly unhistoric, but rather are features of traditional sacramental rituals. In conclusion, there is not a shred of evidence to support the claim that Jesus was an actual person. All evidence suggests that Jesus is a fictional character—a composite myth derived from earlier stories.

Did Jesus's Resurrection Guarantee Eternal Life?

The standard Christian creedal statement asserts that "Jesus died on the cross for our sins so that we can inherit eternal life." From this fundamental postulate, it is evident that Christianity is a self-centered, death-oriented theology. What human motive propels the irrational hope for "life beyond the grave"? The foundation of Christian beliefs is the biological instinct for self-preservation transformed into egocentrism, or self-love that generates the monumental fear of death. The inability to face the most basic fact of life—which is the extinction, obliteration, dissolution, and eradication of human personality—energizes the Christian delusion. But Jesus clearly taught that his followers must deny themselves in this life to achieve everlasting life in the hereafter. Denial of self includes rejection of material possessions and desertion of family. Because almost all people who call themselves Christians disregard or reject Jesus's commandments, they will fail his test on Judgment Day and suffer endlessly for their disobedience.

These ten questions and answers provide a framework for debating Christian fundamentalists on the core issues of their belief system, using historical scholarship and their own holy book to refute their claims.

EIGHTEEN
Who Will Go to Hell According to Jesus?

Jesus—the savior god of Christianity—is obsessed with hell. That's why his primary focus is on everlasting torture for those who do not obey him. He has formulated a theology of punishment that includes a detailed description of eternal torment and a specification of the violations that would result in permanent relegation to this horrific place of infinite suffering.

The real problem for those who call themselves Christians is that very few of them will spend eternity in heaven with Jesus. On the contrary, the large majority will experience endless torture in hell. This is true because Jesus says so—and he explains in detail with considerable redundancy exactly why this will happen.

Jesus, the Gate to Heaven

The foundation of Christian afterlife doctrine is the belief that Jesus will make the final decision regarding eternity in heaven or hell for every person. He captures the detestable dogma of Christian exclusivity in the oft-quoted declaration, "I am the way, the truth, and the life. Nobody comes to the Father except through me" (John 14:6). Moreover, he identifies himself as "the gate" that opens to the Kingdom of Heaven, saying that those who come in by way of the gate will be saved (John 10:9). He reminds his followers on forty separate occasions that he's the Messiah. In other words, those who do not accept Jesus as savior will go to everlasting punishment. Jimmy Swaggart expressed the claim succinctly: It's Jesus or it's hell!

As thoroughly documented below, Jesus fully expected his disciples to obey his teachings as the essential requirement for achieving eternal life. He formulated a logically secure equivalence between loving him and obeying him (see John 14:15–24). He stated repeatedly that his disciples would follow him, by which he meant they would obey his commandments and emulate his life. Isn't this what Christians are referring to when they invoke the guideline of "a Christ-centered life"? What else could the question "What Would Jesus Do?" (WWJD) be addressing? Finally, Jesus the gatekeeper said that he would judge people on their qualifications for heaven according to their deeds (Matthew 16:27; John 5:29).

Jesus Said Most Will Go to Hell

Jesus stated clearly that the vast majority of humankind would go to hell. He apparently realized that the criteria he established would be met by very few candidates. Specifically, he asserted that many will enter the wide gate to destruction, but only a few will enter the narrow gate that leads to life (Matthew 7:13–14). And he concluded the parable of the wedding dinner illustrating what the Kingdom of Heaven is like with the statement "For many are called, but few are chosen" (Matthew 22:14).

It is not unreasonable to suggest that Jesus was being overly optimistic when he indicated that just a few people would qualify for eternal life. As summarized below, the standards of behavior that reflect the total commitment he expected of his followers would be extremely difficult, if not impossible, for most people to satisfy.

Jesus's Binary Afterlife Theology

In Jesus's theology of afterlife reward or punishment, there are only two options: heaven or hell. Reward for the faithful and obedient is life everlasting with the Father and Son in heaven, whereas punishment for the unfaithful and disobedient entails never-ending pain and suffering under the supervision of Satan and his angels in hell. Jesus stressed the binary character of this decision in three well-known formulations: the choice between the wide and narrow gates (Matthew 7:13–14), the separation of the sheep from the goats (Matthew 25:31–46), and the analogy between obeying Jesus's teachings and building a house on a strong foundation (Luke 6:46–49).

Due to the nature of Jesus's theology of the hereafter, it is necessary to consider the stipulated requirements for heavenly reward as well as the specific reasons for sentencing a human soul to everlasting punishment. There are specified behaviors that, if engaged in, will result in eternity in heaven or endless punishment in hell.

Jesus's Description of Hell

Jesus invoked the concept of hell as everlasting punishment in seventy-three gospel verses. The seventy-three verses are distributed as follows: Matthew (thirty-three), Mark (four), Luke (twenty-seven), and John (nine). The hellish expressions are widely varied in language and metaphor, with a total of 104 words or phrases that refer to infinite suffering.

Many are straightforward names or labels, including hell (fifteen), judgment or Judgment Day (twelve), condemnation (five), or end of the world (four). Many others are descriptive phrases, such as eternal fire or burning (ten), weeping and gnashing of teeth (seven), loss of life or doom (6), and absence of forgiveness (four).

Some phrases are framed as Jesus's personal judgments. A few are negative characterizations, such as not fit for the Kingdom of God or outside of the Kingdom's gates.

From Jesus's extensive focus on the primary features of hell, it is a relatively straightforward task to formulate a concise description of this horrific realm of unending torture:

a. *General:* Hell is a real place of terrible suffering, unbearable pain, unimaginable misery, excruciating agony, endless torment, and utter hopelessness.

b. *Specifics:* Hell is a furnace of fire that is never extinguished, where the damned suffer from unquenchable thirst and are infested with intestinal parasitic worms that never die.

c. *Duration:* Hell is the everlasting, eternal, unending expression of God's infinite wrath, revenge, and cruelty. The condemned never experience the relief of death.

d. *Finality:* Hell is an irrevocable judgment that can never be nullified or reversed. No reprieves are ever issued and nobody is ever pardoned. These features are exemplified in Jesus's story about Dives in Luke 16:19–31.

While Christian fundamentalists in particular find much comfort in the idea of hell for sinners, it is only fair to note that other Christians reject this pernicious doctrine partly or entirely. For example, Universalists argue that God will save all people. Jehovah's Witnesses do not believe anyone will go to hell. And the Catholic Church under the doctrine of Baptism by Desire asserts that all sincere believers in God will be saved. Only recalcitrant unbelievers are in danger of hellfire, the Church asserts, a position reiterated by retired Pope Benedict XVI, who assured Christians that hell really exists and should be taken very seriously.

In the larger Protestant community, there has been an ongoing discussion about the meaning and reality of hell. Mainline denominations tend to downplay the issue, referring to hell with the euphemism "separation from God." When evangelical preacher Rob Bell voiced doubts about the traditional Christian position on hell and damnation, suggesting the possibility of universal redemption, he became a controversial celebrity. After Pentecostal Bishop Carlton Pearson disclosed that he could no longer accept Christian dogma about hell because it is inconsistent with a loving God, he was condemned by other clergy, his congregation deserted him, and his ministry went bankrupt.

Jesus's References to Heaven

Contrary to what many Christians believe, Jesus actually spoke of heaven more often than he talked about hell. The false impression is reinforced by the intensity and vividness of Jesus's detailed description of everlasting punishment. In contrast, he did not recite the joys of heavenly existence in the same way that he spelled out the horrors of hell.

A total of 124 verses in the Gospels includes mention of heaven or a word or phrase that clearly refers to heaven. The 124 verses are distributed as follows: Matthew (forty), Mark (eight), Luke (forty-three), and John (thirty-three). In the 124 verses, a total of 143 words or phrases referring to heaven occur with the following frequencies: heaven (thirty-two), Kingdom of Heaven (twenty-six), Kingdom of God (twenty-four), eternal life (twenty-eight), have life, new life, deliverance from life etc. (eight), Heavenly Father, Father's Kingdom, Father's home (six), saved or salvation (five), and various others (ten).

Jesus's Sixteen Commandments about Hell

1. Anyone who disobeys Jesus's teachings or God's commandments or rejects Jesus's message will go to hell.

Supporting verses are:

a. Refusing to obey Jesus's explicit teachings (Matthew 7:24–27, 25:29–30; Luke 6:49; John 8:51, 15:6–7).

b. Refusing to obey God's commandments (Matthew 7:21–23, 19:17–19; Luke 8:21).

c. Rejecting Jesus and his unequivocal message (Mark 8:38; Luke 9:26, 20:16–18; John 12:48).

Not only did Jesus state repeatedly that obedience to his teachings is an absolute requirement to enter the Kingdom of Heaven, he equated loving him with obeying his commands (John 14:15–24) and believing in him with emulating his life (Mark 16:16–18; John 3:15–18; see also 1 John 2:6). Furthermore, he explained that his teachings are actually from God (John 17:8). Also, as documented in the next section, Jesus emphasized that his true disciples would follow him by carrying out his proselytizing mission.

2. Anyone who does not give up everything and follow Jesus will go to hell.

Supporting verses are:

a. Refusing to give up everything and not renouncing one's worldly life for Jesus (Matthew 10:39, 16:25; Mark 8:35; Luke 9:24, 59–62, 14:33).

b. Refusing to devote oneself to Jesus by emulating his exemplary life (Matthew 10:38, 16:24; Mark 8:34; Luke 9:25, 14:27).

c. Loving oneself more than Jesus (Luke 14:26; John 12:25).

Jesus demanded total commitment from his disciples, requiring that they deny themselves by exhibiting complete selflessness and demonstrating utter disregard for their families—as Jesus did himself. Giving up everything or surrendering one's life to Jesus refers specifically to abandoning all personal possessions and family responsibilities, as detailed in the sections below.

3. Anyone who does not give away all possessions or accumulates material wealth will go to hell.

Supporting verses are:

a. Refusing to give away all personal possessions (Matthew 19:21; Mark 10:21; Luke 12:32–34, 18:22).

b. Accumulating material wealth (Matthew 6:19–21, 16:26; Mark 8:36–37; Luke 6:24–25).

c. Pursuing earthly success instead of godly goals (Matthew 6:24; Luke 16:13).

Jesus was perfectly clear about the literal application of this commandment. He said that his followers should not worry about the basic necessities of daily life, such as food, clothing, and shelter, because God will take care of their needs if they dedicate their lives to him (Matthew 6:25–34; Luke 12:22–31). By simple extension, Jesus was discouraging people from planning, working, saving, and similar prudent actions, which is entirely unrealistic advice for modern citizens.

4. Anyone who does not leave home and family for Jesus will go to hell.

Supporting verses are:

a. Refusing to leave home and family for Jesus (Matthew 19:28–29; Mark 10:29–30; Luke 18:29–30).

b. Not loving Jesus more than one's family (Matthew 10:37; Luke 14:26).

c. Failing to join Jesus's "family" of disciples (Matthew 12:46–50; Mark 3:31–35; Luke 8:19–21).

Concerns about immediate family members, including parents, siblings, spouse, and children are irrelevant to Jesus (Luke 9:59–62). He said that family members would turn against those who decide to become his disciples, possibly even killing them (Mark 13:12; Luke 21:16–19). Jesus's stated goal was to destroy the nuclear family unit (Matthew 10:35).

5. Anyone who fails to love enemies or engages in violence or does not strive for peace will go to hell.

Supporting verses are:

a. Not loving enemies or helping them (Matthew 5:44–45; Luke 6:27–28, 35).

b. Not rejecting interpersonal violence (Matthew 5:39, 26:52).

c. Not being dedicated to the cause of peace (Matthew 5:9; see also Isaiah 9:6).

Jesus was a pacifist. He condemned interpersonal violence, even in self-defense, saying that those who take up the sword shall perish by the sword, meaning that violence only begets further violence. Some will suggest that Jesus hypocritically incorporated extreme violence into some of his stories, while his defenders will say that the parables should not be taken literally. For example, Jesus will return unannounced and cut the unreliable servant into pieces and send him to hell (Matthew 24:51; Luke 12:46); Jesus will return for the last judgment to destroy the wicked (the rebellious subjects) saying "bring them in and execute them before me" (Luke 19:27); and Jesus the Stone will fall from heaven crushing unbelievers to dust and relegating them to hell (Luke 20:9–18).

6. Anyone who does not forgive others or judges others will go to hell.

Supporting verses are:

a. Refusing to forgive the misbehavior of others (Matthew 6:12, 14–15, 18:21–22, 35; Mark 11:25; Luke 23:34).

b. Judging the perceived faults of others (Matthew 7:1–2, 3–5; Luke 6:37, 41–42).

Jesus obviously granted himself an exemption from this requirement, because he was perfectly willing to send the overwhelming majority of people to hell forever. Also, Jesus condemned the residents of Capernaum, Chorazin, and Bethsaida to hell because they refused to repent after he devoted a significant part of his ministry to them. In his anger, he compared the cities unfavorably to Sodom (Matthew 11:20–24). On the other hand, he had numerous opportunities to denounce the truly evil institution of slavery, and the allegedly sinful activities of prostitution, abortion, and homosexuality, and he did not do so.

7. Anyone who divorces a spouse (except for infidelity) or remarries (except for spousal infidelity) or marries a divorced person will go to hell.

Supporting verses are: Matthew 5:32, 19:6–9; Mark 10:9–12; Luke 16:18; see also 1 Corinthians 6:9–10.

Jesus equated these violations with adultery. Yet many fundamentalist Christian churches disregard this far-reaching commandment by sponsoring divorce recovery seminars and singles groups for divorced persons.

8. Anyone who denies help to the poor, suffering, and less fortunate will go to hell.

Supporting verses are: Matthew 25:31–46; Luke 14:13–14.

Jesus's forceful command to help "the least of those among you" would appear to be totally contradicted by his radical formulation of right-wing economic ethics: To those who have much, more will be given; from those who have little, even that will be taken away (Matthew 13:12, 25:29; Mark 4:25; Luke 19:26).

9. Anyone who makes a public spectacle of prayer rather than praying in private will go to hell.

Supporting verse is: Matthew 6:5–6.

10. Anyone who swears an oath rather than simply affirming or denying will go to hell.

Supporting verse is: Matthew 5:34–37.

11. Anyone who refuses to mutilate one's body to atone for sins by amputating hands or feet or gouging out eyes will go to hell.

Supporting verses are: Matthew 5:29–30; Mark 9:43–47.

12. Anyone who does not cast out demons, speak in tongues, handle venomous snakes, drink poison, and heal by faith will go to hell.

Supporting verse is: Mark 16:17–18.

13. Anyone who publicly denies Jesus or denies that Jesus is the Messiah will go to hell.

Supporting verses are: Matthew 10:33; Mark 13:13, 16:16; Luke 12:8–9.

14. Anyone who is a false prophet, false exorcist, or false miracle worker will go to hell.

Supporting verse is: Matthew 7:22–23.

15. Anyone who does not possess the simple faith of a child will go to hell.

Supporting verses are: Mark 10:15; Luke 18:16–17.

16. Anyone who commits blasphemy against the Holy Spirit will go to hell.

Supporting verses are: Matthew 12:31–32; Mark 3:28–30; Luke 12:10.

Summary

Jesus declared himself to be the gatekeeper for the afterlife. His description of hell betrays a morbid interest in the horrific aspects of torture. He established sixteen behavioral criteria by which his judgments concerning eternal life will be made. It is apparent from these that virtually all who call themselves Christians will not escape the torments of hell.

NINETEEN

Jesus: Prophet of Love or Purveyor of Hate

Multitudes of Christian commentators over the past two millennia have proclaimed the teachings of Jesus of Nazareth to be unsurpassed tenets of spiritual wisdom and unexcelled guidelines for living a morally responsible life. Hundreds of millions of devout believers are absolutely convinced that they will conquer death and attain everlasting life because God sacrificed his son for their sins.

They are also convinced that Jesus didn't really die. He was restored to life and subsequently ascended to heaven to spend eternity with his father, and soon Jesus will return to Earth to judge the wicked and rapture righteous believers up to heaven with him. Countless books have been written extolling the allegedly commendable features of the "Christian worldview" and the "Christ-centered life," but, by contrast, few authors have examined the unsavory side of Jesus's personality and his less-than-meritorious behavior and opinions.

For this chapter, I've formulated, in balanced fashion, two sets of ten principles based on Jesus's pronouncements. Although his directives come from the canonical gospels (the books of Matthew, Mark, Luke, and John), additional documentation is abundant elsewhere in the New Testament epistles and letters. The twenty precepts are listed along with the supporting bible verses from which they derive. This scriptural evidence will enable readers to answer for themselves the binary question that is the title of this chapter.

Prophet of Peace and Love

It's important to recognize that all of Jesus's so-called unsurpassed teachings derive from the Hebrew scriptures or commentaries on them, specifically the Mishna, a fact documented by German biblical scholar Arthur Drews more than a century ago. Because all of the biographical items in the Jesus composite story were taken from the mythical lives of two dozen earlier savior gods, it can be concluded that there is nothing original in Jesus's biography or his teachings.

A pervasive theme in the gospel is the sharing of possessions by Jesus's disciples, which is consistent with his denunciation of wealth and his advice to not worry about the necessities of daily living because matters of this world are unimportant.

1. The universal human duty is to help other people. Everyone has a moral responsibility for the well-being and happiness of others (Matthew 5:42, 25:31–46; Luke 6:30, 14:12–14).
2. The obligation to assist others extends to persons who subscribe to different value systems. They deserve the same treatment as friends and family members (Matthew 5:43–48; Luke 6:27–28, 6:35).
3. The only acceptable form of human interaction is peaceful in nature. There is never any justification for interpersonal aggression or violence (Matthew 5:9, 5:38–39, 26:51–52; Luke 6:29).
4. Regardless of the misbehavior other people may commit, and no matter how serious the damage they may do, the only appropriate response is to forgive them (Matthew 6:14–15, 18:21–22, 18:34–35; Luke 23:34).
5. The goals in life that should be pursued are personal development and community service, rather than the acquisition of material possessions and wealth (Matthew 6:19–20, 6:24; Mark 10:21; Luke 14:33, 18:22).

6. Criticism should be reserved for examination of one's own faults. No person is qualified to judge the motives of others (Matthew 7:1–5; Luke 6:37, 6:41–42).
7. Personal enjoyment is an important aspect of human existence. Ceremonies and celebrations that commemorate major events and milestone occasions give life meaning (Matthew 9:10–13, 26:17–19; Mark 14:12–16; Luke 5:29–32, 22:7–14; John 2:1–10).
8. Spiritual and religious exercises, including prayer, are intensely personal activities that should be conducted in private to be truly meaningful (Matthew 6:5–6).
9. The compassionate society will be realized when self-interest becomes the standard by which concern for other people is measured (Matthew 22:39, Mark 12:31, Luke 10:27).
10. The infallible rule for monitoring individual behavior is the principle of anticipated reciprocity. We should behave toward others as we prefer to be treated (Matthew 7:12, Luke 6:31).

Purveyor of Fear and Hate

Old Testament law constitutes the foundation for the ethical and behavioral pronouncements of Jesus, as evidenced in his Sermon on the Mount where he said, "Do not think that I have come to abolish the Law or the Prophets; I have not come to abolish them but to fulfill them" (Matthew 5:17). With God's severe treatment of children in the Old Testament as the basis (see "God Hates Children," Chapter 8), Jesus commanded his followers to desert their families and abandon their children in order to join his missionary effort. If these Jesus-sanctioned family values were practiced today, a visit from child protective services would result and an arrest would most likely follow.

The Old Testament's patriarchal point of view dominates the sentiments and actions of Jesus that determine the role of women in his ministry. Slaves fared even worse than women, thanks to Jesus's unquestioning acceptance of the institution of slavery. Eight of his forty parables mention but never condemn this immoral human relationship.

Moreover, he explicitly authorized the cruel master-slave relationship when he recommended beating disobedient slaves, even if they are unknowingly disobedient. (Luke 12:47–48: The servant who knows the master's will and does not get ready or does not do what the master wants will be beaten with many blows. But the one who does not know and does things deserving punishment will be beaten with few blows.)

1. The vast majority of humankind faces an irrevocable eternity of horrific torture for failure to obey inviolable biblical commandments and teachings (Matthew 7:13–14, 7:26–27, 19:17; Mark 8:38; Luke 9:26, 13:22–30; John 8:51, 12:48, 15:6).
2. Sacrificial offerings of innocent creatures are efficacious for expiation of sin and for healing disease, especially the shedding of human blood for remission of collective guilt (Matthew 5:23–24, 8:4, 26:28; Mark 10:45, 14:24; Luke 2:22–24, 5:14, 22:20; John 1:29, 3:16, 6:53–54; 1 John 4:10).
3. In order to achieve the highest calling in life, acolytes must permanently separate themselves from family members, including parents, siblings, spouses, and children (Matthew 10:34–37, 12:48–50, 19:29; Luke 8:19–21, 14:26, 18:29–30).
4. Children are the possessions of their parents and should be punished severely for their own misbehavior as well as the transgressions of their ancestors (Matthew 10:21, 15:4, 24:19; Mark 7:10, 10:29–30, 13:12, 13:17; Luke 12:51–53, 19:43–44, 23:28–29).
5. Atonement for sinful thoughts and actions requires the physical mutilation of limbs and eyes, including emasculation to preserve godly purity (Matthew 5:29–30, 18:8–9, 19:11–12; Mark 9:43–49).
6. Divorce and remarriage are prohibited in almost all circumstances, with the single exception of documented spousal infidelity. Marriage to a divorced person is proscribed (Matthew 5:32, 19:9; Mark 10:11–12; Luke 16:18).
7. Demonstrations of religious dedication include exorcising demons, glossalalic possession, viper-tempting, consuming poison, and faith-healing (Matthew 8:16, 8:28–34; Mark 5:9–17, 16:17–18; Luke 10:8–9).

8. People can be forgiven for all of their sins, with the exception of blasphemy against the Holy Spirit, which can never be forgiven, because it is the eternal sin (Matthew 12:31–32; Mark 3:28–30; Luke 12:10).
9. Acceptable human relationships include communal ownership of property, subordinate status of women, involuntary servitude, and collective punishment (Matthew 10:15, 11:20–24, 27:55–56; Luke 8:1–3, 10:38–42, 11:27–28).
10. Those who renounce worldly success, desert family and home, eschew personal needs, and devote one's mortal life to Jesus will be rewarded with everlasting existence (Matthew 6:19–21, 6:25, 10:39, 16:25–26, 19:21; Mark 8:35, 10:21; Luke 9:24, 12:22, 14:33, 18:22).

Analysis and Conclusion

We use logical principles or rules of reasoned thought to reach valid conclusions. One class of strategies for logical reasoning is that of syllogisms, which includes the framework known as the alternative syllogism. In this syllogism, the major premise specifies two alternatives connected by the words "either . . . or," where "either" may be inferred.

If the minor premise affirms one alternative, this does not compel the conclusion that the other alternative must be false. This is because the major premise only restricts the options to two possibilities. Contrary to popular misconception, it does not limit the choice to one alternative or the other. In fact, both alternatives may be true at the same time.

Now we can answer the question posed in the chapter's title. Jesus is *both* a prophet of peace and love *and* a purveyor of fear and hate. Of course, students of the gospel know that both ten-point portraits are thoroughly accurate, scripture-based summaries of Jesus's mandates. This conclusion is fully supported by the verses and passages cited.

It should be pointed out that Jesus did not always obey the instructions he promulgated for others. For example, he exempted himself from the command to forgive others, because he was perfectly willing to send the majority of humankind to hell forever. And while he condemned interpersonal violence, even in self-defense, he hypocritically incorporated extreme violence into his five Matthean slave parables (Matthew

18:23–35, 21:33–46, 22:2–14, 24:45–51, 25:14–30).

While the two sets of Jesus's ethical decrees are clearly not fully compatible moral visions, just a few precepts and directives are explicitly contradictory. As such, they accurately reflect the multiple personality disorder of the mythical central composite character of the gospels. Of course, believers will still refuse to acknowledge this biblical truth even when confronted with the overwhelming evidence that Jesus is not an exemplary role model for humanity.

TWENTY

Does Human Sacrifice Assure Eternal Life?

The foundation of the Christian religion is belief in the efficacy of human sacrifice to confer immortality on faithful adherents. In other words, Christianity requires believers to accept the improbable claim that the atoning blood sacrifice of a living human being can bring about the impossible—a miracle that enables human personality to transcend bodily disintegration, thereby extending conscious existence forever.

Some believe that what the founder of psychoanalysis, Sigmund Freud, called an obsessional neurosis may be alleviated by the Christian promise of everlasting life, reinforced annually in the Easter celebration, which entails reenacting the mythical execution and restoration to life of the Christian savior deity, Jesus of Nazareth.

In this chapter, I articulate the basic premise of Christian theology as the redemptive human sacrifice, document the pervasiveness of animal sacrifice in early Hebrew worship, review the Passover story of the sacrificial lamb, and delineate the critical role of blood in the ritual sacrifice. These four interrelated theological concepts constitute the biblical foundation of the Easter story.

Animal Sacrifice

The prominent feature of ancient Hebrew religious ceremonies was large-scale animal sacrifice, viewed as a gift to God for the purpose of paying homage and winning favorable treatment. The critical aspect was the disposal of blood on the altar, typically by sprinkling or smearing on the sides, although sometimes also on individuals, as in the consecration of priests (e.g., Exodus 29:20–21). This practice was a major determining factor in portraying Jesus's redemptive blood sacrifice as the Lamb of God to take away the sins of the world.

The volume of attention accorded the topic of animal sacrifice in the Old Testament can only be comprehended by way of numerical summary. Thirty-three chapters of seven books specify in exacting detail how animals are to be sacrificed and twenty-three chapters of eight books describe scores of horrific, sacrificial events. These gory episodes each involved hundreds or thousands of animals, in one case destroying more than 100,000 animals (1 Kings 8:62–63).

In addition to the appalling spectacle presented with the sacrifice of huge numbers of innocent animals, two predominant themes recur in Jesus's atoning death. These are the overwhelming focus on blood and the requirement that only animals without blemish or defect may be sacrificed to God (Malachi 1:7–14). Reflecting this mandate, Peter referred to Jesus as "a lamb without blemish or defect" (1Peter 1:19).

Although animal sacrifices in Israelite worship were conceived as gifts to God to curry favor, Jesus's sacrifice completely reverses this causal order. Scripture explains, for instance, that "God gave his Son, that whoever believes in Him shall not perish but have eternal life" (John 3:16). And, to give a couple of additional examples, Paul recounts, "God presented Christ as a sacrifice of atonement, through the shedding of his blood" (Romans 3:25) and "For Christ, our Passover lamb, has been sacrificed" (1 Corinthians 5:7).

Two other accounts suggest that Jesus was responsible for his own deliverance: "Christ gave himself up for us as a fragrant offering and sacrifice to God" (Ephesians 5:2) and "Christ appeared to do away with sin by the sacrifice of himself" (Hebrews 9:26). Interestingly, Jesus seemed to confirm these declarations by his disciples when he said, "For even the Son of Man did not come to be served, but to serve, and to give his life as a ransom for many" (Mark 10:45).

Regardless of whether Father or Son made the sacrificial decision to save sinful humans, it is necessary to go back to the beginning to understand the justification for the action. Death entered the world as a result of Adam and Eve's disobedience in the Garden of Eden, an event called "the Fall," which is detailed in Genesis 3. Paul explained that just as the disobedience of one man, Adam, brought condemnation for all people, God's grace and one righteous act by another man repaired the damage of the Fall and brought eternal life through Jesus Christ (Romans 5:12–21). In Paul's theology of redemption, Jesus is portrayed as "the last Adam."

Lamb of God

The bible's earliest mention of the sacrificial lamb occurs when Isaac asked his father Abraham, "Where is the lamb for the burnt offering?" In this horrific tale, which prefigures God's sacrifice of his only son, Isaac was the instrument of God's "test" of Abraham's devotion to him. Abraham "passed" the test because he was prepared to slay his only son as a sacrificial burnt offering to God. After Abraham demonstrated that he feared God and would obey him, God blessed Abraham and his descendants forever (Genesis 22:1–18).

In the chronicle of the Hebrew captivity in Egypt, the firstborn male offspring of the Israelites were spared from being killed by God's angel of death because their houses were identified with lamb's blood that was smeared on the door frames. The angel or destroyer "passed over" these marked dwellings so that the infant boys were saved by the blood of the lambs. This is the most often cited source for the story of Jesus's atoning death (see Exodus 12 for details). In another Old Testament precursor to the identification of Jesus as the Lamb of God, Isaiah's Suffering Servant "was led like a lamb to the slaughter" (Isaiah 53:7).

In the New Testament, John the Baptist twice greeted Jesus with the symbolic title, "the Lamb of God who takes away the sin of the world" (John 1:29, 36). Extending the allusion, Peter wrote to the persecuted Christians in the Roman provinces, telling them that they were redeemed "with the precious blood of Christ, a lamb without blemish or defect" (1 Peter 1:18–19). Paul's reference to "Christ, our Passover lamb" was cited previously. Finally, John's apocalypse includes several references to "the slain Lamb," the "blood purchase for God," and "the blood of the Lamb," representing Christ who was killed as a ransom for human sin and proclaimed by 100 million angels (Revelation 5:6–14, 7:14, 12:11)!

The Passover festival in Jesus's lifetime involved the sacrifice of lambs and the smearing of blood on the altar, done in remembrance of the divine protection given Hebrew ancestors in Egypt—a symbolic reliving of the Exodus story. The apostle Paul invoked the ritual sacrifice of the Paschal lamb in the declaration above. Contemporary Christian theology incorporates this representation of Jesus as the Lamb of God who serves as a redeeming blood sacrifice to atone for human sin, making possible everlasting life for the faithful.

Blood of Christ

Old Testament theology includes blood as the life source and vehicle of sacrificial atonement. When sprinkled or spread on the altar, it becomes an important expiatory agent in bringing reconciliation with God. The Passover observance focuses on the blood on the door frames of Israelite houses in Egypt and God's deliverance of his people from bondage, based on the blood of the covenant (Exodus 24:6–8).

The New Testament is organized around the shed blood of Christ and its atoning function. Blood established the basis for God's new covenant of grace, which consists of the free and undeserved love of God. Jesus himself announced this relationship, "For this is my blood of the new covenant, which is poured out for many for the remission of sins" (Matthew 26:28; see also Mark 14:24; Luke 22:20; 1 Corinthians 11:25; Hebrews 12:24).

Christians celebrate God's generously given forgiveness and acceptance by participating in the Lord's Supper, made possible through the redeeming power of Christ's blood. As an illustration, Paul testified to the Ephesians that, "In Christ we have redemption through his blood, the forgiveness of sins, according to the riches of his grace" (Ephesians 1:7; see also Colossians 1:14, 20; 1 Peter 1:19).

The sacrament of the Lord's Supper, also called Holy Communion, the Eucharist, or the sacrifice of the Mass, entails the symbolic or literal incorporation of Jesus's physical being when devotees consume his body and blood. Without quibbling about the Catholic doctrine of transubstantiation, we will simply cite Jesus's own words: "Whoever eats my flesh and drinks my blood has eternal life, and I will raise him up at the last day" (John 6:54).

For additional verses that amplify or augment the themes above, also see Acts 20:28; Romans 3:25, 5:9; Hebrews 13:12; 1 Peter 1:2, 19; 1 John 1:7; Revelation 1:5. The longest discourse on the blood of Christ, which serves as a thorough summary of the critical issues, including the unblemished atoning sacrifice, the cleansing function of blood, and the declaration that "without the shedding of blood there is no forgiveness," occurs in Hebrews 9:11–28. The total number of New Testament references to the blood of Jesus is twenty.

Summary

Christians believe that the blood sacrifice of their savior god, the Son of Man Jesus Christ, will bring about for them everlasting life. The four theological concepts outlined above come together in the execution of an innocent human who is offered by his father as a perfect sacrificial lamb, whose blood will redeem sinners from a fate that they are not responsible for causing. If this bizarre theology seems to defy logic, that is because it makes no rational sense, and that is why unquestioning faith is essential to embracing the Christian celebration of Easter.

TWENTY-ONE

Little-known Facts About Jesus for Fundamentalists

Former Republican presidential candidate and current Housing and Urban Development Secretary Dr. Ben Carson has declared that "the bible is a seemingly inexhaustible source of practical wisdom that could serve as a valuable resource for everyday living."

Is this a defensible claim? We can evaluate the validity of Carson's assertion by examining some of the doctor's own publicly expressed thoughts to establish evidence concerning the inexhaustible practical wisdom he believes saturates the bible.

It would be unfair to judge scripture with respect to the accuracy of statements about modern historical events and scientific developments. However, it is not unreasonable to expect that a discerning individual purified in the alleged wisdom of the bible would exercise careful judgment in distinguishing contemporary truth from error and nonsense. Carson's statements suggest otherwise.

Here is a sample of the good doctor's false, bizarre, and prejudicial assertions: Satan inspired Darwin to develop the theory of evolution so that people would believe there is no God; homosexuality is a choice;

the Holocaust would not have occurred if the Jews in Nazi Germany had guns; American Muslims and mosques should be monitored; sessions of the Constitutional Convention began with prayer at Benjamin Franklin's suggestion; and the US Constitution has a Judeo-Christian foundation.

Regardless of the mental confusion and erroneous ideas that characterize Carson's mind, there is no doubt that he is a committed Christian, an orientation in which he has fully immersed himself. To this point, a British newspaper reporter who visited his home described it as "a shrine," with bible verses posted in every room and a life-size centerpiece portrait of the seated doctor with Jesus standing behind him with a loving paw placed on Carson's shoulder.

As a tribute to Carson's Jesus fixation, this review of bible facts is focused on some lesser-known details about the origins and life outlined in the fictional Messiah story.

What Did Jesus Look Like?

The *Smithsonian* magazine cover of the January/February 2016 issue features an artist's interpretation of a sixth-century painting thought to be of Jesus. It actually looks more like a Roman emperor than a Middle Eastern mystic. Nine very different early depictions of Jesus are also reproduced inside. Tens of thousands of visual representations of the gospel Jesus have been generated over the past two millennia. Is there anything approaching a consensus concerning his physical appearance?

Many years ago, the *National Catholic Reporter* sponsored a Jesus 2000 art competition which drew 1,678 entries from nineteen countries. The tremendous variety in artistic interpretations included portrayals of Jesus as a clown, homeless person, carpenter, TV anchor, and a death row inmate. The winning entry by a Vermont painter (a woman) depicted Jesus as a dark-skinned, thick-lipped, broad-nosed peasant with feminine features. After it was revealed that the artist's model was actually a black woman, an avalanche of hate mail and phone threats ensued. While no violent incidents occurred, as with the more recent cartoon depictions of Muhammad, controversies in the Christian world about Jesus's supposed appearance have been frequent and acrimonious.

An authoritative opinion about Jesus's countenance was delivered by the Reverend Russell Moore, head of the Southern Baptist Convention's

Ethics and Religious Liberty Commission. He declared: "The man on the throne in heaven is a dark-skinned, Aramaic-speaking foreigner who is not at all impressed by chants of Make America Great Again."

How can differences of opinion be resolved when nobody could possibly know what the mythical Jesus actually looked like? Jesus scholar John Dominic Crossan explained that the representations reflect the culture that create them, a theological statement of identity, and therefore no portrayal is more right than any other.

Jesus's Historic Template

Two dozen savior gods preceded Jesus of Nazareth by as many as 2,000 years or more. Every prominent biographical item in the Jesus story is found in earlier savior god life histories. Here are some "facts" about one of Jesus's eminent predecessors.

He was said to be born to a virgin and called the son of God. He supposedly cured diseases, restored sight to the blind, and raised people from the dead. He allegedly walked on water and cast out devils. He left no writings; we only know about him through his disciples. He was a political revolutionary who was killed by his enemies.

He advocated forgiveness of enemies, taught respect for parents and elders, and said "blessed are the poor." He renounced ownership of private property and required communism among his disciples. He recommended deserting family and home. He advocated nonviolence and nonresistance. He taught that the soul is immortal and asserted that his doctrines were a revelation from God. He believed in eternal punishment in hell and everlasting reward in heaven.

He was a Greek philosopher and mystic who made important contributions to mathematics, medicine, music, and astronomy. His greatest discovery was that number is the essence of physical reality. He is best known for a geometric theorem that bears his name. Who is this great philosopher?

Answer: Pythagoras, who lived c. 580–500 BCE.

Unanswered Prayers

Jesus was perfectly clear about the benefits of prayer. He said that petitioners must have faith and then requests in his name would be answered (Matthew 21:22; Mark 11:24; John 14:13–14, 16:23). The strongest biblical support for the efficacy of prayer comes from episodes in which life was restored to allegedly dead persons. The most direct plea was formulated by the Hebrew prophet Elijah, who cried out, "O Lord my God, let this boy's life return to him." The Lord heard Elijah's cry and the boy was returned to life (1 Kings 17:21–22). Three other resurrections of corpses included some form of prayer: Elisha (2 Kings 4:33–35), Jesus (John 11:41–44), and Peter (Acts 9:40).

Christians believe in the "power of prayer" on the basis of faith. Unfortunately, the overwhelming empirical evidence thoroughly contradicts their faith-based belief. Specifically, in five independent clinical trials published in medical journals, more than 4,000 hospitalized cardiac patients were randomly assigned to prayed-for and not-prayed-for conditions. The vast majority of the intercessors were Christians, while a few represented other religious traditions. On the ultimate criterion of patient mortality, no more of the prayed-for patients survived than those not prayed for. The only reasonable conclusion is that God does not answer intercessory prayers for healing, in all likelihood because God does not exist. Also, Jesus was wrong!

Crucified on a Cross?

The universal symbol of Christianity around the world is the Latin cross. Every Christian church, school, and hospital is identified with a cross. Catholic institutions prominently display the crucifix, which includes an emaciated Caucasian in a suffering pose. Is this ubiquitous torture device an accurate reflection of the gospel story?

Two Greek words that are routinely translated as "cross" in the bible actually denote an upright stake or vertical pole. Two terms that are used are "torture stake" and "execution stake." The cross is a pagan symbol that predates Christianity by several millennia. Scholars have found no evidence that the cross was used by early Christians. Moreover, scripture does not indicate that Christian worship should include the instrument that was used to execute Jesus.

Crucifixion was invented by the Phoenicians before 1,000 BCE. The original procedure entailed securing the criminal to a vertical stake and allowing him to die slowly of thirst and exposure. This painful form of execution was adopted by the Assyrians, Egyptians, Persians, and later by the Romans.

If Jesus was actually crucified on a stake, why do Christian churches insist it was a cross? Could the reason be that ten pagan savior gods who preceded Jesus by at least 500 years were all crucified on crosses, and two of them between two thieves?

Crucifixion Contradictions

The bible, especially the gospel, is full of confused claims and contradictory testimony. Each of the statements below is both true and false according to scripture.

Even when confronted with overwhelming evidence of contradictions, believers are still capable of defending the divine inspiration and inerrancy of the bible. For example, apologist Father Richard Hansen conceded that there are contradictions in the gospel stories, but said the stories are altered to reveal the true meaning inspired by the Holy Spirit. He concluded that people of faith should appreciate the lessons contained in the diversity. Popular bible writer Alice Parmelee said that the contradictions make the various accounts "far more convincing than if they had been in perfect agreement." Her statement and the comments of Father Hansen demonstrate that committed Christians can explain anything with utterly preposterous excuses.

Fourteen Contradictions

- The infant Jesus was taken to Egypt.
  True (Matthew 2:14–23); False (Luke 2:22, 39).
- Jesus preached his first sermon from a mountain.
  True (Matthew 5:1, 2); False (Luke 6:17–19).
- John the Baptist recognized Jesus as the Messiah.
  True (John 1:29, 34); False (Matthew 11:2, 3).
- Thaddeus was one of Jesus's twelve apostles.
  True (Matthew 10:2–4; Mark 3:16–19); False (Luke 6:14–16).
- The cleansing of the Temple occurred at the end of Jesus's ministry.
  True (Matthew 21:12–13; Mark 11:15–17; Luke 19:45–46); False (John 2:14–16).

- Jesus knew that he was being betrayed by Judas.
  True (Luke 22:47, 48; John 18:4); False (Matthew 26:49, 50).
- Judas betrayed Jesus with a kiss.
  True (Mark 14:44, 45); False (John 18:3–12).
- Jesus carried his cross to Golgotha.
  True (John 19:16–17); False (Luke 23:26).
- Mary Magdalene came to the tomb alone.
  True (John 20:1); False (Matthew 28:1; Mark 16:1; Luke 24:1).
- Two angels were seen at the tomb.
  True (Luke 24:4; John 20:11–12); False (Matthew 28:2–5; Mark 16:5).
- The women told the disciples of Jesus's resurrection.
  True (Matthew 28:8, Luke 24:9); False (Mark 16:8).
- Jesus first appeared to the disciples in Jerusalem.
  True (Luke 24:33–37); False (Matthew 28:16–17).
- All of the disciples were convinced of Jesus's resurrection.
  True (John 21:12); False (Matthew 28:17).
- Jesus ascended to heaven from Bethany.
  True (Luke 24:50–51); False (Mark 16:7, 19; Acts 1:12).

Jesus's Burial Garment

The Shroud of Turin is believed by some Christians to be the burial cloth of Jesus. The shroud is 14 feet long and 3.5 feet wide with a double image (front and back) of a man in the "death pose." It was declared to be a hoax by the Bishop of Lirey in a report to the pope in 1389. The report indicates that the artist who painted or created the double image "confessed" or explained what he had done. The shroud was acquired by the dynastic House of Savoy in 1453 and kept until 1983, when it was given to the Catholic Church.

Could the Shroud of Turin possibly be the authentic burial garment of Jesus? Three primary sources of evidence say no. First, the known history as noted above suggests that the shroud is a fourteenth-century forgery. Second, the four biblical accounts of Jesus's burial and resurrection are inconsistent and contradictory, and the John gospel in particular does not support the claim (Matthew 27:59; Mark 15:46; Luke 23:53; 24:12; John 19:40, 20:5–7). Third, in 1988 the Catholic Church allowed a small piece of the shroud to be snipped from an edge for radiocarbon dating. Three independent laboratories reached similar conclusions that date the shroud to about 1300 CE. In other words, the linen is only about one-third as old as a true shroud would have to be. The authoritative source is Joe Nickell's *Inquest on the Shroud of Turin* (1998). A recently published encyclopedic resource is Andrea Nicolotti's *The Shroud of Turin: The History and Legends of the World's Most Famous Relic* (2020).

Addendum: How Many Biblical Resurrections?

Most Christians believe that only one person in history was restored to life after dying. God's perfect word says otherwise.

- Elijah resuscitated the dead son of the widow of Zarephath (1Kings 17:17–23).
- Elisha raised the dead son of Shunammite woman (2Kings 4:32–37).
- A dead man thrown into Elisha's tomb came to life (2Kings 13:21).
- Jesus restored life to Jairus's daughter (Matthew 9:18–26).
- Jesus raised the son of the widow of Nain (Luke 7:11–15).
- Jesus reanimated dead Lazarus (John 11:38–44).
- Jesus was resurrected (John 20:1–10).
- Peter raised Tabitha (Dorcas) from the dead (Acts 9:36–41).
- Paul restored life to Eutychus (Acts 20:7–12).

The single mass raising of the dead states that "many" were resuscitated (Matthew 27:50–53). At the moment of Jesus's death many dead saints came to life and following his resurrection they were observed in Jerusalem by numerous people. Assuming that "many" is three or more leads to the conclusion that at least one dozen corpses were restored to life in ten biblical episodes.

TWENTY-TWO

Ten Truths about Easter

The foundational belief of Christianity is that Jesus was resurrected from death, an event that is commemorated at Easter each year. As the most important celebration in Christendom, Easter is focused on the risen savior as a guarantee of everlasting life for believers.

The ten themes below provide the historical, cultural, and theological context for understanding this observance.

- The name Easter derives from the Anglo-Saxon goddess of spring—Eostre or Ostara—whereas the Christian festival that celebrates Jesus's resurrection developed from the Jewish Passover and includes prominent vestiges of Roman paganism.
- The annual Christian commemoration of the resurrected savior is held on the first Sunday after the first full moon that occurs on or after March 21 and before April 25, a method of calculation that was decreed by the First Council of Nicaea in 325 CE.
- The Easter celebration evolved from the Jewish Passover observance, which was adapted from earlier Canaanite festivals that in-

cluded the slaughter of a lamb, which was related by the Hebrew priests to deliverance of the Jews from bondage in Egypt, i.e., they were saved by the blood of the lamb.

- Jesus died on Passover after sharing a "Last Supper" or Passover meal with his disciples, thereby serving as a redeeming blood sacrifice represented as the Paschal Lamb or the Lamb of God. Jesus instructed his followers to observe the Lord's Supper on that day in remembrance of him.
- The Christian observance also incorporates major elements of the festival of Attis, which was celebrated in March by Roman pagans. The yearly ritual included the crucifixion of an effigy and the enactment of an empty tomb, demonstrating that Attis was resurrected and providing assurance that devotees would achieve immortality.
- Crucifixion was invented by the Phoenicians and subsequently adopted by the Assyrians, Egyptians, Persians, and later by the Romans. The original procedure entailed securing the criminal to a vertical stake and allowing him to die slowly of thirst and exposure.
- Some scholars assert that Jesus was crucified on a vertical stake, not a cross, because the Greek words used in the bible translate as "torture stake" or "execution stake." Christian tradition says it was a cross because ten pagan savior gods were crucified on crosses, two of them between two thieves.
- The cross was a widely used religious symbol found in various early cultures. There is no evidence of use of the cross by early Christians.
- The empty tomb story presented in the Gospels is not the first report of the Easter event, nor is it conclusive evidence of the resurrection claim. Two decades earlier, Paul described a series of appearances of the risen Jesus to more than 500 followers.
- Jesus's resurrection was not a unique biblical occurrence, because at least twelve and possibly more scriptural characters died and were subsequently restored to life by Jesus, his apostles, Hebrew patriarchs or some unspecified agent (see p. 177). Of course, a dozen pagan savior gods were also resurrected.

V. Biblical Christian America

TWENTY-THREE

The United States Is Not a Christian Nation — It Never Has Been and It Never Will Be

Attempts to acknowledge Christianity as the official religion of the United States date back to the constitutional convention and have erupted at regular intervals for the past 200 years. The current onslaught was initiated by pseudo-historian David Barton in the late 1980s and continues to this day under the banner of Project Blitz, which is his latest brainchild.

Christian Nation Claims

There are twenty-one Christian Nation declarations that advocates have put forward in support of their political theology. The order of the twenty-one claims is partly based on historical occurrence, but also reflects the time when changes were placed into effect, as well as the content of the particular issue. All assertions are preceded by the phrase, "The United States is a Christian nation because . . ."

1. The first Americans were unbaptized Christians.

   Fact: The first human inhabitants of the Americas were Asians who crossed the Bering land bridge beginning 30,000 years ago. The first white people in North America were the Scandinavian Vikings in 1000 CE and the first Christian to set foot in the new territory (the Bahamas) was probably Christopher Columbus in 1492.

2. The early American colonies were chartered as Christian outposts.

   Fact: Yes, most charters for the American colonies did specify a Christian purpose, but it is noteworthy that the New England communities subsequently became intolerant theocracies where dissent was rigorously suppressed. At the beginning of the Revolution, a majority of the new states (ten of thirteen) had established Christian denominations, but all were disestablished by 1833.

3. Prominent US Founders were Christians.

   Fact: The principal framers of the Declaration of Independence, Constitution, Bill of Rights, and related documents were Deists and Unitarians.

4. The Declaration of Independence invokes God four times.

   Fact: Nature's God, Creator, Supreme Judge of the World, and Divine Providence are all Deistic terms. The Declaration's author, Thomas Jefferson, was not an orthodox Christian. To appreciate this truth, it is only necessary to compare his *Life and Morals of Jesus of Nazareth* with the gospel text from which it was extracted.

5. The majority of contemporary Americans are Christians.

   Fact: About sixty-five percent of US residents now identify themselves as Christians. However, even the late evangelical preacher Billy Graham stated that "only a minority are really committed to Christ or seek to follow him." Barely half of Americans are even church members and fewer than one-fourth attend church on a regular basis.

6. The Constitution's Subscription Clause acknowledges Jesus.

   Fact: "In the Year of Our Lord" is a ceremonial dating custom that was used to attest to the authenticity of political documents for several hundred years prior to the US Constitution. For a detailed rebuttal of this Christian Nation claim, see Andrew L. Seidel's article in the Summer 2018 issue of *Constitutional Studies.*

7. The United States was officially declared to be "One Nation Under God."

   Fact: The phrase "under God" was inserted into the Pledge of Allegiance to the flag during the McCarthy era anti-communist hysteria in 1954. The original pledge was written by Baptist minister Francis Bellamy in 1892 and did not contain any religious references.

8. The US Supreme Court declared America to be a Christian nation.

   Fact: In the often misrepresented *Holy Trinity* decision (1892), a single justice (David Brewer) expressed his personal opinion ("dictum") that the United States was a Christian nation. Moreover, advocates of a Christian nation never cite the Treaty with Tripoli (1797), which said just the opposite.[1]

9. The National Day of Prayer was authorized by Congress.

   Fact: Congress designated the National Day of Prayer an annual event in 1952, later setting the first Thursday in May as the regular date. Under the direction of the National Day of Prayer Task Force, a private entity working hand-in-glove with government officials, it has traditionally been fundamentalist Christian in conception, planning, and presentation, with no contributions permitted by any other faith traditions.

10. The US founding documents are based on the bible.

    Fact: The Declaration, Constitution, and Bill of Rights are not based on the bible. (Because this is a central claim in Christian Nation mythology, it is addressed in greater detail in a separate section.)

11. Only Christians may hold public office in the United States.

    Fact: Pat Robertson, Roy Moore, and other extremists have argued for the exclusive Christian qualification for decades. Obviously, such exclusion would violate the Constitution's prohibition on religious tests for office.[2] Yet, even after more than 230 years have elapsed, eight state constitutions still restrict public office holders to candidates who believe in a higher power. Of course, these relics cannot be enforced, except by voters at the ballot box.

12. The US legal system is based on the Ten Commandments.

    Fact: This popular fringe claim survives primarily due to willful biblical illiteracy. The first four edicts violate the First Amendment's guarantee of religious liberty and these and others also endorse collective punishment, patriarchy, and slavery. Only the prohibitions against murder, theft, and perjury are found in US law.

13. Christian symbols are prominently displayed on public property.

    Fact: Indefatigable Christian Nation advocates carry out their relentless campaign to place Ten Commandments monuments, Latin crosses, statues of Mary, and portraits of Jesus in public venues. Most are removed after sometimes lengthy court battles. Unfortunately, this may change with the addition of staunch opponents of church/state separation like Neil Gorsuch and Brett Kavanaugh to the US Supreme Court.

14. The national motto is "In God We Trust."

    Fact: This embarrassing corruption of American history was put into effect by a cowardly Congress in 1956. The original motto, which many people think should be restored, is *E pluribus unum* (from many, one), composed by Adams, Franklin, and Jefferson to celebrate American ethnic and cultural diversity.

15. Only Christian "historical holidays" are officially recognized.

    Fact: This is a disreputable fundamentalist strategy to acknowledge only Christian holidays (Christmas, Good Friday, Easter, Thanksgiving, St. Valentine's Day, St. Patrick's Day) by including them on government and public school calendars. Actually many other religious holidays are usually recognized, such as Passover, Yom Kippur, and Hanukkah.

16. The Constitution's Preamble acknowledges Jesus as Messiah.

    Fact: During the Constitutional Convention, some delegates wanted Christianity to be officially recognized, but the majority rejected the idea. In the 1870s, an organization of Christian ministers attempted to insert into the preamble recognition of Almighty God, Holy Scripture, and Jesus the Messiah. The proposal failed, as have all other similar efforts to date.

17. The United States was founded on the principles of Christian law.

    Fact: This assertion, which is based on the claim that the common law derives from Christianity, was thoroughly debunked by David Koepsell, a lawyer and philosopher, drawing on an earlier analysis by Thomas Jefferson. The alleged principles of Christian law are nonexistent.

18. The Constitution is based on the idea of biblical covenant.

    Fact: No evidence supports the claim.

19. The US presidential oath acknowledges Almighty God.

    Fact: The Constitution does not prescribe any religious declaration or theistic affirmation in the presidential oath of office. However, many US presidents have appended the meaningless expression of divine dependence, "So help me God," in respect of an unworthy custom.

20. Prayers at the Constitutional Convention ensured success.

    Fact: Contrary to this oft-repeated falsehood, Benjamin Franklin's motion to begin each session with prayer was not adopted (it wasn't even seconded) and there were no official prayers during the convention.

21. The current US president is a devout Christian.

    Fact: Franklin Graham and other fundamentalist leaders proudly proclaimed that "God raised up Donald Trump to be president." Also, he is the exemplar of the "Christ-centered life," based on his overwhelming voter support (81 percent) from fundamentalist Christians. The junior Graham had previously falsely asserted that Barack Obama was a Muslim (based on his father's religion of birth). If true, would this make the United States an Islamic nation?

Conclusion

This diverse collection of claims is testimony to the limitless ingenuity of the dedicated Christian Nation advocates. Although some of their assertions require elaboration, clarification, or explanation to be fully refuted, most are plainly false or irrelevant to the intended purpose of demonstrating that the United States is a Christian nation. It's ironic that only a few items actually refer to Jesus or Christianity, with the god introduced typically being that of "ceremonial Deism." It's never the god of contemporary Christian fundamentalism, which is the deity of the Christian Nation proponents.

Political Foundations of Christian Nation Ideology

The ultimate goal of Christian Nation proponents is to implement a fundamentalist Christian theocracy in the United States through constitutional amendments or other forms of legislative action.

The central theological postulates of fundamentalist Christian Nation ideology are:

1. Christian Exceptionalism: Christianity is the only true religion because only acceptance of Jesus as Messiah confers everlasting life, known as the doctrine of exclusive salvation.
2. Scriptural Inerrancy: The Holy Bible (both Hebrew and Christian testaments) is the absolutely accurate word of God, a perfect revelation of his perfect will that is without error.
3. Biblical Dominionism: This is the Genesis-based assertion that God provided all natural resources on the planet for the unrestricted use of believing Christians, as they deem necessary to fulfill God's eschatological promise to the faithful.

These three axioms of fundamentalism have been translated into ten political objectives of this extremist Christian minority, which consists of less than 20 percent of the US population. These objectives, stated in condensed form, are:

1. Establish Christianity as the official religion of the United States.
2. Acknowledge Jesus as the Lord and Savior of the United States.
3. Dispel the myth of separation of church and state.
4. Restrict elected governmental offices to orthodox Christians.

5. Require Christian prayer at all civic events.
6. Institute patriarchy in all aspects of public life.
7. Eliminate public schools and fund only Christian academies.
8. Exempt Christians from all laws that offend their faith.
9. Control women's reproductive healthcare choices.
10. Deny the freedoms and civil rights of LGBTQ persons.

Project Blitz has expanded Christian Nation theology to include the issue of sexuality, focusing on the narrow specification of what constitutes acceptable forms of sexual relations, for the purpose of delegitimizing the LGBTQ community.

In addition to infusing phony Christian history into the public school social studies curriculum, the Project Blitz strategy specifies three objectives:

1. Regulate sexual behavior by restricting lawful relations to heterosexual, married couples.
2. Legalize discrimination against LGBTQ people by enacting "religious liberty" laws that exempt fundamentalists from civil rights legislation.
3. Control the reproductive lives of women by outlawing abortion, morning-after contraception, in vitro fertilization, and other forms of contraception considered to be abortifacients.

Conclusion

The political foundations of Christian Nation ideology are located in the cultural and historical traditions of Christian fundamentalism, including exceptionalism, inerrancy, and dominionism. The specific objectives of this extreme theopolitical program include imposing a Christian theocracy in America, with an obsessive focus on "normal" sexuality and control of women's reproductive lives.

Separation of Church and State

This constitutional principle that is enshrined in the US founding documents and most of the state constitutions is supported by the majority of citizens and contravenes the claim that the United States is a Christian nation. For this reason, fundamentalist activists have to assert that the principle is just a myth.

Clearly, if government is constitutionally prohibited from establishing an official religion, Christianity will never become the recognized national theology. And this is why we are witnessing the continuing assault on the First Amendment by Christian Nation advocates.

It's important to understand the historical and cultural basis for the strong antipathy toward theocracy among the founders of the United States. As educated individuals, they were familiar with the terrible human destruction wrought in Christian Europe by five major crusades, three devastating Inquisitions, and the endless witch hunts that mostly targeted women. They were convinced that the only viable form of government was secular, meaning divorced from religious establishment.

The more recent early American experience with Puritan theocracies in the New England colonies solidified the founders' resolve to eliminate all religious ideas from the Constitution and to explicitly disallow governmental establishment of churches in the Bill of Rights. They realized that religious liberty was dependent on the indispensable principle of separation of church from state.

The initial formulation of this foundational principle of US secular government is properly credited to a Puritan clergyman who settled in the Massachusetts Bay colony in 1630. He was subsequently the victim of religious persecution and banished from the colony, ironically, because of his unwavering commitment to the concept of religious tolerance.

In 1637, Roger Williams issued his seminal declaration referring to the "wall of separation between the garden of the church and the wilderness of the world." The wall of separation metaphor was later made famous by Thomas Jefferson in his 1802 letter to the Baptists of Danbury, Connecticut. His historic statement leads the pronouncements by six other former US presidents and the first attorney general appointed by the current president.

1. Thomas Jefferson (1802): "I contemplate with sovereign reverence that act of the whole American people, which declared that their legislature should 'make no law respecting the establishment of religion, or prohibiting the free exercise thereof,' thus building a wall of separation between church and state."

2. James Madison (1822): "Religion and government both exist in greater purity, the less they are mixed together."
3. Ulysses S. Grant (1876): "Keep the church and state forever separate."
4. John F. Kennedy (1960): "I believe in an America where the separation of church and state is absolute."
5. Richard Nixon (1960): "The separation of church and state is not subject to discussion or alteration."
6. Jimmy Carter (1977): "I believe in the separation of church and state."
7. Ronald Reagan (1984): "We establish no religion in this country . . . Church and state are, and must remain separate."
8. Jeff Sessions (2018): "The principle of separation of church and state is a recent thing that is ahistorical and unconstitutional—an extra-constitutional doctrine."

The last statement is blatantly false, of course, but illustrates how an educated lawyer and mainline Protestant can be influenced by fanatical proponents of a fundamentalist political ideology to make an absolutely ridiculous assertion.

Sessions's fellow Republican and United Methodist, former president George W. Bush, was also an advocate of merging religion and government, which he did through his highly divisive faith-based schemes. He also endorsed another fundamentalist postulate, declaring that "only Christians are saved," for which he later apologized, after the Anti-Defamation League publicly criticized the thoughtless remark.

Continuing with the contemptible theme of fundamentalist exclusivity, Jeff Sessions's replacement, Matthew Whitaker, believed that only Christians should be judges in America! This is another expression of the fundamentalist postulate of Christian exceptionalism, which was cited earlier.

Conclusion

After 200 years of sustained effort, fundamentalist Christian Nation zealots are not going to curtail their relentless assault on US constitutional principles and core American values. Defenders of church/state separation should adopt an offensive posture by aggressively confronting fundamentalists' political hypocrisy and their incessant biblical lies. Because they claim to be victims of religious persecution, it's entirely appropriate to give them justification for their persistent paranoid charges of aggrievement and victimhood. In fact, the fundamentalists are engaged in a program of systematic persecution of everyone else. Their goal is to impose their unbiblical, ungodly, unChristian theopolitical dogma on all Americans.

Christian Nation Mythologist David Barton

For the past three decades, the premier purveyor of Christian Nation mythology has been David Barton. Since the late 1980s, he has tirelessly traveled the country speaking at fundamentalist churches, evangelical conferences, and private Christian academies, promoting the myth that the United States was founded as a Christian nation.

Although Barton is not a professional historian, he did not allow his lack of training or credentials to deter him from conducting a one-man war on American history. He produced and distributed scores of booklets, brochures, pamphlets, posters, and videos promoting revisionist Christian Nation theology, through his publishing empire, Wallbuilders, while under continuous criticism by legitimate historians.

Four major episodes that constitute milestones in his career are reviewed below.

1. Barton initiated his program of unhistoric revisionism with a self-published treatise titled *The Separation Myth* (1989). After a dozen fake quotes attributed to US Founders were uncovered by readers, Barton recalled and reworked the volume, deleting the bogus quotes which he labeled "questionable," and adding some material. Then he released the revised book with a new title, *Original Intent* (1994).

In fairness to Barton, it should be stated that he did not fabricate the fake quotes himself, but rather he failed to verify their authenticity after locating them in the fundamentalist fringe literature.

The most popular of the false citations was attributed to James Madison:

> We have staked the whole future of American civilization, not

> upon the power of government, far from it. We have staked the future of all of our political institutions upon the capacity of each and all of us to govern ourselves according to the Ten Commandments of God.

All experts in American political history and constitutional studies have concluded that Madison never said it! But authors ranging from the Legal Training Institute of America to Bill O'Reilly have erroneously quoted the Founding Father.

2. Barton concluded that the Supreme Court decisions in 1962/1963 declaring mandatory prayer and required bible reading in the public schools to be unconstitutional precipitated a monumental moral decline in the United States.

In his book *Original Intent*, graphs that depict five social variables (unwed mother birth rate, violent criminal offenses, gonorrhea cases, SAT total scores, single parent female households) plotted over time (1951–1993) are used to conclude that the accelerating values of the variables were caused by the two court decisions.

There were several major methodological flaws in his retrospective post hoc analysis, which are summarized as follows:

- Barton identified an alleged cause and then searched for effects retroactively, without proposing hypotheses about variables that should and should not be influenced.
- Barton failed to formulate differential hypotheses about the numerous possible alternative causes, such as the Vostok space flights and JFK's assassination.
- Barton did not report results for the scores of other indicators of social pathology, health diagnoses, criminal activity, and economic changes that he should have examined.
- Barton could commission a multivariate longitudinal analysis by qualified investigators who could design and conduct an appropriate analysis more than a half century later, because all of the relevant data are available in government archives. Why not do it? He could confirm or disconfirm the original claim.

3. Barton spent several years preparing his masterpiece, *The Jefferson Lies* (2012), in which he argued that Thomas Jefferson was really an orthodox Christian who did not advocate separation of church and state. Scholars recognized immediately that these conclusions were false. After two conservative Christian college faculty members documented Barton's numerous errors and misrepresentations, reputable evangelical publisher Thomas Nelson recalled the unauthentic tract from bookstores and libraries. It should be emphasized that it was not godless, anti-Christian, secular historians who took down this guru, but two persons of faith who were embarrassed by his endless misconceptions and embellishments of American religious history.
4. Barton miraculously emerged from *The Jefferson Lies* debacle as the creative genius behind the newest Christian Nation theopolitical program, known as Project Blitz. Most of his fundamentalist followers apparently accepted his explanation that he had been the unwitting, innocent victim of a liberal conspiracy. However, Hobby Lobby did not, and quickly dissolved its partnership with him. Although some observers were convinced that his fragile credibility was permanently compromised by Thomas Nelson's decision to withdraw the Jefferson screed, "Professor" Barton (his academic title was conferred by former Fox News host Glenn Beck) has risen from the grave, indeed. Project Blitz updates and incorporates many of Barton's earlier strategies into a comprehensive Christian Nation playbook. These include Christianization of public schools by posting "In God We Trust" and teaching bible courses, as well as issuing proclamations recognizing Christian Heritage Week, Year of the Bible, and Christmas Day. The truly despicable assaults on the LGBTQ community and women's reproductive rights were mentioned earlier.

Conclusion

David Barton's schemes have given fundamentalist Christians a focus for their never ending frustrations with the requirements of a secular government. His legacy, while certainly not favorable for Christian Nation proponents, is one of ongoing controversy that has drawn attention to the destructive potential that Christian fundamentalism has for democracy.[3]

Were the Founders Christians?

In February 1994, Acting Arkansas Governor Mike Huckabee signed one of the first Christian Heritage Week proclamations asserting that George Washington, Thomas Jefferson, James Madison, and Benjamin Franklin were "Christian statesmen of caliber and integrity who did not hesitate to express their faith."

The only problem with Huckabee's proclamation was that these four prominent Founders were not Christians! As I show in the thumbnail sketches of ten eminent Founders below, they were actually Deists. The brief profiles provide a factual background against which to judge the highly misleading characterizations of these men presented by Christian Nation proponents.

1. George Washington was nominally an Episcopalian. He was accused of being an agnostic and even an atheist because he seldom attended church and was not a communicant. He denounced the Calvinist doctrine of original sin, he never mentioned Jesus in his writings, and he used the term Providence as synonymous with destiny or fate. He had a low opinion of religion because of the "incessant acrimony and irreconcilable hatreds." His so-called personal prayer book that is routinely cited by revisionists was judged by experts to be a hoax and his prayer at Valley Forge (kneeling in the snow) is now acknowledged to be a fabrication. He was a Deist.

2. John Adams studied for the ministry at Harvard. Doubts about his Christian convictions led him to shift to the law. Although he generally wrote favorably of Christianity and Jesus throughout his life, he rejected orthodox Christian dogma, including the Trinity and the doctrine of eternal damnation. In his diary, he wondered how the Judeo-Christian scriptures came to be "the most bloody religion that ever existed." He also called the cross "the most fatal example of the abuses of grief which the history of mankind has preserved." He did not declare Christmas to be a national holiday. He was a Unitarian.

3. Thomas Jefferson authored the Declaration of Independence and coined the oft-repeated phrase, "the wall of separation between church and state." Political opponents called him a "champion of atheism and immorality" because he denied the deity of Jesus, he did not think the bible was God's word, and he rejected the Christian concept of hell as a state of everlasting punishment. Yet, he greatly admired Jesus's secular teaching and assembled them into a small book referred to as *The Jefferson Bible*. He was a Deist.
4. James Madison, the Father of the US Constitution, did not attend church, but he spoke out repeatedly on behalf of freedom of conscience, which he believed was a basic right of citizenship. He opposed any form of government support for religion, because history demonstrates that established Christian churches tend to produce "superstition, bigotry, and persecution." He declared that "religious bondage shackles and debilitates the mind and unfits it for every noble enterprise." His alleged quote about "the Ten Commandments of God" that is popular with the revisionists is a verified fake. He was a Deist.
5. James Monroe attended an Episcopal church, but never talked about his religious beliefs because he considered religion to be a private matter. A reference to the Divine Author of All Good in his second annual message to Congress suggests that he may have been a Deist.
6. John Quincy Adams was not a regular churchgoer, causing some religious people to call him an atheist. Ironically, he read at least three chapters of the bible each day and read through the entire bible every year. He wrote "Civil liberty can be established on no foundation of human reason which will not at the same time demonstrate the right to religious freedom." A lifelong opponent of slavery, he severely criticized clergy and parishioners for not condemning slavery on religious and moral grounds. Like his father, he attended the United First Parish Unitarian Church in Quincy, Massachusetts, and he was a Unitarian.
7. Benjamin Franklin rejected nearly all doctrinal aspects of Christianity. While he doubted Jesus's divinity, he applauded his ethical

teachings. He considered morality to be independent of religion and stressed the cultivation of civic virtue in his writings. Contrary to the revisionists' dishonest assertion, his motion to begin daily sessions of the Constitutional Convention with prayer was not approved; it was tabled without a vote. He opposed oaths and religious tests for public office. He was a Deist.

8. Thomas Paine is best known for his immensely popular booklet, *Common Sense*, which developed the argument for independence from England. In another persuasive volume, *The Age of Reason*, he demonstrated that the bible's claims could not be true and he ridiculed Christianity, which he regarded as an obstacle to social and political reform. He said that more than half of the bible contains "obscene stories, voluptuous debaucheries, cruel and tortuous executions, and unrelenting vindictiveness," and for this reason it should be called "the word of a demon." The charge that he was an atheist is false; he believed in God and an afterlife. He was a Deist.

9. Ethan Allen was a military hero of the American Revolution, best known for conquering the British stronghold at Fort Ticonderoga. He formulated a Deistic philosophy based on reason, disavowing revelation and miracles. His treatise, *Reason the Only Oracle of Man*, was the first openly anti-Christian book published in the United States. He was a Deist.

10. Joel Barlow was a revolutionary political writer and diplomat. As US consul to Algiers, he authored and negotiated the Treaty with Tripoli which assures that "the government of the United States is not, in any sense, founded on the Christian religion." The treaty was approved by the US Senate and signed by President John Adams, thus making it the supreme law of the land. He was later US minister to France, and died in Poland during Napoleon's retreat from Moscow. Based on his extensive poetry, it is apparent that he was a Deist.

What can we conclude about the religious views of these ten American founders? First, eight were Deists and two were Unitarians. Second, all were advocates of religious tolerance and freedom of conscience. Third, ironically, most were themselves targets of religious bigots. Fourth, none was an orthodox Christian. And fifth, none was even remotely close to the modern day fundamentalist revisionists who attempt to expropriate them for partisan political purposes.

Obviously, it is essential to know something about Deism to fully appreciate American history.[4] Deism was a religious philosophy popular among educated people living in the seventeenth and eighteenth centuries. It was referred to as a rational religion, meaning that it was based on science and reason, explicitly rejecting all forms of revelation, and arguing that God's existence is manifest in the natural world.

Deists believed in God as a celestial explanatory mechanism or first cause, but disaffirmed all claims of divine authority, including the deity of Christ. Yet, Deists endorsed the ethical teachings of Jesus, as well as those of other religious prophets. Deists also denounced all religious dogma and creeds, were strong supporters of religious liberty, and emphasized civic morality and ethical responsibility instead of personal salvation.

The modern equivalent of Deism is Unitarianism. All of the above tenets of Deism also characterize Unitarianism. Several of the Founders, including Jefferson, Adams, Madison, Franklin, and Paine, were strongly influenced by Unitarian ideas, through friendship with the English scientist Joseph Priestly, a Unitarian minister, who lived in America from 1794 to 1804.

A major consequence of the adoption of the religious philosophies of Deism and Unitarianism was the emergence of the principle of separation of church from state in the US founding documents, which was the basis for the American concepts of freedom of conscience and religious liberty. The rejection of creedal statements and emphasis on ethical behavior transformed Unitarianism into alignment with humanism.

Conclusion

It should be emphasized that while none of the prominent US Founders discussed above were even close to being orthodox Christians, they were not opposed to religion. In fact, they considered the promotion of religious belief and practice to be beneficial to society and, therefore, the responsibility of political leaders. They thought that religious faith could foster ethical conduct, create goodwill in the community, generate respect for the rights of others, and diminish antisocial behavior. Were they just hypocrites? It is more likely that they sincerely viewed religion pragmatically as a useful instrument for maintaining civil peace and public amity. Political philosophers since Plato have shared this perspective.

Are the US Founding Documents Based on the Bible?

The overarching historical assertion by Christian Nation advocates is that the United States was founded on Judeo-Christian principles. If this were demonstrably true, it would constitute strong evidence for the Christian Nation claim.

However, it is a nonspecific supposition that is not directly amenable to objective evaluation, primarily because the oft-cited Judeo-Christian precepts have never been fully enumerated. Put simply, there is nothing approaching an agreed-upon set of principles.

But, a more precisely specified assertion that is amenable to objective assessment is that the US founding documents are based on the bible. We can examine the documents and scripture together, so the requisite task becomes that of identifying the bible themes, principles, and events that are represented in the founding charters.

The focus will be the three basic documents: the Declaration of Independence (1776), the US Constitution (1787), and the Bill of Rights (1791).

The first step in any historical analysis is to ask if there exists direct evidence in support of the claim. Are there any references to Jesus, Christianity, or the bible in the three primary founding documents? Did Thomas Jefferson, author of the Declaration, or James Madison and Alexander Hamilton, the principal writers of the Constitution and Bill of Rights, ever say that they relied on the bible in composing the founding documents? The answer to both questions is negative.

The second critical step is to search for those themes, principles, and events in the bible that appear in the founding documents and those that do not. Our initial concern will be with four themes that are arguably represented both in the bible and these documents, followed by a listing of ten prominent themes and events that are excluded.

1. The major theme that predominates in the founding documents and the bible is patriarchalism. The doctrine that men are superior and women are subservient is explicit in holy scripture, at one point quantified in God's differential valuation of men and women (Leviticus 27:1–7). Also, only one title is given to women, that of "helper."

How is the pernicious doctrine of patriarchalism manifested in the founding documents? Three questions frame the answer: Who wrote the documents? Who signed and approved them? Who was allowed to vote in the new republic? The answers are, of course, men only.

2. Another significant theme in common is slavery. The doctrine that one race or ethnicity is superior to others, which may be owned as property (chattel) pervades scripture. Ownership of slaves was categorically approved by Jesus, Paul, and Peter. The US Constitution legally permitted the importation of black slaves until 1808. For the purposes of enumeration, slaves were counted as three-fifths of a person. The dehumanizing institution of slavery was legal in "Christian America" for almost a quarter of a millennium (1619–1865). Another expression of racism appears in the Declaration of Independence, where the native inhabitants of the continent are referred to as "merciless Indian Savages."
3. The constitutional principle of separation of church and state received clear support from Jesus himself, when he said, "Render unto Caesar that which is Caesar's and unto God that which is God's" (Matthew 22:21). While scholars of different persuasions disagree on this interpretation, a useful discussion is provided by Herbert Titus in *The US Constitution: A Christian Document* (1997).
4. The constitutional option of affirming rather than swearing an oath occurs twice in the document. Jesus also unequivocally prohibited swearing an oath: "Do not swear an oath at all, simply say Yes or No, anything else comes from the Devil" (Matthew 5:34–37) and was repeated by his alleged brother James (5:12). Virtually all Christian politicians disregard this unambiguous scriptural teaching.

Listed next are ten major biblical themes, precepts, and events not included in the founding documents:

1. The Ten Commandments, the so-called quintessential guidelines for civilized living.
2. The death penalty, required for two dozen contemporary transgressions.

3. Collective punishment, which entails execution of innocent family members of guilty parties, including children.
4. Recognition of Jesus as Messiah and obedience to his teachings, the essential requirement for salvation.
5. Jesus's detailed description of the horrors of hell, essential knowledge for encouraging good citizenship.
6. Biblical history, including the creation, Noah's flood, Sodom and Gomorrah, and the Conquest of Canaan.
7. God's murderous behavior toward the unborn, infants, babies, children, adolescents, adults, women, and homosexuals.
8. The compelling biographies of the patriarchs and prophets, like Moses, Joshua, Samuel, Elijah, David, Jesus, Paul, and Peter.
9. Animal sacrifice, which is a central component of Godly worship, detailed in fifty-six chapters of fifteen books of scripture.
10. Three supreme Christian doctrines, original sin, punishment for disobedience, and human sacrifice guarantees immortality.

Conclusion

Although it is not true that the US founding documents were based on the bible, it is accurate to say that the Declaration, Constitution, and Bill of Rights do incorporate four basic themes that occur in the bible: patriarchalism, slavery, separation of church and state, and affirmation of oaths. It is also obvious that the vast majority of themes, principles, and events that are central to the bible story are absent from the founding documents.

Social Pathology in Christian America

If we define a Christian nation as a political entity under the authority of God the Father and his son Jesus the Savior of humankind, then we can reasonably ask: Why is there so much social pathology in the United States? Doesn't Christianity engender moral behavior in believers? Isn't that the primary claim that Christian pastors and preachers make? Can't we live ethical lives through acceptance of Christian faith? What does the objective evidence tell us?

Compared to thirty other modern Western industrial countries, the

United States has by far the highest rates (per capita) of social pathology, as documented by the following indicators:

1. Homicide rate: Fifteen to twenty times higher.
2. Execution rate: All others have abolished capital punishment.
3. Incarceration rate: More residents in jails, prisons, and penitentiaries.
4. Suicide rate: Driven by stress, depression, and drugs.
5. Drug abuse rate: World's number one illegal drug market.
6. Maternal mortality rate: Mothers dying during childbirth.
7. Infant mortality rate: Newborns do not survive.
8. Military budget: Exceeds the next fifteen countries combined.
9. Military sales: Exceeds the next eight countries combined.
10. Teenage pregnancy: Unwed teen birth rate.
11. Children living in poverty: Infants, babies, children in poverty.
12. Marital infidelity: Divorce, adultery, abuse.
13. Sexually transmitted diseases: All STDs.
14. Sex industry: Prostitution, pornography, trafficking.
15. Sexual assault: Physical abuse, harassment.
16. Violence in entertainment: Sports, television, movies.
17. Gambling: Legal, illegal, government sponsored.
18. Financial crimes: Business fraud.
19. Political corruption: Dishonesty.
20. Economic inequality: Disparity between wealthy and poor.
21. Fundamentalist religion: Intolerance, discrimination, hate.

Many additional indicators could be listed, such as highest obesity rate, highest abortion rate, highest drunken driving fatality rate, highest child gun death rate, lowest life expectancy, and lowest equality of opportunity, among others. While the United States may not be the worst in all categories every year, it is at the top or close on each variable, and the aggregate or composite ranking is far and away numero uno for the modern Western world.

What are the causes of this monumental epidemic of social pathology in an allegedly Christian nation? It is an undeniable fact that Americans are an incorrigibly violent people. The country was founded on the evils of forcible conquest, bloody massacres, chattel slavery, and conscripted labor.

The North American continent was taken from the native inhabitants by violent, murderous expropriation, decimating the Indian tribes (of Asian descent), destroying their cultures, and imprisoning survivors on "reservations." Ironically, the later westward expansion of the United States depended upon conscripted Asian workers.

The nation was built initially by enslaved Africans transported to the colonies beginning in 1619. Enslavement of black captives as the foundation of the Southern economy continued for two and one half centuries. Only a bloody Civil War terminated this God-ordained practice.

Another insult to human dignity occurred during World War II when 100,000 US citizens of Japanese descent were incarcerated in "internment camps," not because they committed any crimes, but due entirely to their ancestry. A government film produced at the time declared that the action was taken "without violating the principles of Christian decency."

Conclusion

The US was birthed in violence and the tradition continues to this day. How do Christian Nation advocates reconcile these horrific historical embarrassments and the dismal statistical evidence of social pathology with their assertion that the United States is a Christian nation? Are these terrible historical events and social data indicative of Christian godliness? Do they reflect Christian exceptionalism? What would the Prince of Peace say? Fundamentalist doomsday preachers tell us that Satan is alive and well in America and this frightening evidence confirms their allegation!

Absence of Christian Consensus in America

The fundamentalist promoters of Christian Nation ideology assume that there exists a consistent set of "pro-family values" that have the overwhelming support of the Christian community.

All available evidence flatly contradicts their assumption. In fact, disagreement within the Christian community is almost as large as in the greater US population. It is the huge divide between fundamentalist and mainline Christians on the moral issues that accounts for most of the differences.

If the United States were truly a Christian nation, then it follows that those who identify as Christians would agree completely on the central moral issues. The clear absence of consensus, with fundamentalists typically in the minority, contradicts the very idea of a nation committed to a unified series of Christian values.

Outlined next are one dozen major moral issues that thoroughly divide the Christian community, with the mainline Protestants' majority position (with substantial Catholic support) given first in the contrasting viewpoints.

1. Abortion rights: Freedom of choice in women's reproductive health care *versus* outlaw and criminalize abortion and related procedures for women and doctors.
2. LGBT rights: Equal rights and legal protections for all sexual minorities *versus* ban same-sex marriage and legalize discrimination against LGBT persons for religious reasons.
3. Sexuality education: Comprehensive sexuality education including thorough explanation of contraception *versus* abstinence-only until marriage to an opposite sex mate.
4. Science education: Indoctrination in the philosophy, methods, and findings of scientific investigation *versus* denial of human evolution, climate change, vaccination efficacy, and prayer failure.
5. Capital punishment: Abolish state-sponsored killing as immoral *versus* execute criminals expeditiously because the death penalty is an effective deterrent.
6. Gun ownership: Implement strong public safety requirements such as universal background checks *versus* any restrictions in access to firearms is a violation of the Second Amendment.
7. Right-to-die: Individuals have the right to choose assisted death with dignity *versus* individuals do not have the right to accelerate dying and must accept "natural death."

8. Ordination of women: All persons should be eligible to assume all ecclesiastical responsibilities *versus* women should be restricted to those statuses that scripture approves.
9. Drug use: Individuals should have freedom of choice in use of recreational drugs *versus* drugs are a societal scourge and all use should be strongly discouraged or outlawed.
10. Gambling activity: Wagering is a generally harmless recreational activity that must be regulated *versus* all gambling should be abolished because it is morally destructive.
11. Public schools: Public education is the foundation of the community and should focus on the acquisition of knowledge, skills, and social development *versus* public schools should be replaced by private religious academies and home schooling.
12. Public religion: Expression of religious faith is a private matter that is best left to home and church *versus* public religious exercises, such as invocations and prayers, are essential for strengthening Christian commitment.

Conclusion

The United States cannot be a Christian nation if Christians do not agree on the central moral values that Christian Nation advocates argue are the foundation of the alleged national faith. In other words, the complete absence of anything even approaching a Christian consensus on basic moral issues demonstrates that there are no definitive Christian values or Godly principles and renders the concept of a "Christian nation" incoherent and utterly meaningless.

Summary

Regardless of the total lack of support for their claim, Christian Nation advocates will not stop their obsessive activities aimed at achieving the goal of having Christianity officially recognized and proclaimed America's religion, with all others excluded. Most authorities say this will not happen because the First Amendment protects citizens from government establishment of any religion.

Many fundamentalists still regard David Barton to be the living savior of the Christian Nation dream. The *Jefferson Lies* debacle should have been the end of his journey of historical distortion and corruption. But despite his public exposure and disgrace, millions of believers accept the Christian Nation theopolitical myth as an article of faith, rather than rejecting it as the product of fraudulent scholarship.

Their hopes have been revived by a recent episode in Israel, in which Benjamin Netanyahu and his cronies railroaded through a new law that declares Israel to be "The nation-state of the Jewish people" and contends that "The right to exercise national self-determination in the state of Israel is unique to the Jewish people." In other words, it asserts that Israel is now a Jewish nation! Interestingly, Israel's founding Declaration of Independence guaranteed complete equality of social and political rights for all residents, regardless of religion.

Could it happen in America? With Netanyahu's fellow demagogue in the White House, endlessly pandering to the fundamentalist far right, almost anything is possible.[5] Only the entirely secular US Constitution stands between the vast majority of American citizens and the small minority of Christian Nation zealots.

Chapter 23 Endnotes

1 Contrary to the standard misrepresentation by David Barton and Hobby Lobby, the Supreme Court did not declare the United States to be a Christian nation. Yet, court rulings that proscribed mandatory prayer, bible reading, moments of silence, graduation prayers, pledging allegiance to the flag, and teaching creationism in public schools are never mentioned by Christian Nation advocates. Nor are the decisions that legalized abortion and same-sex marriage ever celebrated.

2 Three Williamson County, Texas, commissioners did not believe that the prohibition against religious tests for public office applied to them. They interrogated candidates for a constable position about their views on abortion and same-sex marriage as well as their church attendance. As a consequence, they were convicted in federal court of violating the constitutional rights of a job applicant.

3 Barton also believes that giving women the right to vote weakened the family and contributed to the alleged moral decline of the nation, because granting female suffrage was contrary to God's will. His propensity for denying reality is illustrated by his delusional belief that The Jefferson Lies will be reissued in the near future. Of course, no responsible publisher would touch it, but he could sponsor distribution himself under the Wallbuilder imprimatur.

4 For an excellent discussion of Deism in revolutionary America, see Kerry S. Walters, *The American Deists: Voices of Reason and Dissent in the Early Republic* (1992).

5 The common themes in the political strategies of Donald Trump and Benjamin Netanyahu reflect their shared authoritarian values: both embrace ultraright racist hatemongers, both call legitimate investigations into their corrupt activities "witch hunts," and both blame the free press and liberals for their problems.

TWENTY-FOUR

Herbert Titus and Christian Nationalism

Herbert W. Titus was an outstanding student, graduating as co-valedictorian of his Baker (Oregon) high school class, Phi Beta Kappa at the University of Oregon, and cum laude from Harvard Law School (1962). For fifteen years, he was a professor of law at state universities in Oklahoma, Colorado, and Oregon. During this time he opposed the war in Vietnam, supported abortion and homosexual rights, and was a cooperating attorney with the American Civil Liberties Union.

Then, on the last weekend of July 1975, Titus was "dramatically converted to Christ" (his words). The following year, he studied with evangelical theologian Francis Schaeffer in Switzerland. In 1979, he joined the Christian law school faculty at Oral Roberts University. Three years later, he moved to Pat Robertson's Regent University, where he served in several administrative positions, including founding dean of the law school. He left Regent in 1993 after a disagreement with Robertson.

Since then, Titus has been active in a number of conservative religious causes. He established a journal that focuses on biblical and constitutional analysis of public policy issues; he conducts training seminars on law from a biblical perspective; he wrote two booklets asserting that the Declaration of Independence and the US Constitution are Christian documents; he was the vice presidential candidate on the Constitutional Party ticket in 1996; and he was an attorney for Ten Commandments Judge Roy Moore after his removal from the Alabama Supreme Court.

Titus's views would appear to have become progressively more extreme, culminating in an association with survivalist and longtime Christian Reconstructionist "Scary Gary" North. (North is a former son-in-law of Rousas Rushdoony, the late founder of the modern Reconstructionist movement.) But this would not be entirely accurate because Titus's affiliation with Reconstructionism can be traced back to his attendance at a small Reconstructionist-affiliated Orthodox Presbyterian church in Oregon, where North's father was a member.

Christian Reconstructionists believe that (a) American law should be based on the legal code of the Hebrew Testament, requiring the death penalty for eighteen specific offenses, such as adultery, homosexuality, witchcraft, and blasphemy; (b) abortion should be outlawed, with execution the punishment for the woman and physician; (c) the American system of public education and the current program of government entitlements should be abolished; (d) an unregulated system of economic capitalism should be implemented; (e) the Genesis version of creation is the only acceptable doctrine of origins; and, most important, (f) democracy as we know it should be eliminated, e.g., most Americans would not be able to vote. In summary, Reconstructionists propose to replace our constitutional democracy with a bible-based theocracy.

It is only fair to note that Titus does not agree with all Reconstructionist positions. However, he does believe that only born-again Christians should be eligible to hold public office in America, a view he shares with his former mentor Pat Robertson. He also would like to see the Ten Commandments posted in courthouses across the country, the public school system and welfare abolished, and Mosaic Law incorporated into the US legal code.

The fundamental premise underlying Reconstructionist political philosophy is the assertion that America was founded as a Christian nation. Titus's contribution to the Christian Nation proposition was published in the aforementioned booklets that claim to demonstrate that the Declaration of Independence and the US Constitution are Christian documents. Among the numerous distortions, misrepresentations, and fallacies presented in the two publications, four points merit comment because they are found throughout the Christian Nation mythological literature.

First, Titus repeatedly attempted to diminish Thomas Jefferson's role as author of the Declaration, stating instead that it was "produced by the combined efforts of five men." In fact, Jefferson wrote a draft of 1,806 words, which was edited to 1,322 by the appointed committee and Congress. Fully 90 percent of the words in the final version came from Jefferson's draft. Why do Christian Nation advocates dislike Jefferson? Because he denied the divinity of Jesus. How could a man who held the basic Christian dogmas (virgin birth, resurrection, miracles, trinity, and original sin) in contempt have written a Christian document?

Second, Titus cited a total of forty-nine bible verses that he claims constitute the Christian foundation of the Declaration. Two-thirds of the citations are Hebrew Testament verses and one-third are from the Christian Testament. However, three-quarters of the latter are Paul's statements, and none derives from the Gospels. In other words, Titus assembled a Hebrew/Paulist foundation for the Declaration, with Jesus's teachings contributing nothing to the argument. The truth is that the Declaration is a deistic formulation authored by Thomas Jefferson with valuable editorial input from others.

Third, concerning the alleged Christian basis of the US Constitution, Titus declared that the subscription clause ("in the year of our Lord") attests to the "authenticity" of the document and guarantees that it is "genuine." Of course, the subscription clause has been a ceremonial formality in English-speaking countries for a thousand years. For example, many state universities in the United States granted diplomas as recently as the 1970s with the subscription clause preceding the date of award.

Fourth, Titus argued that the "no religious test" clause permits but does not require a religious oath, which is proved by the practice of many American presidents taking the oath of office with his hand on the bible and uttering "so help me God." What Titus fails to mention is that Jesus himself prohibited *all* oaths (Matthew 5:34–37).

It is difficult to understand the personality dynamics that caused an accomplished individual to go from dedicated civil libertarian to staunch proponent of theocracy. Of course, Herbert Titus was not the first person to experience a dramatic conversion to Christ. He testified that Jesus appeared in the attic of his home in Oregon, a precipitating event in his spiritual journey. It is apparent that superior intellectual abilities coexist with bizarre ideas in his mind. Not only did his conversion to radical Christianity constitute a loss of talent to the cause of social justice, Herbert Titus's extreme political theology represents a potential threat to the freedom of nonbelieving Americans.

Prominent Conversions to and from Christianity

Prominent examples of dramatic conversion begin with Saul of Tarsus (St. Paul) and include well-known Christian writers C.S. Lewis and Malcolm Muggeridge. It should also be noted that many contemporary humanists have gone the other direction, i.e., they "lost the faith." Examples are Dan Barker, Jerry Coyne, Bart Ehrman, A.J. Mattill Jr., Gregory Paul, Michael Shermer, and Thomas Vernon. Based on anecdotal stories and personal testimony, it seems that there are numerous paths to and from supernatural belief.

TWENTY-FIVE

Christian Heritage Week — More Fundamentalist Dishonesty

At a news conference in the Capitol rotunda in February 1994, Arkansas Lieutenant Governor Mike Huckabee defended his signing of a "Christian Heritage Week" proclamation. He said that he would be willing to sponsor similar declarations for other religions.

Speaking at a Republican Party dinner a few days later, Huckabee decreed: "In America, we ought to be open and tolerant of various religious viewpoints." And he again said that he would support official recognition of contributions made by other religious groups.

But his utterances are insincere. I had requested that Huckabee proclaim Humanist Heritage Week by signing a declaration modeled after the Christian proclamation. Interestingly, the humanist proclamation included quotations from four of the six American founders cited in the Christian declaration. Huckabee declined to sign the humanist proclamation for various reasons. For example, he said that the quotes from the six founding fathers were not documented so that their accuracy could be verified and that my request had not first been presented to the governor.

The justification given by Huckabee for not signing the humanist declaration was a transparent subterfuge. Governor Jim Guy Tucker had a well-known policy of not issuing proclamations favoring specific religious groups. In fact, he had rejected the Christian proclamation in October 1993!

Nevertheless, I addressed each of Huckabee's concerns. References for the quotes by the six humanist founders were provided and I asked Tucker to sign the humanist proclamation. After the governor predictably declined, I again requested that Huckabee endorse the humanist declaration.

In his hostile reply, Huckabee once more refused to sign the humanist proclamation. He listed several reasons to rationalize his decision.

For example, Huckabee characterized the humanist proclamation as consisting of "out of context and isolated statements by various historical figures." Ironically, this describes exactly the Christian declaration. Furthermore, four of the six founders quoted in the Christian proclamation and commended as "Christian statesmen" were not even Christians! They were humanists.

Another charge by Huckabee was that I had not demonstrated how humanism "has benefited our culture or our society in a significant way." I had assumed that an educated individual would be acquainted with the milestone intellectual epochs in the history of Western civilization.

Humanism originated in classical Greek and Roman antiquity and reemerged in the fifteenth century literary and philosophical movement called the Renaissance. The values and attitudes of Renaissance humanism were amplified in the eighteenth-century Enlightenment. For over two millennia, the religious philosophy of humanism has contributed substantially to the intellectual and moral foundation of Western thought.

The American Founders were products of the Enlightenment, as evidenced by their allegiance to the naturalistic religion of Deism. Language in the Declaration of Independence and other source documents indicates the pervasive influence of Deism ("Nature's God").

Humanism is the philosophical precursor of Deism and thus constitutes the historical basis for many American political principles. The religious philosophy of humanism embraces many contemporary groups and denominations, such as Religious Humanism, Humanistic Judaism, Ethical Culture, Freethought, Unitarianism, Secular Humanism, Rationalism, and Christian Humanism.

Huckabee also rejected the humanist proclamation because he "could not recall having seen hospitals, homeless shelters, and educational institutions built in the name of advancing humanism." What the Rev. Huckabee has done, of course, is to enumerate a set of exclusionary criteria that eliminate all minority religious views from consideration for official state recognition.

More than 80 percent* of Americans identify themselves as Christians, with one-fourth associated with fundamentalist theologies. So the dozens of small faiths like Bahaism, Buddhism, Hinduism, Islam, Mormonism, Scientology, and Unity, as well as the Humanist denominations noted above, are dismissed by Huckabee as undeserving of official recognition because they don't satisfy his personal requirements.

This is simply religious bigotry. How ironic that the nation's founders, who were misrepresented in the Christian proclamation that Huckabee signed, were staunch advocates of religious tolerance, respect for the beliefs of others, and freedom of conscience in matters of faith.

Huckabee has routinely used his office to promote his own fundamentalist views while denigrating the values and beliefs of citizens with whom he disagrees. For example, he asserted that April 1st ("Fool's Day") should be celebrated as "Atheist Day." And during his first year in office, Huckabee's income from Religious Right activities exceeded his taxpayer-supported salary.

It's no wonder that Huckabee was unwilling to support a humanist declaration.

Brian Bolton's Proclamation

> WHEREAS, the US Constitution contains no mention of God or Christianity and states specifically that "no religious test shall ever be required as a qualification to any office or public trust" (Article VI); and
>
> WHEREAS, Benjamin Franklin, American statesman, asserted: "When a religion is good, I conceive it will support itself, and when

it does not support itself, and God does not take care to support it so that its professors are obliged to call for help of the civil power, 'tis a sign, I apprehend, of its being a bad one"; and

Whereas, under George Washington, first President of the United States, the Treaty of Tripoli was written, with the assurance that "the government of the United States is not, in any sense, founded on the Christian religion"; and

Whereas, Thomas Jefferson, author of the Declaration of Independence, wrote: "Question with boldness even the existence of God; because if there be one, He must approve the homage of Reason rather than that of blindfolded Fear"; and

Whereas, James Madison, Father of the US Constitution, stated: "During almost fifteen centuries has the legal establishment of Christianity been on trial. What has been its fruits? More or less, in all places, pride and indolence in the clergy; ignorance and servility in the laity; in both, superstition, bigotry and persecution"; and

Whereas, John Adams, second president of the United States, declared that "I almost shudder at the thought of alluding to the most fatal example of the abuses of grief which the history of [hu] mankind has preserved—the Cross. Consider what calamities that engine of grief has produced!"; and

Whereas, Thomas Paine, author of *Common Sense*, wrote: "Whenever we read the obscene stories, the voluptuous debaucheries, the cruel and tortuous executions, the unrelenting vindictiveness with which more than half the bible is filled, it would be more consistent that we call it the word of a demon than the word of God. It is a history of wickedness that has served to corrupt and brutalize [hu]mankind"; and

Whereas, These, and many other truly great men and women of America, giants in the structuring of American history, were humanists of the Deist, Freethought, and Unitarian persuasions, and staunch advocates of religious tolerance and freedom of conscience;

Now, Therefore, I do proclaim Humanist Heritage Week.

* *Christian Heritage Week has been resurrected as a major component of Project Blitz's campaign to Christianize the United States. Also, 65 percent of Americans now self-identify as Christians, down more than 15 percentage points since the article was first written and down 30 percentage points since 1950.*

VI. Biblical Ten Commandments

TWENTY-SIX
Questioning Those Ten Commandments

The US Supreme Court, in the 1980 case *Stone vs. Graham*, declared that the Ten Commandments is "undeniably a sacred text" and ruled that posting it in public schools is unconstitutional.

In past decades, more than two dozen cases dealing with displays of the Hebrew decalogue in public schools, courtrooms, and other government buildings have been addressed by the US judicial system. The vast majority of the decisions have concluded that displays of the Ten Commandments in public venues violate the US Constitution.

Yet, the Ten Commandments devotees persist. A survey of American adults, conducted for the First Amendment Center, found that 61 percent of respondents thought that the decalogue should be posted in the public schools! They are encouraged by irresponsible statements by judges and state attorneys general that the Ten Commandments is the moral foundation of US law and culture.

Although this assertion is absolutely false, most Americans have not taken the time to read the full text of the Ten Commandments and decide the issue for themselves. The following sixteen questions and answers outline why the Ten Commandments should be rejected. They demonstrate that the Mosaic decalogue is not an exemplary behavioral code that will make America a better society.

1. Does the Ten Commandments constitute a set of philosophical precepts?

Former cable television news commentator Bill O'Reilly asserted that the decalogue summarizes "Judeo-Christian philosophy" and therefore is not an establishment of religion. To counter this claim it is only necessary to cite three facts: The commandments are taken from the Holy Bible, they were issued by the Hebrew god Yahweh ("I am the lord thy god"), and the first four are clearly theological edicts. The Ten Commandments is obviously a religious code.

2. Does the Ten Commandments acknowledge the Judeo-Christian god?

The decalogue was authored by Yahweh, the Hebrew god who liberated the ancient Israelites from slavery in Egypt (Exodus 20:2). The Christian savior-god story was not assembled until more than 1,000 years after the Mosaic rules were formulated. In fact, there is no Judeo-Christian god and no evidence that Jews were enslaved. This deity was invented to suggest a unified biblical history and theology which does not exist.

3. Is the Ten Commandments the moral foundation of American law, government, and culture, as Roy Moore, Bill Pryor, Greg Abbott, and other fundamentalists have repeatedly stated?

A distinguished committee of legal historians recently concluded that American law is not based on the Ten Commandments. The US Constitution is the foundation of American law, which derives in good part from English common law. Interestingly, Thomas Jefferson reached this conclusion more than 200 years ago. A cursory review of the Ten Commandments reveals that only the unoriginal prohibitions against murder, stealing, and perjury are reflected in current US law.[1]

4. What is the prescribed punishment for violators of the first nine commandments?

Infractions of any one of the first nine commandments require imposition of the death penalty—typically by stoning to death, but occasionally by burning alive or strangulation. Are the pious religionists who want to post God's laws in public buildings willing to apply God's ordained punishment to violators? If the decalogue is posted anywhere, then the associated penalties with mode of administration should also be displayed. After all, it's God's word!

5. Does the first commandment acknowledge the existence of multiple gods?

"Thou shalt have no other gods before me" (Exodus 20:3) unambiguously recognizes the existence of competing gods—the basis of polytheism. This commandment orders adherents to worship only the Hebrew God and relegates the others to a lesser status. It is entirely inappropriate for this religious directive to be displayed on any public property in the United States, because it constitutes exclusive approval of one among many acknowledged gods.

6. Does the second commandment enunciate a religious principle that is repellent to all civilized people?

The first part of the second commandment prohibits the making of graven images (Exodus 20:4). However, the second part contains jealous Yahweh's promise to "visit the iniquities of the fathers upon the children unto the third and fourth generation of those that hate me" (Exodus 20:5). Is punishing the innocent descendants of violators an acceptable principle of justice? Is this one of the "foundational principles of Western legal codes and culture" that (the then) Texas Attorney General Greg Abbott considers worthy of defense? Critics should demand that the full text of the Ten Commandments be reproduced in all public displays.

7. Does the fourth commandment endorse slavery?

The fourth commandment forbids working on the sabbath: Thou shalt not do any work on the seventh day, nor thy manservant nor thy maidservant (Exodus 20:10). Manservant and maidservant are euphemisms for male and female slaves. It should also be noted that while there is some disagreement about which day is the sabbath (Friday, Saturday, or Sunday), outlawing all work on any day would virtually destroy the US economy. Furthermore, enforcement would entail executing millions of

Americans—professional athletes, Walmart employees, restaurant workers, and others. It is blasphemous to post Yahweh's sacred rules and then disobey them.

8. Does the fifth commandment promise a reward for honoring one's parents?

The fifth commandment is another rule that is almost always listed in abbreviated form. The phrase "that thy days may be long upon the land which Yahweh giveth thee" (Exodus 20:12) is usually omitted. This commandment explicitly appeals to the selfish motives of offspring.

9. Does the tenth commandment further diminish the status of women?

"Thou shalt not covet thy neighbor's house, wife, servants, animals, or anything else" (Exodus 20:17). This godly law clearly classifies a man's wife as one of his possessions, reinforcing the view that women are property. The subservient status of women is a dominant theme in several religious denominations in the United States, e.g., Southern Baptist, Catholic, and Muslim. The tenth commandment also approves of slavery.

10. Is the Ten Commandments posted in the US Supreme Court building?

George W. Bush's recess judicial appointee (to a circuit court judgeship), former Alabama Attorney General Bill Pryor, asserted that the Hebrew decalogue is displayed in the US Supreme Court building. The fact is that Moses is depicted on a frieze with several other historical and nonhistorical lawgivers, including Hammurabi, Solomon, Confucius, Muhammad, Napoleon, and Augustus. Moses is holding two tablets that contain only a few Hebrew characters, not the entire Ten Commandments.

11. Does a Ten Commandments monument on public property constitute a religious endorsement?

In his decision supporting a Ten Commandments monument (donated by the Fraternal Order of Eagles) on the capitol grounds in Austin, Texas, Judge Harry Hudspeth declared that "no reasonable person would consider the display to be a religious endorsement." How could any reasonable person read the first line ("I am the lord thy god") and conclude otherwise? No less an authority than Roy Moore said that the public display of the decalogue "recognizes the sovereignty of God." Unbelievably, the local newspaper (the *Austin American-Statesman*) agreed with Hudspeth, opining that anyone offended by the monument should just not look at it!

12. Does advocacy of the Ten Commandments promote religious bigotry?

Under questioning by Judge Myron Thompson of the US District Court, former chief justice of the Alabama Supreme Court Roy Moore stated that Buddhism, Hinduism, and Islam are not religions under the First Amendment of the US Constitution because they do not recognize the God of the holy scriptures. Moore also said that his judicial duty under the Constitution was to acknowledge the Judeo-Christian god, that only the Judeo-Christian god allows for freedom of conscience, and that America was founded on the law of the Holy Bible. Thompson found these assertions to be incorrect and religiously offensive.

13. Are there actually twelve commandments in the decalogue?

All presentations of the Ten Commandments end with the tenth. But, two additional commandments are given in chapter 20 of Exodus. First, do not make or worship silver or gold idols (Exodus 20:23). Second, construct sacrificial altars of earth or uncut stone without steps (Exodus 20: 24–26). Why do the fundamentalist advocates of posting Yahweh's holy word omit these important rules?

14. Does proscribing unacceptable behavior develop commendable character?

Nine of the Ten Commandments are stated as prohibitions—they tell us what not to do; only one is phrased affirmatively (honor your parents). We know that a useful ethical code tells us how to behave properly—not just to avoid being bad. In other words, the absence of antisocial behavior does not constitute good citizenship. Instead of posting the decalogue, schools and courtrooms should display the Affirmations of Humanism, a series of philosophical principles that promote ethical living.

15. What did Moses do with the stone tablets on which Yahweh wrote the Ten Commandments?

Moses broke the stone tablets in anger when he saw the Israelites dancing, fornicating, and worshipping the golden calf that Aaron had created (Exodus 32:6, 19, 25). Then, under Yahweh's instruction, Moses ordered the righteous Levites to kill their ungodly kinsmen—about 3,000 were slaughtered. Yahweh sent a plague to punish the surviving people for worshipping the golden calf (Exodus 32:27–35).

16. Is the popular version of the Hebrew decalogue the true biblical Ten Commandments?

A careful examination of the Exodus story indicates that the true biblical Ten Commandments are found in Exodus 34:14–26. The key verses that support this conclusion are Exodus 31:18; 34:1; 34:28. The true biblical decalogue consists of theological edicts, purity laws, and festival requirements—only three overlap with the popular version of the Ten Commandments. However, because it is the Cecil B. DeMille version that Christian fundamentalists want to post in schools, courtrooms, and government offices, this is the set of Ten Commandments that should be the target of critics.

Summary

The US Bill of Rights guarantees religious freedom for all Americans and prohibits the government from promoting religious rules of any kind. If the advocates want to display the Ten Commandments in their homes, businesses, or churches, that's their constitutional right.

However, if fundamentalist fanatics continue to publicly impose the abbreviated version of the Hebrew decalogue on everyone else, then I have a reasonable proposal. See the next chapter.

Chapter 26 Endnotes

1 Forty-one law professors and legal historians, who were convened by Steven Green of the Willamette University College of Law, prepared scholarly arguments to be used in friend-of-the-court briefs for the federal lawsuit against Roy Moore and McCreary County, Kentucky Supreme Court case. The committee demonstrated that American law was based on English common and statutory law, Roman law, and the laws of other European nations, as well as the writings of William Blackstone, John Locke, and Adam Smith. They concluded that nothing in the nation's legal history supports the false claim that the Ten Commandments are the foundation of American law.

TWENTY-SEVEN
Display the Ten Commandments Now!

Opponents of Ten Commandments displays in public venues have been reasonably effective in keeping them out of capitols, courthouses, and classrooms. Yet these successful efforts have only served to further enrage fundamentalist activists and cause them to intensify their spurious schemes. What is needed is a new approach that will thwart this obsession with the Hebrew Decalogue. Remember, Christian fundamentalists relegate Jews to eternal suffering for refusing to acknowledge Jesus as messiah. Why, then, are they so enamored with the Hebrew scriptures?

A rational approach to addressing this fundamentalist fetish entails a complete reversal from the current strategy. Supporters of church/state separation should strongly endorse public display of the Ten Commandments, with three specified provisos that would surely have God's approval, because they are entirely consistent with the letter and spirit of his divine word.

1. The full text of the Hebrew decalogue must be reproduced exactly as god dictated it to Moses.

2. The punishments ordained by God for violators must be listed with each of the commandments.
3. The commandments must be incorporated into the US legal code and enforced in a manner consistent with God's will.

This chapter summarizes basic facts about the ancient Hebrew decalogue and outlines the impact of enforcement on the US population. The biblical justification, with detailed scriptural documentation for this proposal, follows.

Historical Perspective

The most celebrated Ten Commandments battle in recent US history was initiated in 2001 when Alabama Supreme Court Chief Justice Roy Moore secretly installed a two-ton granite decalogue monument in the rotunda of the Judicial Building. Two years later, after a federal judge ruled "Roy's rock" to be unconstitutional, it was removed, and Moore was thrown out of office. A fitting epitaph for his tombstone would be his statement: "If they want to get the Commandments, they're going to have to get me first." Moore was reelected to the bench in 2012 but suspended *again* by the state's Judicial Inquiry Commission in 2016.

Over the past ten years, more than a dozen attempts to display the Ten Commandments have been undertaken by state legislators, county commissioners, district judges, and school officials. The targeted locations have included state capitols, county courthouses, public schools, municipal parks, and other government offices. The states involved have been Alabama, Arkansas, Florida, Georgia, Michigan, Ohio, Oklahoma, Tennessee, Texas, Utah, and Virginia. Almost all of these efforts failed, although in some cases the proponents are still fighting on behalf of their sacred symbol.

A major judicial confrontation occurred in Oklahoma and has some amusing similarities to Alabama's melodrama from years earlier. In 2012, a granite Ten Commandments monument was erected on the Capitol grounds in Oklahoma City after being authorized by the state legislature. Citing the state Constitution's "no-aid" clause, which bars taxpayer dollars from funding religion, the Oklahoma Supreme Court ruled 7–2 in 2015 that this contemporary megalith was unconstitutional. Shortly after

Governor Mary Fallin vowed not to move the shrine, it was relocated to a private setting. More encouraging news came in November 2016, when Oklahoma voters rejected a ballot measure that would have removed the "no-aid" clause.

And at the time of writing, it seems likely that the next Ten Commandments showdown will occur in Arkansas. In 2015, a bill authorizing a decalogue commemorative on the state Capitol grounds was signed into law by Governor Asa Hutchinson. Unlike the Oklahoma monument, the proposed Arkansas display will be modeled after the one on the grounds of the Texas Capitol, where the Ten Commandments are included in a much larger arrangement of seventeen separate markers situated on a twenty-two-acre lawn. The Texas decalogue display was deemed constitutional by the U S Supreme Court in 2005.

I will give Scott Teague of Mountain City, Tennessee, the final word in this review. In defending a decalogue display at the Johnson County Courthouse, he intoned, "God have mercy on the soul of any person who attempts to have these documents removed from this courthouse or any courthouse in America." It should be noted that Teague is a professional undertaker.

Indisputable Facts

- The Ten Commandments is clearly a religious code with the first four presenting theological edicts. It derives from a sacred text that was issued by the Hebrew god, known as Yahweh.
- The first commandment unambiguously acknowledges the existence of multiple competing gods, who are relegated to inferior status. Americans know that their government has no authority to tell citizens which of these gods, if any, to worship.
- In addition to prohibiting idolatry, the second commandment contains God's explicit promise to punish the innocent descendants of those who violate this injunction. In fact, God often punished children for the sins of their parents (e.g., Numbers 16:25–34; Joshua 7:13–26; Daniel 6:24).
- The fifth commandment to honor one's parents explicitly appeals to the selfish motives of offspring by promising a reward of long life

for obedience. Shouldn't this be a sacred duty motivated by intrinsic values?

- Both the fourth and tenth commandments endorse slavery, and the tenth diminishes the status of women by classifying a man's wife as one of his possessions, reinforcing the view that women, just like slaves and livestock, are property.
- Legal scholars have demonstrated that the foundations of American jurisprudence are the Constitution, the Bill of Rights, and English common law—not the Ten Commandments and not the bible. This is the false premise on which the entire public display scheme is based.
- The decalogue is not a useful ethical code. Nine of the commandments are stated as prohibitions against extreme behavior and don't tell us how to act ethically. It's worth repeating that the absence of antisocial behavior does not constitute good citizenship.

Capital Punishment for Violators

The following list provides a comprehensive biblical justification for enforcing the death penalty for violators of the first nine commandments. The death penalty is required for violating:

Commandment one—Anyone who worships or sacrifices to gods other than Yahweh (Exodus 22:20; Leviticus 20:1–2, 5; Numbers 25:1–9; Deuteronomy 17:2–7; 2 Kings 10:24–28; 2 Chronicles 24:17–26) or encourages others to worship heathen gods (Deuteronomy 13:6–17, 2 Chronicles 21:11–19).

Commandment two—Anyone who worships idols or the sun, moon, or stars (Exodus 32:27–29, 35; Deuteronomy 17:2–5; 2 Kings 17:13–20; 2 Chronicles 21:13–21) or engages in occult practices (Exodus 22:18; Leviticus 20:6, 27; Deuteronomy 18:10–12; 1 Samuel 28:9; 2 Kings 23:5–7, 20–24; 1 Chronicles 10:13–14).

Commandment three—Anyone who curses Yahweh (Leviticus 24:10–23; 1 Kings 21:8–13) or engages in false prophecy (Deuteronomy 13:5, 18:20; 1 Kings 18:40).

Commandment four—Anyone who works on a sabbath day (Exodus 31:14–15, 35:2; Leviticus 23:30–31; Numbers 15:32–36).

Commandment five—Anyone who strikes or curses their parents (Exodus 21:15, 17; Leviticus 20:9; Matthew 15:4; Mark 7:10).

Commandment six—Anyone who murders (Genesis 9:6, Exodus 21:14, Leviticus 24:17–21, Numbers 35:16–34, Deuteronomy 19:11–13) or kidnaps (Exodus 21:16, Deuteronomy 24:7).

Commandment seven—Anyone who commits adultery or fornication (Leviticus 20:10–12, Deuteronomy 22:22–27) or engages in homosexual acts (Genesis 19:23–25, Leviticus 20:13, Romans 1:26–32).

Commandment eight—Anyone who steals from Yahweh (Joshua 7:1–26) or the Christian community (Acts 5:1–11).

Commandment nine—Anyone who gives false testimony when the defendant is facing the death penalty (Deuteronomy 19:21).

Commandment ten is the only one that appears not to require the death penalty if violated. It is also the only edict that involves no more than an "improper" attitude of envy or desire rather than an explicit action or behavior.

It should be stressed that both Jesus (Matthew 5:17, 15:4, Mark 7:10) and Paul (Romans 1:26–32, 1 Timothy 1:8–11) unequivocally endorsed the death penalty as promulgated in Mosaic Law.

Who Would Be Executed in the United States?

We know from long experience that chronicling moral directives without imposing punitive sanctions on transgressors has minimal benefit. So shouldn't we expect that those who propose displaying the Ten Commandments would also endorse Yahweh's punishment scheme? What impact would enforcing the Mosaic death penalty in the United States have on the population? What would the execution rate be under strict adherence to the capital punishment requirements associated with the Hebrew decalogue?

The first commandment orders residents to worship only Yahweh and relegates all other gods to prohibited status. About one-tenth of the population would be immediately executed unless they renounced their false gods. If Paul's directive concerning the applicability of the death penalty to irreligious citizens is accepted, then an additional fifth of the nation's people would be eliminated.

Correctly punishing violators of the second and third commandments, which forbid idolatry and blasphemy, respectively, would exterminate the Deists, Wiccans, sculptors, astrologers, and mediums among us.

While there is some disagreement about which day is the sabbath, in almost all US communities it is Sunday ("the Lord's Day"). Outlawing all work on the traditional day of rest as required by the fourth commandment would cause a major disruption of the US economy. Furthermore, enforcement would involve executing millions of Americans, including entire hospital staffs; firefighters; police officers; paramedics; 911 dispatchers; security guards; professional athletes; store clerks; restaurant workers; customer service representatives; and many, many others.

Regarding the fifth commandment, which counsels respect for parents, it is a sad fact that abuse of the elderly is a serious problem. The explicit appeal to the selfish motives of offspring doesn't seem to enhance compliance with the directive. Likewise, it is doubtful that capital punishment for those who strike or curse parents would improve the situation, but they still must be killed.

The US judicial system, with the overwhelming support of the citizenry, already does a great job of punishing violators of the sixth commandment, which prohibits murder, by invoking the biblical dictum of "a life for a life." America is the only Western democracy that has not abolished state-sanctioned execution of its murderers, with Texas in first place among the states that allow the death penalty.

Uniform enforcement of the seventh commandment, which condemns adulterers, would result in a substantial reduction in the US population, because one-third of married residents engage in at least one extramarital affair. If Jesus's equating of remarriage after divorce with adultery is included, along with the addition of homosexuals and fornicators, the lives of one-half of all Americans would be in jeopardy.

The application of the death penalty under the eighth commandment, which prohibits theft, would entail careful analysis of the crimes to determine just what constitutes stealing from Yahweh or the Christian community. While very few witnesses commit perjury in capital punishment trials, they would have to be executed in accordance with the ninth commandment.

Recommendations

First, we should demand that the full text be included in all displays, so that the truly offensive elaborations cannot be omitted. Commandments two, four, five, and ten are absolutely essential to any exhibit endorsed by critics. To abbreviate any of god's edicts is blasphemy and should be punished just as scripture mandates.

Second, we need to demand that God's ordained penalties for violators of the first nine commandments be prominently displayed on all monuments and plaques. The compelling argument is that publicizing the required punishments will have a much stronger deterrent effect; moreover, this is God's will.

Third, we must demand that God's sacred law as embodied in the decalogue be enforced precisely as god intended. This will necessitate prompt action by lawmakers, who will have to quickly enact legislation that incorporates the Ten Commandments into the US legal code.

Will the fundamentalist Christian advocates of displaying the Decalogue also insist that the required penalties be applied as God ordained? Of course not. These pious proponents of public posting want to impose their sanctified rules on everybody else without assuming any responsibility for enforcement.

Their fanatical promotion of publicly recognizing God's moral mandates is selective, cowardly, and dishonest. Furthermore, anything less than total implementation and enforcement of the Ten Commandments is willful disrespect for God's word and therefore constitutes blasphemy, a crime that requires and deserves the death penalty.

What the Monuments Won't Tell You: The Ten* Commandments in Their Entirety Exodus 20:1–17

Then God spoke all these words:

> I am the Lord your God, who brought you out of the land of Egypt, out of the house of slavery;
>
> You shall have no other gods before me.
>
> You shall not make for yourself an idol, whether in the form of anything that is in heaven above, or that is on the earth be-

neath, or that is in the water under the earth. You shall not bow down to them or worship them; for I the Lord your God am a jealous God, punishing children for the iniquity of parents, to the third and the fourth generation of those who reject me, but showing steadfast love to the thousandth generation of those who love me and keep my commandments.

You shall not make wrongful use of the name of the Lord your God, for the Lord will not acquit anyone who misuses his name.

Remember the Sabbath day, and keep it holy. Six days you shall labor and do all your work. But the seventh day is a Sabbath to the Lord your God; you shall not do any work—you, your son or your daughter, your male or female slave, your livestock, or the alien resident in your towns. For in six days the Lord made heaven and earth, the sea, and all that is in them, but rested the seventh day; therefore the Lord blessed the sabbath day and consecrated it.

Honor your father and your mother, so that your days may be long in the land that the Lord your God is giving you.

You shall not murder.

You shall not commit adultery.

You shall not steal.

You shall not bear false witness against your neighbor.

You shall not covet your neighbor's house; you shall not covet your neighbor's wife, or male or female slave, or ox, or donkey, or anything that belongs to your neighbor.

**With an addendum a few verses later re: idols and altars (Exodus 20:23–26)*

TWENTY-EIGHT

Ten Facts About the Ten Commandments for Justice Gorsuch

Justice Neil Gorsuch does not understand that the constitutional principle of separation of church and state is the foundation of religious freedom in America. In fact, he seems to hold the essential First Amendment principle in contempt, if we rely on two dissenting opinions written when he was a judge on the United States Court of Appeals for the Tenth Circuit.

Gorsuch apparently believes that governments should be able to endorse religion, Christianity in particular. Specifically, he has argued that decalogue monuments on public property are acceptable because they are more than religious symbols and that standing Latin crosses don't promote Christianity.

His views should be a matter of concern to everyone because his decisions will influence the lives of all US citizens for decades to come. But his opinion about Ten Commandments displays also raises questions about his knowledge of scripture, certainly a serious issue for a jurist who is embraced by conservative Christians.

In the case *Green v. Haskell County [Oklahoma] Board of Commis-*

sioners, then-Judge Gorsuch wrote a dissent, stating that public decalogue displays communicate a "secular moral message," in addition to the clear religious directives. Although his claim is factually accurate, the "moral ideals" expressed in the Ten Commandments are offensive to many Americans.

Gorsuch should read the full text of the Judeo-Christian decalogue before recommending public posting and thus government endorsement of the Mosaic edicts.[1]

Ten Problems with the Decalogue

1. The first commandment forbids worship of any god other than Yahweh, the god of the ancient Israelites. This blanket prohibition effectively establishes the religion of the early Hebrew people, in violation of the First Amendment to the US Constitution.[2] It also violates the free exercise clause by restricting religious practice. Governments have no business telling citizens which gods, if any, they should worship or what constitutes acceptable religious practice.
2. The second, third, and fourth commandments, which prohibit idolatry, blasphemy, and Sabbath breaking, respectively, clearly violate the First Amendment by imposing limits on the free exercise of religion. No government entity should interfere with citizens' rights by proscribing idol worship, blasphemous utterances, and labor on holy days, especially in a secular democracy. Interestingly, the last blasphemy conviction in the United States occurred less than a century ago, but the charges were later dropped.
3. The second commandment also features God's explicit promise to punish the descendants of Israelites who worship or sacrifice to idols. Penalizing innocent offspring for the crimes of their progenitors is called collective punishment and is condemned by all modern societies. In fact, the biblical god routinely engaged in the detestable practice of punishing children for the sins of their parents (e.g., Numbers 16:25–34; Joshua 7:13–26; Daniel 6:24).
4. The fourth commandment endorses involuntary servitude or slavery, in the context of prohibiting sabbath breaking. The sacred scriptures, both Hebrew and Christian testaments, strongly support the

horrific institution of chattel slavery. In particular, Jesus, Paul, and Peter were unwavering advocates of this approved Christian practice. Moreover, the largest US Protestant denomination was formed as a direct consequence of the bible's sanction of slavery.

5. The fifth commandment, which requires children to demonstrate respect for their parents, expressly appeals to the selfish motives of offspring. The responsibility to care for one's parents should not be contingent on the promise of long life for compliance. An authentic ethical code encourages good behavior because it's intrinsically correct, not because benefits may accrue for actions taken.
6. The tenth commandment endorses involuntary servitude or chattel slavery again—see point 4 above. It should also be noted that this God-ordained human institution provided the labor force for the Southern economy for almost a quarter of a millennium, giving problematic meaning to the term "American exceptionalism."
7. The tenth commandment also endorses patriarchalism, the scriptural principle which holds that men are superior and women are subservient. Specifically, the status of women is diminished by classifying a man's wife as one of his possessions, reinforcing the view that women, just like livestock, are men's property.
8. Biblical law mandates the death penalty for violators of the first seven commandments, with no exceptions. Transgressions specified in scripture include: worshipping or sacrificing to other gods; encouraging worship of heathen gods; worshipping idols or the sun, moon, or stars; engaging in occult practices; cursing Yahweh; engaging in false prophecy; working on the sabbath; striking or cursing one's parents; committing murder; kidnapping another person; committing adultery or fornication; engaging in homosexual acts.[3]
9. Biblical law requires the death penalty for some violations of the eighth and ninth commandments. Those who steal from God or the Christian community or who give false testimony when the defendant is facing the death penalty must be executed.

10. Biblical law explicitly prohibits modifying God's commandments by either adding to or subtracting from the sacred text, especially the Mosaic decalogue (Deuteronomy 4:2; Revelation 22:18–19). Because all current public decalogue displays, as well as those previously posted and subsequently removed, include only the seventy-five to one hundred word abbreviated versions, rather than the 300-word original text, most of the offensive material summarized above is omitted.[4] This huge discrepancy is probably the source of Gorsuch's erroneous claim about the desirability of the secular morality expressed in the Ten Commandments.

Six Additional Facts About the Decalogue

In addition to the ten problems detailed above, the Ten Commandments include six other shortcomings that deserve mention.

11. The tenth commandment is unique in that it does not require the death penalty if violated. This may be because it is the only one that does not address an observable behavior. Coveting, wanting, or desiring someone else's property is an attitudinal disposition that may or may not lead to overt action.

12. The sixth, eighth, and ninth commandments, which prohibit murder, theft, and perjury, respectively, are included in every legal scheme enacted by modern societies. Furthermore, these prohibitions were not original to Mosaic Law, but are found in much earlier Egyptian, Babylonian, and Assyrian legal codes.

13. The seventh commandment prohibits adultery, which refers to having sexual relations with someone other than a marital spouse. This definition extends adultery to include fornication and homosexuality. At one time these were illegal acts, but Western attitudes have changed and they are now considered to be permissible, if not always approved, adult relationships.

14. A primary reason that the decalogue is not a useful ethical code is that nine of the commandments are stated as prohibitions against extreme behavior and therefore don't tell us how to act ethically. The absence of anti-social behavior is not the equivalent of good citizenship.

15. The foundation of American jurisprudence is not the Ten Commandments. Yet, many citizens believe this, including President Truman, who asserted that "the fundamental basis of this nation's law was given to Moses on the Mount." In fact, the US legal system is based on the Constitution, the Bill of Rights, and English common law.
16. Decalogue ignorance can be found in every US community. For example, the mayor of Georgetown, Texas, declared that America "would be a better country if we governed with the Ten Commandments." An opinion writer for the local newspaper disagreed, but then proclaimed the commandments to be "the quintessential guideposts for our lives." Why don't believers just read the bible to dispel their ignorance?

Gorsuch's Egregious Error

Gorsuch should have realized when he dissented in the Oklahoma case that the first four Mosaic commandments contradict both the establishment and free exercise clauses of the First Amendment (problems 1 and 2 above), and this fact alone renders decalogue monuments entirely inappropriate for placement on public property.

If he had been familiar with the complete text of the Ten Commandments and the rest of the Hebrew testament as well, Gorsuch would have realized the problems with the punishments ordained if you break the commandments. Regardless, we can state unequivocally, based on what scripture actually says, that there is no commendable secular moral message communicated by the Ten Commandments.

For advocates of public posting of the Ten Commandments who say the full 300-word text is too long, an acceptable alternative is the following seventy-word abbreviated version.

A Seventy-Word Fully Accurate Version of the Ten Commandments

I. Do not worship other gods.

II. Do not worship idols; if you do, I will punish your children for your sins.

III. Do not misuse my name.

IV. Do not work on the sabbath, nor your slaves.

V. Honor your parents; if you do, your reward will be long life.

VI. Do not murder.

VII. Do not commit adultery.

VIII. Do not steal.

IX. Do not commit perjury.

X. Do not covet your neighbor's wife, slaves, or livestock.

Chapter 28 Endnotes

1 The Ten Commandments addressed herein are located in Exodus 20:1–17 and Deuteronomy 5:6–21 of the Protestant Bible. Not included are the true Ten Commandments found in Exodus 34:10–27, or the slightly different versions in the Catholic Bible and other Hebrew translations, or the Ten Commandments for slave owners embedded in Exodus 21:2, 3, 4, 5–6, 7–8, 9, 10–11, 20–21, 26–27, 32.

2 It could be argued that the first commandment does not ban atheism or any nontheistic religion. Moreover, polytheism is endorsed because the existence of other gods is acknowledged. In fact, three dozen competing gods are identified by name in the scripture. God's initial commandment simply prohibits worship of these foreign gods. On this general issue, Gorsuch is a committed theist, maintaining that faith in God is a positive attribute.

3 It should be noted that these violations do not begin to encompass all of the "crimes" for which God requires execution of transgressors. Although Gorsuch is a passionate defender of the death penalty, it is doubtful that he endorses all sixty biblically mandated applications, as the Christian Reconstructionists do. Also, he opposes assisted dying and elective abortion, both of which involve individual liberty issues.

4 Seven prominent decalogue monuments currently displayed on public property are located in Austin, Texas, Bradford County, Florida, Hobbs, New Mexico, La Crosse, Wisconsin, Little Rock, Arkansas, Nueces County, Texas, and Somersworth, New Hampshire. Many others have been placed by zealous supporters and then removed by court order, the best known being at the Alabama Supreme Court building, the Oklahoma Capitol, and the Haskell County Courthouse. The Austin, Texas and Little Rock, Arkansas monuments include selfish motivation, slavery endorsement, and patriarchalism sanction. In conjunction with a dispute over a decalogue display in Levy County Florida, the commissioners approved a new requirement that monuments "reproduce the entire text" of any documents displayed. Not surprisingly, their Ten Commandments monument did not satisfy this new standard!

VII. Biblical Christian Prayer

TWENTY-NINE

Does God Answer Christian Prayer?

Every survey conducted during the past decade indicates that between 80 percent and 85 percent of Americans believe in a god or some form of higher power.[1] Virtually the same proportion of respondents affirm a belief in the efficacy of prayer—which refers to communication with the god or higher power. More specifically, prayer is defined as a petition or request for intercession based on an unquestioning faith that is characterized by complete trust, confidence, and reliance on the deity.

From a methodological perspective, three types of prayer can be distinguished: personal prayer, interpersonal prayer, and intercessory prayer. The alleged benefits of personal prayer (for oneself) and interpersonal prayer (with or for others who are present or know that they are targets) are difficult to isolate because of the confounding effects of belief (or placebo effect) and interpersonal support, respectively.

In contrast, intercessory prayer (for others who are not present and do not know they are intended recipients) is amenable to scientific investigational strategies. Consequently, the focus of this review is on research studies that have addressed the utility of intercessory prayer (which is also called "distant healing" in the literature).

Anecdotal Evidence of Prayer Efficacy

Before summarizing the scientific studies, it is appropriate to consider a category of evidence that encompasses the numerous events that are reported regularly in the print and television news. For example, an eleven-year-old boy was found alive after spending four days lost in the rugged Utah wilderness in June 2005. His mother declared that the family's prayers were answered.

During the very same week, three boys were found dead in the trunk of a car in New Jersey after a five-day search. Yet there were no public laments about the futility of the fervent prayers by family and friends. Situations like these occur daily and raise the obvious question: Why would a loving God return the Utah boy to his family while allowing the New Jersey boys to slowly suffocate to death?

Regardless of the nature of the tragedy, whether lost or abducted children, patients with serious illnesses, or victims of natural disasters, the reaction is always the same. Family, friends, and strangers pray for a happy outcome. When the prayed-for individual survives, all credit is given to God, and the power of prayer is acclaimed ("Praise the Lord, our prayers were answered"). But when the prayed-for person dies, the inevitable response is "She has gone to be with Jesus" or "God has called him home." Clearly, the traditional religious framework does not permit prayer to fail. The infallibility of prayer is an article of faith that cannot be questioned.

Even overwhelmingly negative evidence does not cause believers to doubt the value of prayer. After a reader's brother died of cancer, Billy Graham explained in a 2001 column that God *did* answer the family's prayers—because the brother was now perfectly healed and free of illness in heaven! The Reverend Graham told the surviving sibling to rejoice that the brother was beyond all sickness and pain.

Another strategy for avoiding the obvious conclusion that prayer fails on a regular basis is to restrict requests for intercession to the generic prayer, "Thy will be done." So, no matter what the outcome, it is always god's will.

Experimental Studies of Intercessory Prayer

The first major experimental investigation of intercessory prayer (called a randomized double-blind clinical trial) was conducted by Randolph Byrd and reported in the *Southern Medical Journal* in 1988. A total of twenty-nine diagnostic and outcome variables were recorded for 393 coronary patients who had been randomly assigned to prayed-for and not-prayed-for groups. Christian intercessors prayed daily for the patients in the experimental group. Statistically significant differences were obtained on six variables and also on a global judgment of improvement. However, Dr. Byrd subsequently revealed that his study contained two serious procedural violations. The global judgment of improvement was made *after* the data were unmasked, and the study coordinator knew which patients were assigned to the prayer group. These compromises could easily account for the slightly favorable results.

A decade after the Byrd study was published, William Harris and nine colleagues attempted to replicate Byrd's findings in the *Archives of Internal Medicine*. Thirty-five variables, including all of Byrd's, were recorded for 990 cardiac patients who had been randomly assigned to prayed-for and control groups. None of Byrd's 29 variables or his global judgment of progress was statistically significant. Clearly, the attempted replication completely failed. Contrary to the original report, less than 1 percent of the variance in overall recovery was explained by prayer—hardly evidence for the power of an omnipotent god.

The third large-sample investigation of intercessory prayer was carried out by Jennifer Aviles and six colleagues in the journal *Mayo Clinic Proceedings in 2001*. Five primary outcome variables were assessed at a six-month follow-up for 762 coronary patients who had been assigned to prayed-for and not-prayed-for groups. Christian intercessors initiated prayers for patients in the experimental group at the time of hospital discharge. No statistically significant differences were obtained for the total group comparisons or for subgroups of high-risk and low-risk patients.

A more recent major study of intercessory prayer was conducted by Mitchell Krucoff and 14 colleagues in *Lancet in 2*005. Four outcome variables, in-hospital and six-month follow-up, were recorded for 748 coronary patients who were treated at nine medical centers. Participating prayer groups encompassed Christian, Muslim, Jewish, and Buddhist traditions. There were no statistically significant differences between the randomized prayed-for and control patients. It is noteworthy that Dr. Krucoff is an enthusiastic advocate of the use of prayer in conjunction with standard medical treatment.

Of the several published small-sample studies, one deserves mention because of the wide public attention it initially received and the later revelation that research malpractice was involved.

Fred Sicher and three colleagues, including the late Elisabeth Targ, designed and conducted a controversial investigation in the *Western Journal of Medicine in* 1998. Forty advanced AIDS patients were randomly assigned to prayer or control groups. Christian, Jewish, Buddhist, and secular healers served as intercessors. Of the eleven outcomes measured, six were statistically significant. Unfortunately, these seemingly favorable results were illusory. An article in *Wired* magazine by a journalist detailed the numerous violations of accepted research methodology.

While there are many ways to evaluate the benefits of prayer, observable outcomes such as recovery from illness provide the strongest evidence. Because the four major investigations were carried out in hospitals with coronary patients, a quick recovery with minimal complications was the focus of the prayers for intercession. Of course, the ultimate complication and indicator of failure in medicine is patient death. Contrary to believers' hopes and expectations, the mortality rates were virtually identical for prayed-for and control patients in the four studies (overall, 7.1 percent versus 7.4 percent). Why would god allow a total of 100 patients in the four studies who were recipients of Christian prayers to die, when Jesus promised: "If you ask anything in my name, I will do it" (John 14:12–14)?

Christian Reactions to Prayer Failure

The most predictable reaction to the thoroughly negative results of the scientific prayer studies comes from believing professionals: They dismiss the disappointing findings by invoking a variety of ecclesiastical excuses. For example, John Chibnall and colleagues claim in *Archives of Internal Medicine* that God is outside the domain of science and that it is a violation of faith to test god. Specifically, Chibnall et al. outlined a theological argument, with a series of pseudoscientific misrepresentations of measurement and statistical issues—all for the purpose of denying the validity of the intercessory prayer investigations. Why? Because, as true believers, they simply cannot accept the unequivocally negative research results. Chibnall has flatly stated, "Studies cannot be designed in a scientific way." In other words, Drs. Byrd, Harris, Aviles, Krucoff, Targ, and Dossey are scientific and theological illiterates!

Other dogmatic religionists have also made public statements rejecting the negative findings of the intercessory prayer studies. *Newsweek* quoted Cynthia Cohen of Georgetown University as declaring that the research is "based on a total misconception of how god responds to prayer" (*Newsweek*, November 16, 2003). Greg Plotnikoff of the University of Minnesota said, "I don't believe that we can randomize god or truly understand his will." In his popular book, *The Healing Power of Faith* (1999), Harold Koenig asserted that "research can neither prove or disprove the reality of answered prayers or divine intervention." Then why conduct the research? Interestingly, Dr. Koenig coauthored the Krucoff et al. study!

In contrast to the religiously motivated dissenting opinions, the acknowledged guru of distant healing, Larry Dossey, has repeatedly affirmed the validity of intercessory prayer research. For example, he declared that "Byrd deserves credit for establishing the principle that prayer can be tested scientifically, Krucoff's study deserves high marks for methodological soundness, and Targ's study of HIV patients sets the gold standard." In numerous articles and books, Dr. Dossey has cited the results of intercessory prayer research as scientific evidence supporting the distant healing hypothesis (such as in *Reinventing Medicine*). Ironically, Dr. Dossey has been called an agnostic by Christian fundamentalists because he believes that all prayers (e.g., Hindu, Buddhist, Christian, and Native American) are equally valuable, and God is not required in his conceptualization of distant healing.

Several popular news magazines (e.g., *Newsweek, U.S. News, Reader's Digest,* and *Parade*) have published many articles touting the alleged connection between religiosity and health. The topic of prayer is inevitably addressed, usually under headings like "New Proof Prayer Works" and "The Healing Power of Prayer." Writers typically rely on believers as their sole source of information and never devote equal time to rational skeptics. It is abundantly clear that the major news media in the United States irresponsibly distort the evidence for the purpose of promoting the myth that God answers prayer. The conservative charge that the so-called liberal media harbor an antireligious bias is simply false.

Summary

Faith in God and belief in the efficacy of prayer are virtually synonymous. Hence, religious faith does not permit the possibility that prayer fails, despite the overwhelmingly negative evidence of everyday experience. Four large-sample experimental investigations of Christian intercessory prayer, conducted by evangelical Christians for the purpose of demonstrating God's power, produced negative results. The few instances of statistical significance were due to chance or admitted research malpractice. Apparently god was not motivated to respond to altruistic prayers for strangers with serious medical conditions. The only rational conclusion supported by the studies is that the God of religionists does not answer intercessory prayer, most likely because God does not exist, except in the imaginations of believers.

Chapter 29 Endnotes

1 At the time this chapter was written, the figures for "belief in a god or some form of higher power" were accurate. As discussed in several other chapters, the current rate of belief in deities or supernatural influence is considerably lower.

THIRTY

God Does Not Answer Christian Prayer

A prominent skeptic's article "Prayer and Healing" reached two completely unwarranted conclusions: that scientific prayer research is "bad science and worse religion." Concerning the first conclusion (bad science), it should be pointed out that the randomized double-blind clinical trial has established the respected and useful body of knowledge known as evidence-based medicine. The second conclusion (worse religion) is premised on his declaration that the ultimate flaw in all studies is theological, because an omniscient and omnipotent God already knows who needs healing, suggesting that prayer is superfluous.

With regard to the skeptic's assertion that "scientific prayer makes God a celestial lab rat," it is apparent that the devout Christian investigators who designed and conducted the five major experimental evaluations of intercessory prayer disagree with him. For example, Dr. Randolph Byrd, a cardiologist at San Francisco General Hospital, thanked God for responding to prayers for patients in his study. Dr. Mitchell Krucoff, a surgeon and director of interventional clinical trials at the Duke University

Medical Center, expressed confidence that his research would put prayer on a scientific foundation.

Because his short summary of what he calls the most significant flaws in prayer studies intermixes criticisms of randomized prayer experiments and observational studies of various issues in religion and health, the skeptic's first conclusion inappropriately denigrates the unequivocal findings of the former category of research. Also, it should be noted that his conclusions essentially repeat an allegation made previously by Richard Sloan in the *New England Journal of Medicine* (2000): "Combining religion and medicine leads to weak science [and] watered-down religion." However, Sloan's statement followed a comprehensive review of methodological problems associated almost entirely with epidemiological studies published previously in *The Lancet* (1999).

The skeptic's conclusions contain the clear implication that the more than three dozen researchers who carried out the major experimental prayer studies are not only theologically naive, but, even more importantly, are scientifically unsophisticated. To address the latter charge, it will be helpful to briefly summarize the key features of the five large-sample randomized clinical trials that were designed to document the value of intercessory Christian prayer that have been reported in the medical literature.

In these five studies, 4,094 hospitalized cardiac patients were randomly assigned to prayed-for and not-prayed-for conditions. The intercessors represented a variety of religious and spiritual backgrounds, but the vast majority came from Christian denominations. While frequency and duration of prayers differed across investigations, the focus was consistently on patient recovery with minimal complications. Although a wide range of measures of clinical progress and outcome were recorded in the five studies, one critical indicator was common to all investigations: patient mortality. This definitive criterion of success or failure of healing prayers can be assessed reliably and possesses indisputable validity, reflecting directly the primary concern and emphasis of prayers for recovery.

Furthermore, the intervention has excellent generalizability. Intercessory prayers for healing are a central activity in almost all theistic religious traditions, including regular services, prayer circles, and continuous (24/7) prayer ministries that address the health circumstances of members, community leaders, and national figures. Finally, it should be recognized that the principal investigators of the five major studies are either outspoken advocates of the healing potential of Christian prayer or sympathetic to the value of prayer and spiritual support in medical practice.

The results of the five experimental investigations of intercessory prayer were uniformly negative. This series of carefully conducted clinical trials did not produce any evidence in support of the proposition that hospitalized patients derive benefit from the altruistic prayers of committed intercessors. Specifically, the mortality rates were very similar for the prayed-for and not-prayed-for patients (5.75 percent versus 5.97 percent). Of course, these findings are entirely consistent with the evidence of everyday experience: God disregards fervent prayers for recovery from accidents and disease just as often as favorable outcomes occur. In other words, restoration to good health is a matter of competent hospital care and good luck.

So how did ardent physicians and other believers in the power of prayer react to the disappointing results of the studies? Typical reactions were that the research is premised on a misconception of how God responds to prayer and that it is a violation of faith to test God. Dr. Gregory Plotnikoff, medical director for the Center for Spirituality and Healing at the University of Minnesota, asserted that it is not possible to randomize God or truly understand his will. Another physician, Dr. Harold Koenig, who has written extensively about religion and medicine, said that research cannot prove or disprove the reality of answered prayers. Then why did he serve as a co-investigator on the Krucoff study?

A legitimate theological question that the skeptic might have posed is: Why would an omnipotent, omniscient, omnibenevolent God not respond to healing prayers for cardiac patients? The alleged scientific and theological defects of the studies would not preclude an all-powerful God from directly intervening in the investigations. Or, if God objects to randomization, then why didn't he instantaneously cure all patients in both the prayed-for and not-prayed-for groups? Also, while the skeptic cited methodological critiques by Sloan and Chibnall, he neglected to mention that physician and prominent prayer author Dr. Larry Dossey has repeatedly praised the scientific quality of the intercessory prayer experiments.

In summary, five large-sample investigations of intercessory prayer were carried out for the purpose of establishing a scientific foundation for Christian faith. These studies satisfied the methodological requirements of the randomized clinical trial just as well as other published research in evidence-based medicine. More than 2,000 randomly assigned cardiac patients were the recipients of healing prayers by mostly Christian intercessors. On the crucial criterion of patient mortality, no more of the prayed-for subjects survived than those not prayed for. The five studies provided no support for the hypothesis that hospitalized cardiac patients benefit from Christian prayers for them. The only reasonable inference is that God does not answer intercessory prayers, in all likelihood because God does not exist.

THIRTY-ONE

Have Christians Accepted the Scientific Conclusion That God Does Not Answer Prayer?

In 1982, a young cardiologist at the San Francisco General Medical Center named Randolph Byrd had a brilliant insight that would motivate several important investigations of prayer during the following two decades. He realized that the standard research paradigm known as the double-blind randomized clinical trial could be used to test the efficacy of intercessory prayer with medical patients in the hospital setting.

Dr. Byrd, who identified as a born-again Christian, believed that he could put (heretofore faith-based) prayer on a solid scientific foundation by implementing rigorous study procedures within an experimental framework. In his groundbreaking investigation, 400 cardiac patients were randomly assigned to prayed-for and not-prayed-for conditions. The prayers offered by Christian intercessors requested a quick recovery with minimal complications.

A variety of intermediate measures of medical progress, as well as the ultimate indicator of patient success—recovery versus mortality—were objectively recorded for all subjects, prayer recipients and control subjects alike. After the data were analyzed, Byrd erroneously concluded that the results supported the hypothesis that intercessory prayers to the Judeo-Christian god have a beneficial therapeutic effect on cardiac patients. He thanked God for responding to the prayers for healing. Byrd's landmark study was published in the *Southern Medical Journal* in 1988.

While the initial results did suggest the possibility that prayer conferred only a small benefit, the subsequent revelation that a major violation of experimental protocol had occurred cast even this modest ray of hope into doubt. Later studies confirmed the correct inference, namely, that God does *not* answer intercessory prayer.

After mixed reactions from research specialists, medical personnel, and religious believers, four new major investigations incorporating the same procedures Byrd had followed were carried out at other medical centers. The principal investigators of the four replication studies, with their affiliations and publication dates for their articles, are: William Harris, Saint Luke's Hospital (1999); Jennifer Aviles, Mayo Clinic (2001); Mitchell Krucoff, Duke University Medical Center (2005); and Herbert Benson, Beth Israel Deaconess Medical Center (2006).

Why Investigate Intercessory Prayer?

If we begin with a general definition of prayer as a petition or request for assistance directed to a higher power, then we can distinguish between three types of prayer: personal, interpersonal, and intercessory. Why not investigate the first two types of prayer?

The alleged benefits of personal prayer (for oneself) and interpersonal prayer (with or for others who are present or know that they are targets) are difficult to isolate because of the confounding effects of belief (or placebo effect) and interpersonal support, respectively.

In contrast, intercessory prayer (for others who are not present and do not know they are intended recipients) is amenable to scientific investigation. It was this critical recognition by Byrd that intercessory prayer could be studied objectively that established the conceptual basis for his visionary project. (Note: Intercessory prayer is sometimes referred to as "distant healing" in the literature.)

Critical Features of the Investigations

All five of the large-sample randomized trials of intercessory prayer with hospitalized cardiac patients shared a set of attributes that justify confidence in the findings obtained from the studies.

1. Careful random assignment of subjects to the prayed-for and not-prayed-for conditions ensured that groups were equivalent (within the limits of statistical sampling fluctuation) on all relevant variables.
2. The double-blind requirement, in which neither patients nor hospital personnel knew which condition (prayer or nonprayer) to which subjects had been assigned, prevented contamination. This was the flaw in Byrd's project—the study coordinator *did know* which patients were receiving prayers at the time she interacted with them.
3. The principal investigators were all committed Christian advocates of the healing power of prayer or (in the fifth study) a physician sympathetic to the value of prayer and spiritual support in medical practice. It should be emphasized that none was an unbeliever or skeptic.
4. The overwhelming majority of the members of the teams of intercessors came from Christian backgrounds, including various Protestant denominations and Catholic traditions, with a small number of Jews, Muslims, and Buddhists participating in some studies.
5. The critical outcome indicator common to all investigations was patient mortality, a definitive criterion of success or failure that reflected directly the primary focus of the intercessory prayers for speedy recovery with few complications.

Unambiguous Experimental Results

Refuting the sincere beliefs and hopes of the dedicated researchers and funding agencies, the results of the five investigations of intercessory prayer were uniformly negative. This series of carefully conducted clinical trials did not produce any evidence in support of the proposition that hospitalized cardiac patients derive benefit from the altruistic prayers of committed intercessors.

Table 1: Patient Mortality Rates for Prayer and Control Subjects

	Prayed-For Patients			Not Prayed-For Patients		
Study	**Total**	**Died**	**Percent**	**Total**	**Died**	**Percent**
Byrd	192	13	6.77	201	17	8.46
Harris	466	42	9.01	524	46	8.78
Aviles	383	31	8.09	379	34	8.97
Krucoff	371	14	3.77	377	13	3.45
Benson	604	16	2.65	597	14	2.35
Total	**2016**	**116**	**5.75**	**2078**	**124**	**5.97**

Specifically, the mortality rates listed in Table 1 were very similar for the prayed-for and not-prayed-for patients. The outcomes of three of the individual studies slightly favored the *not*-prayed-for patients, although none of the five differences was statistically significant. The total comparison (a simple meta-analysis) is not statistically significant even with the huge aggregate samples, and the effect size is miniscule—mostly due to Byrd's study, which accounted for 80 percent of the difference—and obviously not the achievement of an omnipotent God.

It is apparent that the Judeo-Christian god disregards fervent prayers for recovery just as often as favorable outcomes occur. In other words, restoration to good health is a matter of competent medical care and good luck. Intercessory prayer does not improve the probability of survival. Why would God allow 116 patients in the five study samples who were recipients of Christian prayer to die, when Jesus promised, "If you ask anything in my name, I will do it" (John 14:10–14)?

One anomalous finding from the Benson study that, after a dozen years, continues to be cited by prayer articles in popular magazines is that a third group of participants, composed of patients who *knew* that they were receiving intercessory prayer, exhibited significantly more post-operative complications during the recovery period. However, the overall mortality rate for this group (2.16 percent) was very similar to the other two study groups, indicating that the higher level of complications did not manifest as an increased probability of death.

The database here is truly remarkable. These are the mortality statistics for 2,000 recipients of intercessory prayer and 2,000 not-prayed-for cardiac patients in *five major investigations* conducted over a span of *twenty years*. This level of documentation is unparalleled in the history of prayer research.

Excuses, Denial, Ignorance

How did Christian medical personnel and other believers in the healing power of prayer react to the disappointing results of the five scientific prayer studies? Six assertions capture the range of excuses and denials expressed by ignorant critics of the investigations:

- The research is premised on a misconception of how God responds to prayer.
- God is outside the domain of science and therefore is not amenable to experimental evaluation.
- It is not possible to randomize God or truly understand his will.
- Research can neither prove nor disprove the validity of divine intervention.
- Because God already knows who needs healing, prayer is superfluous.
- It is a corruption of faith, if not willful blasphemy or sacrilege, to test God.

All six of these rationalizations entail the invocation of theological dogma in an attempt to explain away the irrefutable evidence that the Judeo-Christian god does not answer prayer. It is important to note that these worthless explanations from the dumbfounded religious community only emerged *after* the negative results of the clinical trials were thoroughly replicated. Two legitimate questions that prayer advocates should have addressed are:

1. Why would an omnipotent, omniscient, omnibenevolent God refuse to respond to altruistic healing prayers for cardiac patients (or anyone else)?
2. Why didn't God instantaneously cure *all* patients in *both* the prayed-for and not-prayed-for groups? This miraculous mediation

> would have demonstrated conclusively that God really does intervene supernaturally to heal disease and illness.

Illustrating just how far removed from reality prayer advocates can be, the principal investigator of one major study asserted that prayer could conceivably overdose the human body with fatal consequences! He then declared that if prayer were as powerful as he believed it to be, prayer interventions and therapies would be taught in all medical schools. (These extremely optimistic comments were made before the negative results of his study were known.)

The most bizarre reaction to the results of the prayer studies was published in an evangelical Christian magazine. The following quotes demonstrate the devout authors' utter confusion: "The real scandal is that the not-prayed-for group received just as much, if not more of God's blessings; True to his character, God appears inclined to heal and bless as many as possible; His answers often don't give us the where, when, or how that we originally sought; We know that prayer works: The real question is, are we prepared for God's answer." These comments exemplify the fundamentalist rejection of science. (Christianity Today, 2009)

A Common Criticism of the Studies

An oft-voiced criticism of the investigations is that patients in the not-prayed-for condition were recipients of prayers from family, friends, and churches. In other words, all study participants, including those in the control groups, received healing intercessory prayers from others.

Christian defenders of the studies explained that patients in the prayed-for experimental groups actually received supplemental or incremental prayers of a more carefully focused nature, in addition to prayers from family, friends, and church. Based on the assumption of a positive dose-response relationship, supporters of the investigations expected patients in the prayed-for condition to experience greater healing benefit.

Of course this criticism would be moot if the presumed omnipotent, omniscient, omnibenevolent Judeo-Christian god had simply eliminated all human illness in the first place. But remember that God routinely inflicts disease on his children and their enemies as punishment for disobedience or to test their faith.

Small Sample Studies

Many articles continue to assert that the results of research on prayer have been mixed, with some investigations finding that prayer *can* improve disease outcomes and prolong survival. This misleading and unwarranted conclusion is typically based on the uncritical acceptance of claims from various small sample studies of intercessory prayer, all spawned by Byrd's innovative research project.

For example, a study of intercessory prayer with advanced AIDS patients in *Western Journal of Medicine* appeared to have generated positive findings until several egregious methodological violations were exposed, rendering the results meaningless.

Another investigation that received much attention was subsequently labeled the "Columbia Miracle Prayer Study" (*Journal of Reproductive Medicine*). The researchers purportedly used intercessory prayer with infertile women, producing such an amazing outcome that independent reviewers eventually concluded that the data were contrived, because there were no records indicating that the study was ever carried out.

Yet at the time, prominent prayer advocates and "distant healing" gurus touted these and other investigations as evidence for a scientific revolution in healing modalities. Investigations inspired by "the Byrd effect" included intercessory prayer interventions with rheumatoid arthritis patients, patients with common skin warts, and alcoholic patients. After these and other similar studies were carefully examined, it became apparent that the hoped-for healing breakthroughs attributable to prayer simply did not occur.

Some Skeptics Were Confused

While it is obvious from their comments that many devout believers in the power of prayer refused to accept the unequivocal results of the prayer studies, it is also true that even some rational observers had difficulty appreciating the very important contribution that intercessory prayer research made to the scientific study of supernatural claims.

For example, one prominent skeptic reached two completely unwarranted conclusions, declaring that scientific prayer research is "bad science and worse religion." Of course, it was clearly not bad science, because the randomized double-blind clinical trial has established the respected and highly useful body of knowledge known as evidence-based medicine. Nobody argues with the scientific success of this endeavor.

Elaborating his allegation of defective religion, the skeptic propounded the colorful charge that "scientific prayer makes God a celestial lab rat." It is apparent that the committed Christian investigators who carried out the studies were convinced that their research procedures were theologically sound, or they would not have undertaken their projects in the first place.

Distrust of Scientific Methodology

More than a decade after results from the last of the five replicated studies were reported in the medical literature, no additional efforts to document the benefits of healing prayer have been implemented. This suggests that believers may have seen the "handwriting on the wall"—or that they followed the logic of mathematical induction and gave up on their goal of putting prayer on a scientific foundation.

Is this because Christians have accepted the verdict of science and dismissed the value of intercessory prayer? No. When science fails to support faith, it is science that is rejected, not faith, as has been well-documented in books such as Shawn Otto's *The War on Science* and Antony Alumkal's *Paranoid Science: The Christian Right's War on Reality*. The numerous excuses proffered by Christian believers summarized above amply testify to this pervasive distrust of science.

What sustains belief in the efficacy of intercessory prayer in the face of overwhelming negative scientific evidence? The simple fact is that Christians are much more likely to absorb uncritically the claims of anecdotal accounts in newspapers, on television, and in personal testimonials, rather than to accept the replicated results of randomized clinical trials.

For example, after a prominent actor's twelve-day-old twins recovered from a massive accidental medication overdose, he announced that "the power of prayer from so many is what saved them." At about the same time, in an unrelated tragedy, a young man died of incurable cancer.

Situations such as these, which occur daily across America, raise a perplexing question: Why would a benevolent deity save the actor's infant twins but allow a young man to die of cancer? In trying to rescue prayer from failure, the young man's obituary asserted that "many prayer requests by Christian intercessors were miraculously answered along the way" (to death)!

Regardless of the nature of the tragedy—whether lost or abducted children, patients with serious illnesses, or victims of natural disasters—the reaction is always the same. Family, friends, and strangers pray for a happy outcome. When the prayed-for individual survives, all credit is given to God and the power of prayer is acclaimed. But when the prayed-for person dies, God is never blamed for the negative outcome. Typical responses are "God has called him home" and "She has gone to be with Jesus." The infallibility of prayer is an article of faith that cannot be questioned.

In plain language, the traditional Christian framework does not permit prayer to fail.

Believers are quick to cite cases where prayer is associated with positive results, while they steadfastly disregard those circumstances where prayer is followed by unfavorable outcomes. It is this selective attention to everyday events that helps sustain faith in the power of prayer.

Is there any reason to think that the unequivocal negative outcome of the prayer studies has resulted in any diminishment of prayer activity in the United States? No. Surveys indicate that the vast majority of Americans still believe in the value of prayer, which is virtually identical to belief in the existence of God, because prayer is simply communication with the deity.

Moreover, intercessory prayers for healing continue to be a critical feature of many Christian activities, including regular worship services, the ubiquitous prayer circles, and continuous ("24/7") prayer ministries that address health problems of parishioners, community leaders, and national figures. In other words, despite the disconfirming scientific evidence, Christians have not lost faith in the power of prayer for healing.

Another strong indicator of the undiminished Christian belief in the value of prayer is the huge volume of books on the subject published over the past decade exceeding 1,000 titles per year.

Popular magazines routinely publish articles touting the alleged connection between religiosity and health. The topic of prayer is inevitably addressed under headings such as "New Proof Prayer Works" and "The Healing Power of Prayer." Writers typically depend on believers as their sole source of information and never devote equal time to skeptics.

It is obvious that Christians have not accepted the scientific conclusion that God does not answer intercessory prayer, demonstrating again that faith surpasses evidence in the religious mind, especially when reinforced by irresponsible propaganda generated by major news outlets for the purpose of perpetuating the dominant religious mythology.

Implications for Larger Issues

Despite the endless excuses generated by fundamentalist believers, the only rational conclusion supported by the five replicated studies is that God does not respond to altruistic prayers for hospitalized cardiac patients. This conclusion can be reasonably generalized to non-hospitalized patients and those with other medical conditions and to all forms of prayer to all gods under all circumstances. Put simply: *God does not answer prayer*. What does this conclusion mean for two larger issues of Christian faith?

First, it thoroughly undermines the indispensable axiom of so-called "theistic science," which is that the supernatural realm actually exists and therefore supernatural causation is a legitimate scientific explanation. The replicated failure of the attempted intercessory prayer demonstrations constitutes the strongest rebuke yet to this doctrinal claim, which derives from a universal religious belief.

Second, it casts substantial doubt on the foundational claim of theology, which is that the postulated God has independent existence in objective reality. In other words, theology asserts that God actually exists outside of the human mind, rather than just being a figment of the imagination. A reasonable inference from the failed prayer investigations is *that the allegedly omnipotent Judeo-Christian god does not exist*. We are reminded of Mark Twain's astute aphorism, "Faith is believing what you know ain't so."

Scientific Credibility of Prayer Studies

Believers in the value of prayer, which include virtually all Christians and members of other churches, as well as many people who are not religious, have not only rejected the overwhelmingly negative findings of the five replicated intercessory prayer studies, they have accepted the false conclusion that the investigations are not credible.

It's essential that all Americans, believers and nonbelievers alike, appreciate the critical importance of these experimental studies in demonstrating that God does not answer intercessory prayer. This could be because God doesn't care about his children, or that he doesn't exist, except in the imaginations of believers. Regardless of the explanation, the incontrovertible fact is that God does not respond to Christian healing prayers.

The definitive statement of rationale for the five replicated prayer experiments was formulated by Dr. Mitchell Krucoff, a cardiologist and director of interventional clinical trials at the Duke University Medical Center. He was the principal investigator for the fourth prayer study which was published in 2005. Before the results of his major controlled trial were known, he was interviewed for an article in *Hippocrates* magazine (August 2000). The following statements summarize his justification:

- The question whether prayer "works" cannot be addressed scientifically. As prayer is going on all the time, there is no true control group to study.

  Note: In his 2005 report, Krucoff uses the terms "scientifically structured," "control group," and "no prayer controls," suggesting that his earlier statement involved an idiosyncratic use of language.

- What we can ask is if there is a measurable incremental therapeutic benefit to sending prayer from all over the world to people undergoing angioplasty for heart attack or risk of heart attack.
- We are actually studying supplemental prayer—the prayers of designated groups in addition to those of whoever else might be praying for the patients.
- There is nothing in the history of therapeutic medicine that has not been shown to be toxic in someone at sometime in some dose. There is no reason to imagine prayer would be different. In some situations, prayer could conceivably overdose a human body.

  Note: Distant prayer authority Dr. Larry Dossey recommended that investigators keep track of how much and how often the intercessors prayed, because "you wouldn't give a medication without recording the dose."

Thus, we see the logic of Krucoff's framework of incremental benefit from supplemental prayer as an additional healing component, which results in a larger dose of prayer for patients in the experimental group, which, in turn, produces more therapeutic benefit.

It can be reasonably assumed that the principal investigators and their colleagues who carried out the other four major prayer trials agreed with Krucoff's conceptualization. Their standard design includes random assignment of patients to E and C groups to control for the effects of all potentially confounding variables, except the experimental intervention, which is focused intercessory prayer by teams of pray-ers.

The last word on this subject is appropriately given to the late Victor Stenger, an experimental physicist who dedicated the final 25 years of his career to exposing the false claims of religionists. In his book *God—The Failed Hypothesis* (2008), he carefully examined the published literature addressing the question of prayer efficacy and reached a series of definitive conclusions:

- Unfortunately, the prayer literature is marred by some very poor experimental work. But in reading the best of the published papers you will witness all the indications of proper scientific methodology at work. If they are not science, then I do not know what is.
- Many popular books and articles have been published claiming that science has shown that prayer has positive healing value. Every published claim for a positive effect of which I am aware fails to satisfy one or more requisite methodological conditions.
- Two well-executed experiments [Krucoff and Benson] seem to meet all the requirements of a proper investigation. Both find no evidence that prayer improves health.
- Since he signed the paper, Krucoff is now apparently satisfied with the published conclusion that no effect of prayer has been observed.
- Father Dean Marek and other investigators at one site in the Benson study have tried to account for why prayers do not work within a theological context, but they are to be commended for accepting the data and admitting prayers did not work in their particular experiment.

- It does not appear—based on the scientific evidence—that a God exists who answers prayers in any significant, observable way.

VIII. Biblical Capital Punishment

THIRTY-TWO

Does the Bible Require the Death Penalty?

The United States is the only Western nation that still inflicts capital punishment on its citizens. Judeo-Christian America, the fundamentalists' favorite label, finds itself in the disreputable company of major authoritarian nations, including China, Russia, Iran, Iraq, Saudi Arabia, and North Korea. Ironically, these are countries that the United States relentlessly reprimands for committing various human rights violations! What is the basis for the hypocritical US position? What explains the disparity between the ethical standards demanded for others and America's own behavior? The answer is simple: the Holy Bible.

Why are the majority of Americans so dedicated to the death penalty, when it is obvious that the practice does not deter even the most serious capital crime: murder? The astronomical homicide rate in the United States is fifteen to twenty times higher than that of other Western democracies. In other words, the only country that executes murderers on a regular basis also has by far the highest homicide rate. Furthermore, the United States is indisputably the most overtly devout Christian enclave in the West. Reasonable observers ask: How can these apparent contradictions be explained? The title of former Arkansas governor and one-time Republican presidential wannabe the Reverend Mike Huckabee's new publication provides a clue: *God, Guns, Grits, and Gravy*. Again, the answer is the horrific impact of the Holy Bible.

This chapter identifies the biblical offenses that require the death penalty, reviews Jesus's and Paul's positions on the death penalty, determines whether unbelievers are subject to the death penalty, and estimates the impact on the US population of the strict application of the death penalty.

Which Crimes Warrant the Death Penalty?

According to Mosaic Law, Yahweh requires the death penalty for about sixty specified "crimes." Many of these entail violations of rules of religious ritual and dietary practice and are generally not applicable today. However, other offenses have direct parallels in contemporary America. In this section, a subset of infractions for which Yahweh mandated the death penalty is listed with scriptural citations.

The Ten Commandments (Exodus 20:1–17) provides a highly useful framework for organizing these punishable sins, because the Hebrew decalogue is revered by fundamentalist bible believers. Former Alabama Supreme Court Chief Justice and failed senatorial candidate Roy Moore gave the fundamentalist rationale to justify the death penalty when he declared that public display of the decalogue "recognizes the sovereignty of God." He further asserted that his judicial duty under the US Constitution was to acknowledge the Judeo-Christian God and that America was founded on the law of the Holy Bible.

Fundamentalist devotees continue to fight in communities across the country to place their cherished Ten Commandments on monuments and plaques in town squares, courthouses, and public school classrooms. A decalogue monument at the Oklahoma Capitol is the most recent of numerous attempts to display the ancient Hebrew edicts on public property. Amusingly, the Oklahoma decalogue display has inspired applications for religious monuments from the Satanic Temple, the Freedom From Religion Foundation, and the Universal Society of Hinduism, among others.

The following list of Yahweh's death penalty mandates is organized under the traditional Ten Commandments with references that establish the scriptural justification for the penalties. The real or replacement set of commandments is found in Exodus 34:14–26. There is an important distinction between the abstract declaration of the biblical rules or laws and the actual implementation of the punishments. Generally, the Pentateuch promulgates the rules and the Histories demonstrate their application to wrongdoers.

The unwritten initial clause for the first nine commandments below is: The death penalty is required for . . .

1. Anyone who worships or sacrifices to gods other than Yahweh (Exodus 22:20; Leviticus 20:1–2,5; Numbers 25:1–9; Deuteronomy 17:2–7, 18:10; 2 Kings 10:24–28; 2 Chronicles 24:17–26) or encourages others to worship heathen gods (Deuteronomy 13:6–17; 2 Chronicles 21:11–19).

2. Anyone who worships idols or the sun, moon, or stars (Exodus 32:21–29,35; Deuteronomy 17:2–5; 1 Kings 13:34, 21:25–29; 2 Kings 17:13–20; 2 Chronicles 21:13–21) or engages in occult practices (Exodus 22:18; Leviticus 20:6,27; Deuteronomy 18:10–12; 1 Samuel 28:9; 2 Kings 23:5–7,20–24; 1 Chronicles 10:13–14).

3. Anyone who curses Yahweh (Leviticus 24:10–23; 1 Kings 21:8–13) or engages in false prophecy (Deuteronomy 13:5; 18:20; 1 Kings 18:40).

4. Anyone who works on the Sabbath (Exodus 31:14–15, 35:2; Leviticus 23:30–31; Numbers 15:32–36).

5. Anyone who strikes or curses parents (Exodus 21:15,17; Leviticus 20:9).

6. Anyone who commits murder (Exodus 21:14; Leviticus 24:17–21; Numbers 35:16–34; Deuteronomy 19:11–13) or kidnapping of another person (Exodus 21:16; Deuteronomy 24:7) or rape under limited circumstances (Deuteronomy 22:13,22,25–27).

7. Anyone who commits adultery or fornication (Leviticus 20:10–12; Deuteronomy 22:22–27) or engages in homosexual acts (Genesis 19:23–25; Leviticus 20:13).

8. Anyone who steals from Yahweh (Joshua 7:1–26) or the Christian community (Acts 5:1–11).
9. Anyone who gives false testimony when the defendant is facing the death penalty (Deuteronomy 19:21).
10. The Tenth Commandment is the only decalogue commandment that, if violated, appears not to require the death penalty. It is also the only edict that involves no more than an improper attitude (envy) rather than an explicit action or behavior.

Five additional sinful behaviors beyond the Big Nine that also require the death penalty illustrate just how unforgiving Yahweh's mandates can be: Anyone who owns a dangerous, uncontrolled animal that kills someone (Exodus 21:28–29); a son who is stubborn, rebellious, disobedient or a drunkard (Deuteronomy 21:18–21); a daughter who is not a virgin at marriage (Deuteronomy 22:13–21); a daughter of a priest who becomes a prostitute (Leviticus 21:9); and a man who has sexual relations with a woman and her mother (Leviticus 20:14). For the last two infractions, burning alive is the prescribed mode of execution. There are other Mosaic Laws that mandate the death penalty, including for being a witch or a wizard (Exodus 22:18; Leviticus 20:27).

There are two major issues that opponents of public exhibition of the decalogue should stress in their efforts to thwart this obsessive fundamentalist Christian activity. First, biblically illiterate advocates of displaying the standard Ten Commandments typically don't know that all but one require the death penalty for violators. Opponents of posting the decalogue on public property should adopt the strategy of demanding that the Mosaic punishments for offenders be listed on all monuments, plaques, and similar displays. This action would shift the burden of justification to supporters of decalogue exhibits. Adversaries should argue that disclosing the required penalties along with the commandments would have a stronger deterrent effect. Moreover, advocates should be eager to acknowledge and publicize God's ordained punishments.

The First Commandment (worship of any god other than Yahweh is forbidden) is reiterated more than 300 times by Yahweh in the Hebrew Testament. Decalogue opponents should emphasize that government approval of the Mosaic First Commandment clearly violates the First

Amendment of the Constitution, which prohibits the government from endorsing religion. In a nation in which scores of different gods are venerated, the government has no authority to tell citizens that just one god (Yahweh) is preeminent and solely worthy of adoration.

Did Jesus Endorse Capital Punishment?

It is obvious that Yahweh the Father was a fanatical proponent of the death penalty, especially for those people who disrespected him by worshipping or sacrificing to other gods. But what about Jesus the Son? Did he endorse the death penalty? The answer to this question is not entirely clear, with arguments and bible verses supporting both sides of the debate among Christians of different persuasions.

First, Jesus stated unequivocally that he fully endorsed Mosaic Law: "Do not think that I have come to destroy the Law or the Prophets. I have not come to destroy, but to fulfill" (Matthew 5:17). But a little later in the Sermon on the Mount, he repudiated at least a few applications of the law of retribution (Matthew 5:38–48). However, some death penalty advocates argue that Jesus was rejecting only personal revenge. Yet the rule of retaliation was actually a criminal law. Finally, Jesus did specifically endorse the death penalty for one crime: that of cursing parents (Matthew 15:4; Mark 7:10).

On the other hand, in addition to his advice to love enemies from the Sermon on the Mount cited above, Jesus disavowed all forms of interpersonal violence, even actions taken in self-defense (Matthew 26:51–52). Furthermore, in the only episode in which Jesus dealt directly with the death penalty (an apprehended adulteress), he rejected its use (John 8:3–11). Based on these verses, many Christians say that any suggestion that the Prince of Peace endorsed state-sanctioned executions for the purpose of achieving societal justice is nothing less than blasphemy.

This is certainly a major reason that many mainline Christian denominations have consistently opposed capital punishment, including Episcopalians, Methodists, and Quakers. Of course, many non-Christian faiths such as Unitarians, Baha'is, and some Jewish denominations also reject the death penalty. But it also should be noted that most fundamentalist Christian denominations, such as the Southern Baptist Convention, wholeheartedly support capital punishment.

The fundamentalist churches find biblical backing for their pro-death penalty stance in Romans 13:4, which says, "But if you do wrong, be afraid, for he does not bear the sword in vain; he is the servant (or revenger) of God to execute his wrath on the wrongdoer." The problem with this ambiguous verse is that if "bearing the sword" refers to killing, then it would appear to apply to all wrongdoers, which could be all capital crimes listed in the Pentateuch. Liberal Christians respond that Romans 13:4 simply directs Christians to obey the legal system and that "bearing the sword" is a metaphor that refers to an appropriate penalty for the particular violation committed. They also cite Romans 12:19, which suggests that God will deal with wrongdoers.

One more excursion into the non-gospel Christian testament captures the views of Jesus's foremost apostle, Paul, on the correct punishment for the alleged sin of homosexual behavior. We have already seen that Mosaic Law mandates the death penalty for homosexual acts (Leviticus 20:13; Genesis 19:23–25). In two separate statements (Romans 1:26–32; 1 Timothy 1:8–11), Paul affirmed the Mosaic decree that homosexuals, whom he calls immoral, evil, and wicked and compares to murderers, kidnappers, and parent-killers, should be executed. Jude (in verse 7) presented a reinforcing opinion by invoking God's punishment by heavenly fire for the so-called sexual perverts living in Sodom and Gomorrah. It is apparent that Paul also approved the death penalty for murderers, parent-killers, kidnappers, adulterers, perjurers, atheists, and, possibly, other sinners.

The most unyielding institutional opponent by far of capital punishment has been the Catholic Church, and the outstanding Vatican spokesperson against state-sponsored executions was the late Pope John Paul II. The pontiff never missed an opportunity to condemn the death penalty. As the direct spiritual descendant and earthly representative of Jesus (the pope is the Vicar of Christ) and the preeminent moral authority in all Christendom, John Paul II denounced capital punishment as a monstrous perversion of the Savior's instruction for humankind.

Interestingly, the pope's forceful position was not convincing enough to sway all devout Catholics. In 2003, then-Supreme Court Justice Antonin Scalia asserted: "To believing Christians, death is no big deal—and that's why Christians favor the death penalty." In fact, Scalia even favored execution for murderers under eighteen years of age—children, in other words. Also his assertion that death is no big deal for Christians is patently false: It is fear of death and the subsequent state of eternal nonexistence that motivates Christian faith (John 3:16). Christians like Scalia are simply denying the reality of death and projecting their immense existential fear onto criminals, thereby justifying their claim that death is the "ultimate punishment."

To return to the original query: Did Jesus endorse the death penalty? As with so many questions about Jesus's views on important controversial issues, such as slavery, homosexuality, abortion, poverty, adultery, and divorce, the bible is typically ambiguous and generally unhelpful. However, the preponderance of the scriptural evidence indicates that Jesus accepted as necessary or inevitable the death penalty, as well as slavery and poverty. Regardless, readers can always select passages that support their own faith-based ideologies, and this is why the bible is worthless as an ethical guidebook.

Do Unbelievers Qualify for the Death Penalty?

Are atheists, agnostics, freethinkers, humanists, rationalists, and other unbelievers subject to the death penalty under Mosaic Law? There is no doubt that Muslims, Hindus, Buddhists, and those who worship gods other than Yahweh must be killed. The status of Deists, Wiccans, and other nature worshippers is not clear, because while these devotees do not venerate other gods, they may be guilty of idolatry as it is construed in the Hebrew testament.

Unbelievers obviously do not pay homage to gods of any kind, nor do they engage in idolatry or practice the occult arts. Thus, they might be spared from death under the first two commandments. However, refusing to worship the God of the bible certainly constitutes disobedience, and denying the existence of Yahweh could easily be deemed blasphemy. But failing to recognize Yahweh as the only deity does not in strict terms violate the prohibition against worshipping gods other than Yahweh.

On the other hand, there are three instances in the Hebrew Bible that may serve to convict unbelievers. First, Deuteronomy 13:5 indicates that "prophets" who speak against Yahweh must be killed. Do unbelievers qualify as prophets, and do they advise believers to disobey Yahweh or stop worshipping him? Yes: by their example of rejecting Yahweh and his law and denouncing all forms of superstition, unbelievers might reasonably be regarded as false prophets and therefore deserving of the death penalty.

The second and third instances suggest that unbelievers may be subject to the death penalty under Mosaic Law, with the second being more compelling than the third. Because King Ahaziah doubted (or denied) the existence of the Israelite Deity, Yahweh punished him with death (2 Kings 1:1–18). When the Assyrian colonists were relocated to the cities of Samaria, they refused to praise or exalt Yahweh, so he sent lions to kill some of them. The surviving colonists and their descendants compromised by worshipping their own gods *and* Yahweh (2 Kings 17:24–25).

At this point there doesn't appear to be a definitive answer to the question posed at the beginning of this section. However, the views of the eminent legalist and acknowledged founder of the church, Apostle Paul, about the applicability of Mosaic Law are perfectly clear and unequivocal: the ungodly and irreligious (also called God-haters) should be executed along with murderers, kidnappers, adulterers, homosexuals, perjurers, and various other criminals (Romans 1:26–32; 1 Timothy 1:8–11). In this connection, it should be noted that two of the greatest philosophers in history, one pagan (Plato) and the other Christian (Thomas Aquinas), both advocated death for incorrigible atheists.

Finally, while there may be some residual doubt about the death penalty question, it is an absolute certainty that unbelievers who reject Jesus will go to hell. According to Matthew 10:33, Mark 13:13, 16:16, Luke 12:8–9, and John 3:18, anyone who publicly denies Jesus or denies that Jesus is the Messiah will be dispatched to hell. Based on Jesus's horrific descriptions, it can be concluded that an eternity of suffering and agony is infinitely worse than death!

Who Would Be Executed in the United States?

We know from long experience that chronicling moral directives without imposing punitive sanctions on transgressors has minimal benefit. So shouldn't we expect that those who propose displaying the Ten Commandments would also endorse Yahweh's punishment scheme? What impact would enforcing the Mosaic death penalty in the United States have on the population? What would the execution rate be under strict adherence to the capital punishment requirements associated with the Hebrew decalogue?

The first commandment orders residents to worship only Yahweh and relegates all other gods to a prohibited status. About one-tenth of the population would be immediately executed unless they renounced their false gods. If Paul's directive concerning the applicability of the death penalty to irreligious citizens is accepted, then an additional fifth of the nation's people would be eliminated.

Correctly punishing violators of the second and third commandments, which forbid idolatry and blasphemy, respectively, would exterminate the Deists, Wiccans, sculptors, astrologers, and mediums among us.

While there is some disagreement about which day is the Sabbath, in almost all US communities it is Sunday. Outlawing all work on the traditional day of rest as required by the fourth commandment would cause a major disruption of the US economy. Furthermore, enforcement would involve executing millions of Americans, including professional athletes, Walmart employees, restaurant workers, and many others.

Regarding the fifth commandment, which counsels respect for parents, it is a sad fact that abuse of the elderly is a serious problem. It is doubtful that capital punishment for those who strike or curse parents would improve the situation, but they still would have to be killed.

The US judicial system, reflecting the overwhelming support of the citizenry, already does a great job of punishing violators of the sixth commandment, which prohibits murder, by invoking the biblical dictum of "a life for a life." America is the only Western democracy that has not abolished state-sanctioned executions of its murderers, with Texas among the leading states.

Uniform enforcement of the seventh commandment, which condemns adulterers, would result in a substantial reduction in the US population, because one-third of married residents reportedly engage in at least one extramarital affair. If Jesus's equating of remarriage after divorce with adultery is included, and with the addition of homosexuals and fornicators, the lives of one-half of Americans would be in jeopardy.

The application of the death penalty under the eighth commandment, which prohibits theft, would entail careful analysis of the crimes to determine just what constitutes stealing from Yahweh or the Christian community. While very few witnesses commit perjury in capital punishment trials, they would have to be executed in accordance with the ninth commandment.

Will the fundamentalist Christian advocates of displaying the Ten Commandments also demand that the required penalties be applied as Yahweh ordained? No, of course not! These pious proponents of public posting want to impose their sanctified rules on everybody else without assuming any responsibility for enforcement. They could learn a lesson about courage and fidelity to God's Word from the Christian Reconstructionists, who propose that Mosaic Law be subsumed in the US legal code.

Should Rationalists Oppose the Death Penalty?

Rationalists, humanists, and others of similar persuasion do not form their opinions on the basis of alleged holy books or sacred texts. Rather, they rely on empirical evidence and philosophical arguments to determine their positions on social and political issues. Summarized below are six reasons to oppose capital punishment.

First, the death penalty is applied unfairly. Individuals who commit capital crimes often receive very different punishments, e.g., some are executed while others are eventually paroled. Furthermore, economically disadvantaged persons and racial and ethnic minorities are disproportionately sentenced to death.

Second, the death penalty is premised on a logical contradiction. When our judicial apparatus executes a convicted murderer for the premeditated killing of another person, we collectively engage in the very behavior that we condemn: intentional, willful killing.

Third, the death penalty is based on an erroneous psychological assumption. The United States is a death-denying society that projects fear of annihilation onto criminals, thus falsely concluding that death is the ultimate punishment. This is untrue because everyone dies, typically a slow, painful demise. The most severe punishment we can impose instead is permanent loss of freedom.

Fourth, the death penalty is immoral. Since the advent of DNA testing, scores of death row inmates have been exonerated. Because capital punishment is irreversible, there is no possibility of correcting judicial errors. The justice system is obviously not perfect and therefore execution is immoral.

Fifth, the death penalty does not serve as a deterrent to future criminals. Several sophisticated statistical studies have attempted to establish empirical support for the claim that use of the death penalty reduces the probability that others will commit serious crimes. None has produced convincing evidence of a deterrent effect. Rather, state-sponsored executions serve as a terrible example for violence-prone individuals by giving official sanction to killing within the legal framework.

In addition to the specific reasons to question the morality and efficacy of capital punishment enumerated above, there is an overarching issue. In an attempt to instill terror in criminals by legally terminating life, we diminish our purported commitment to life-affirming values. The only ethical course of action is to abolish the death penalty, as all Western nations except the United States have already done.

THIRTY-THREE
Let's Use Biblical Execution Methods

In recent years, several US states that regularly carry out the death penalty have had difficulty obtaining the requisite drugs for lethal injection. Many pharmaceutical manufacturers don't want to supply the drugs because they fear retaliation by death-penalty opponents, while others simply want to avoid the negative publicity, and some actually have ethical concerns.

Exacerbating the situation were the well-publicized cases of "botched" executions, where condemned persons were literally tortured to death. Of course, some death-penalty advocates believe that this is not only acceptable, but desirable, because criminals deserve to suffer like their victims. They say the greater the suffering, the better the quality of justice that is realized. Fundamentalist Christian legislators seem especially keen on capital punishment.

Some state legislatures have revived old "tried and true" methods of execution, such as firing squads, while others have proposed refurbishing electric chairs and gas chambers. But the lawmakers who get their morality from the bible are forgetting that their holy book is a resource rich with alternatives to lethal injection.

This chapter provides a catalog of biblically approved methods for killing convicted criminals. All techniques are endorsed by the God of the bible, Almighty Yahweh, and were used by him on numerous occasions. Bleeding-heart liberals may be uneasy when contemplating these procedures, but they should understand that Yahweh has personally approved these modes of eliminating evildoers from among us and, therefore, any objections or criticisms constitute blasphemy, a violation that requires and deserves the death penalty. This compilation is organized into handy categories that are ordered according to Yahweh's expressed preferences and includes the transferability of the procedures to the contemporary American justice system.

Stoning

This method of execution serves a cathartic function for the community, with all members participating in the meting out of justice. Also, it is readily adapted to collective punishment, which is strongly endorsed and widely practiced by Yahweh.

Yahweh decreed stoning to death by community members for the following: disobeying an order not to keep booty from the destruction of Jericho (Joshua 7:10–26), blaspheming the Lord (Leviticus 24:10–16,23), gathering firewood on the Sabbath (Numbers 15:32–36), and unpopular preaching (2 Chronicles 24:21).

Stoning was carried out even when the victim was falsely accused, as Naboth was by evil Jezebel (1 Kings 21:8–13). Of course, we know that many innocent men and women have been convicted and served lengthy prison terms and have even been executed by the American judicial system.

Other violations that specify stoning as punishment include: worshipping other gods (Deuteronomy 17:1–7), encouraging the worship of other gods (Deuteronomy 13:1–11), sacrificing children to Molek (Leviticus 20:1–2), and communicating with the dead (Leviticus 20:27).

Burning Alive

It could be reasonably argued that the electric chair constitutes a modern version of burning alive, which is possibly more humane. However, the procedure is not necessarily recommended here. After all, wrongdoers deserve to suffer maximally for their crimes against Yahweh.

Yahweh burned sinners alive for sexual immorality in the massacre of Sodom and Gomorrah (Genesis 18–19), for specified sexual misbehaviors (Leviticus 20:14, 21:9), and for offering incense without proper authorization (Leviticus 10:1–2, Numbers 16:35). Jephthah sacrificed his only daughter as a burnt offering to Yahweh (Judges 11:29–40). King Abimelech burned alive one thousand residents who had taken refuge in the tower of Shechem (Judges 9:49).

King Manasseh sacrificed his son as a burnt offering on a heathen altar (2 Kings 21:6). King Ahaz (2 Kings 16:3) sacrificed his son as well, and countless Israelites sacrificed both their sons and daughters (2 Kings 17:17). Two other stories that involve burning people alive are found in Judges 15:6 and 2 Kings 1:10–12.

Stabbing and Impaling

Some of the earliest instruments of attack and defense were sharp implements, including knives, daggers, swords, and spears. These weapons were designed to cause lethal damage by penetrating the body and therefore may be viewed as the precursors of guns. This suggests a possible biblical justification for execution by firing squad. Hence, the relevance of this mode of killing.

At Yahweh's behest, the Levites used their swords to kill three thousand fellow Israelites for worshipping the golden calf (Exodus 32:27–29). Phinehas murdered a fornicating Israelite man and his consort by driving a spear through both of them (Numbers 25:1–18).

Acting as Yahweh's messenger, Ehud killed King Eglon of Moab by plunging a sword into the king's belly, causing his entrails to ooze out (Judges 3:12–25). Four similar killings by stabbing in the abdomen are reported in 2 Samuel 2:23, 3:27, 4:5–6, and 20:8–10. Three additional gruesome killings by bodily penetration are reported in Judges 8:19–21, 2 Samuel 18:14–17, and 2 Kings 9:24.

General Sisera was killed by Jael, who hammered a tent peg through his skull and into the ground while he was asleep, as prophesied by Deborah (Judges 4:17–22). This classic tale played out more recently at the

New Mexico State Penitentiary when rioting inmates killed each other in similar fashion in 1980.

Finally, two of King Xerxes's officers were impaled alive on poles because they had conspired to assassinate him (Esther 2:21–23, NIV). The villain Haman was also impaled (Esther 7:5–10, NIV), as were his ten sons (Esther 9:13–14, NIV).

Drowning and Suffocation

There is no doubt that drowning and suffocation are methods close to Yahweh's heart, so it is entirely appropriate to honor the Lord's predilection by recognizing that the gas chamber also involves asphyxiation. Yahweh drowned all living people except eight adults for incorrigible wickedness (Genesis 6–8). He also drowned Pharaoh's charioteers, their horses, and the Egyptian cavalry to bring glory to himself (Exodus 14:21–31). Yahweh buried alive three disobedient Israelites, as well as their wives and children (Numbers 16:31–35), and Hazael suffocated King Ben-Hadad (2 Kings 8:15).

Wild Animals

This is another mode of execution favored by Yahweh. However, it strikes most civilized people as too barbaric to even seriously consider. But with the expansion of zoos, wildlife parks, and exotic animal exhibits, the means are readily available and rather inexpensive. In fact, lions, alligators, sharks, and other large predators have to eat, and they are not vegans. So, this may be a truly cost-effective deterrent for potential evildoers.

Yahweh killed disobedient Israelites—including children—using venomous snakes (Numbers 21:6), lions (1 Kings 13:23–26, 2 Kings 17:24–25), and bears (2 Kings 2:23–24). Daniel's false accusers, along with their wives and children, were also permitted by Yahweh to be ripped to shreds by lions (Daniel 6:24).

It should be noted in the interest of thoroughness that if Jezebel didn't die from her fall, she was trampled to death by horses, and dogs subsequently ate everything except her skull, feet, and hands, as had been prophesied by Elijah (2 Kings 9:30–37).

Beheading

Although beheading or decapitation is an age-old mode of killing, it does not appear to rank among Yahweh's preferred methods. In fact, he never specifically ordered beheading as punishment for any violation. Maybe if the guillotine had been invented three thousand years earlier, Yahweh would have been more favorably disposed to beheading. Of the seven episodes of cutting off heads described in holy scripture, only two are unequivocal beheadings, while the others involve hacking off heads after killing. In all cases, the severed head is regarded as a trophy to be displayed disrespectfully or (in one situation) treated with reverence.

David slew Goliath, cut off his head, and delivered it to Saul (1 Samuel 17:50–57). The Philistines cut off Saul's head after he killed himself, and they hung up his head in the temple of Dagon (1 Samuel 31:9–10; 1 Chronicles 10:9–10). Other postmortem beheadings are described in Judges 7:25 and 2 Samuel 4:5–12.

It is not entirely clear whether Ahab's seventy sons were slaughtered before their heads were removed, but the description of the event suggests that they were killed first (2 Kings 10:6–8). On the other hand, the account of Sheba's death indicates that he was most probably beheaded (2 Samuel 20:20–22). Finally, John the Baptist was almost certainly executed by beheading (Matthew 14:6–12; Mark 6:22–29).

Ripping Open Pregnant Women

To acknowledge the erroneous political viewpoint of fundamentalist Christian antiabortion zealots, it is necessary to address this truly unpleasant biblical reality. Three uses of this grisly mode of killing indicate Yahweh's approval, whereas the last provoked Yahweh's anger. Elisha prophesied that King Hazael would rip open pregnant Israelite women (2 Kings 8:12), King Menahem of Israel ripped open all of the pregnant women of Tiphsah with a sword (2 Kings 15:16), and Yahweh promised that the pregnant women of Samaria would be ripped open with a sword (Hosea 13:16).

However, after the Ammonites ripped open the pregnant women of Gilead with swords, Yahweh declared that he would destroy the Ammonites (Amos 1:13). Despite Yahweh's strong endorsement of the killing of pregnant mothers-to-be (and their unborn children) by ripping them open, this biblically approved method of execution should probably be rejected. In broader context, it should be emphasized that the bible does not prohibit abortion, and Yahweh loves neither unborn nor living children.

Throwing from Heights

Another method that may be applicable today is that of throwing condemned people from great heights to their deaths. This gruesome spectacle permeates urban mythology surrounding violent drug gangs and infuses prison lore about inmate punishment. The fear of falling from dizzying heights ranks up there with snakebites and public speaking as causes of irrational anxiety and panic attacks.

Of course, some thrill-seeking convicts might actually opt for this mode of execution, for the same reason that sky-diving enthusiasts like to jump. The two examples in the bible are the ten thousand Edomite men who were thrown from the top of a cliff (2 Chronicles 25:11–12) and the wicked woman Jezebel, who was thrown out of a window (2 Kings 9:30–37).

Scraping to Death

Gideon killed seventy-seven leaders of Succoth by scraping them to death with thorns and briars (Judges 8:16). Fans of the classic western series Gunsmoke will remember the episode in which the good guy was dragged through a patch of spiny cactus in order to be taught a lesson. Happily, he was rescued by Marshall Dillon before sustaining serious injuries. Were the script writers inspired by the gory bible story?

Miscellaneous Methods

Yahweh also relied on several killing strategies that are probably not realistic options for the American judicial system. For example, sending plagues to punish disobedient Israelites was a favorite Yahwehean technique (Numbers 11:31–35, 16:46–50, 25:9; 1 Samuel 5:6–12; and 2 Samuel 24:15). Causing a deadly hailstorm (Exodus 9:13–35) and inflicting incurable bowel disease on Jehoram (2 Chronicles 21:13–19) were imaginative—but not easily applicable—methods.

Of course, Yahweh could always use direct execution, as when he struck Ananias and Sapphira dead after they lied to the Holy Spirit (Acts

5:1–11) and when he turned Lot's wife into a pillar of salt for looking back (Genesis 19:26). Included in this category of inapplicable methods are Samson's use of a donkey's jawbone to kill one thousand Philistines (Judges 15:15–16) and his causing the temple collapse in order to crush to death 3,005 Philistines (Judges 16:25–30). The latter incident reminds us that some Salem witches were pressed to death, a common mode of execution by slow torture in the late Middle Ages.

Going Forward

It is my fervent hope that these scripturally based suggestions will be of valuable assistance to fundamentalist Christian legislators who are searching for biblically approved methods for state-sponsored executions. This information may also be a useful resource for dedicated Sunday school teachers who strive to implant the fear of the Lord in their pupils.

THIRTY-FOUR

Does the Bible Prohibit Feticide?

In recent years, Republican-controlled legislatures in Texas, Wisconsin, Ohio, North Carolina, and many other states have passed new laws restricting access to abortion. These include the requirements that women view an ultrasound image of the fetus, clinics meet the standards for surgery centers, and doctors have admitting privileges in a local hospital. These laws, which can be accurately characterized as legislative harassment, constitute the primary focus of the continuing assault by ultra-fundamentalist Christians on women's reproductive rights. The ultimate goal of the antiabortion zealots is to outlaw and thereby criminalize all abortions, with no permissible exceptions.

It is a fact that the vast majority of antiabortion activists are fundamentalist Christians and that their views predominate in the Republican Party. Their strident rhetoric suggests that opposition to abortion derives from the bible, and they routinely assert that "God loves the unborn." Nothing could be further from the truth. The purpose of this chapter is to review what the bible actually says about abortion, providing arguments and scriptural documentation so that advocates of reproductive choice can be prepared to confront and refute the claims of antiabortion Christian extremists.

Definitions, Misconceptions, Disagreements

A preliminary issue that needs attention is that of proper terminology. Antiabortion devotees prefer to call themselves pro-life or defenders of life, while labeling pro-choice advocates as "pro-abortion." Pro-choice individuals should be accurately described as abortion rights advocates or defenders of reproductive freedom. Furthermore, antiabortion fundamentalists are *not* pro-life, because they typically endorse the biblically mandated death penalty, unrestricted access to guns, and preemptive military attacks on non-Christian nations.

The antiabortion crusaders suggest in their arguments and propaganda that opposition to abortion derives from a Judeo-Christian principle they characterize as "respect for the sanctity of life." The implication is that all authentic Christians and Jews oppose reproductive choice. The truth is that many religious denominations, churches, and organizations representing mainline Christian and Jewish faith traditions support abortion rights, including Episcopalians, Jews, Lutherans, Methodists, Presbyterians, and Unitarians.

The Religious Coalition for Reproductive Choice, an interfaith assembly of religious people who support a woman's right to choose, lists more than three dozen denominations and organizations as members. If the bible prohibited abortion, it is doubtful that these faith groups would advocate for abortion rights. It is obvious that there is no unified Judeo-Christian position on abortion and that the Religious Right does not speak for all people of faith. Moreover, the antiabortion fundamentalists represent a minority viewpoint in the US religious community.

One issue that divides the antiabortion community concerns which, if any, abortion exceptions can be tolerated. The hardliners say that absolutely no exceptions can be permitted, while a slightly more moderate faction believes that situations where the life of the pregnant woman is endangered warrant the option of abortion. Allowing the choice of abortion in cases of rape and incest generates a much more contentious argument. In 2012, Republican senatorial candidate Richard Mourdock in

Indiana infamously declared: "If a woman becomes pregnant as a result of rape—then it's God's will." He was defeated, and the Republican distinction between legitimate rape and illegitimate rape quickly dissolved.

Perhaps the most difficult ethical dilemma for the antiabortion movement concerns the status of "unborn children" that are not developing normally. Is there a point at which the abnormal development is so severe that abortion is justified? According to Texas law, which includes an exception after twenty weeks for "severe fetal abnormality," the answer is yes. It is possible that economic considerations trumped "pro-life" values in legislative debates concerning these tragic circumstances, because most severely developmentally compromised fetuses that survive end up being warehoused for life in state institutions for profoundly disabled people at substantial cost to the taxpayers.

Finally, the antiabortion extremists regularly attempt to impose their dogmas of political correctness on other less extreme members of their coalition. An amusing example occurred when Anita Perry (the then-Texas governor's wife and a nurse) stated in an interview her entirely reasonable position on abortion: "I see it as a woman's right—that is her decision. I don't agree with it, but I am not going to criticize [a pro-choice woman]." The next day Governor Perry publicly rebuked his wife, announcing in a televised statement that she had "misspoken." The poorly informed governor also declared that "abortion is the second most conducted surgical procedure in the US," a falsehood that earned him another "Pants on Fire" rating from PolitiFact.

Statistics and Opinions

To provide context for the discussion that follows, some data about the frequency of abortion in the United States and how people regard abortion are presented. Since abortion was legalized in 1973 with *Roe v. Wade*, more than seventy million abortions have been performed.

It should be emphasized that more than 90 percent of planned abortions occur within the first trimester (thirteen weeks), while only 2 percent occur after twenty weeks, which is congruent with the *Roe* criteria. It is also a very safe procedure. Pregnancy and childbirth were thirty-four times more likely than an abortion to result in a woman's death in Texas, for instance, based on data for a decade (2000–2011) compiled by the state health department. Why don't Texas legislators enact new regulations to make childbirth safer for women?

A very different and disturbing statistical reality is that the United States has the highest unintended pregnancy rate of any Western industrialized nation. Most Americans understand that comprehensive sexuality education stressing the importance of contraception would reduce the number of abortions—a causal relationship denied by antiabortion activists, who promote abstinence-only ignorance.

Surveys of national samples conducted over the past decade indicate strong support for legal abortion as operationalized in *Roe v. Wade*. Typically about two-thirds approve of the *Roe* criteria, while less than one-third want *Roe* overturned and all abortion criminalized.

A final set of statistics testifies to the propensity for violence among a small minority of antiabortion Christian extremists. In the forty years since *Roe v. Wade* was decided, twelve abortion providers have been murdered and seventeen have been maimed or seriously injured in attempted murders. More than 6,000 acts of violence have been perpetrated, including fire bombings, arsons, kidnappings, assaults, and death threats. A prominent victim was Dr. George Tiller, who was assassinated in the lobby of his church in Wichita, Kansas, after the murderer had spent three months engaged in daily bible reading preparing for his mission.

When Does Life Begin?

Antiabortion activists assert that life begins at the moment of conception when the sperm penetrates the egg. This is the basis for the personhood argument, which states that the fertilized egg is a human person with all the constitutional rights of living people. One fact that is overlooked in this formulation is that the sperm and the egg separately are living organisms, and thus the fertilized egg is a biological transformation of elemental life components. Life does not begin at this point because it already exists in the elemental components.

But a much more substantial problem with the personhood claim is encompassed in the following facts. While it is true that all human lives must originate with a conceived embryo, it is also true that most fertilized eggs do not become living human infants nine months later. As a result of natural reproductive processes, between one-half and three-quarters of fertilized human eggs or conceived fetuses are spontaneously aborted.

Specifically, about one-third of fertilized human eggs fail to implant in the uterine wall and thus are destroyed. A much smaller fraction of fertilized eggs that do implant terminate before a pregnancy is recognized. Of the clinically verified pregnancies, a substantial number end in the premature birth of the fetus long before survival is possible. Two million miscarriages or spontaneous abortions occur annually after pregnancy is confirmed in the United States and constitute a great disappointment to prospective parents.

For rational people, the three categories of unsuccessful outcomes of pregnancy reflect the result of natural processes but must be considered to be God's abortions from the perspective of theists. In other words, spontaneous abortions are an expression of God's plan of divine design. What does the fact that the majority of conceived embryos do not become human beings say about the personhood dogma? Either God kills human persons for some unknown sacred reason or advocates of personhood are knowingly advancing a theological fiction that is contradicted by medical knowledge.

Lastly, what does the bible say about the question of when human life begins? Holy Scripture is perfectly clear about this event: God breathed into man's body the breath of life and man then became a living person (Genesis 2:7). At least a dozen additional verses indicate that breath is synonymous with life (Genesis 6:17, 7:22; Job 12:10, 17:1 [KJV], 33:4; Psalms 104:29, 146:4; Isaiah 2:22, 42:5; Jeremiah 51:17; Ezekiel 37:6–10; Acts 17:25).

On the other hand, many abortion opponents believe that several verses referring to the development of the fetus in the woman's uterus establish the continuity of human existence from the womb to life following birth, which they consider to be an argument against abortion (Psalms 22:10, 58:3, 139:13; Isaiah 49:5; Hosea 12:3; Luke 1:41). Examination of these half-dozen verses reveals that they contain undeniable poetic and some literal truth. But while they illustrate why abortion may be an emotional and controversial issue, they do not provide an explicit prohibition against it. Moreover, we know that God murdered tens of millions of unborn children and hundreds of millions of living children, because the bible says so, as documented in the next section. Of course, any estimates like these depend on Christian assertions about the age of the Earth, which range from 6,000 years to 4.5 billion years.

Does the Bible Condemn Abortion?

Abortion is unequivocally a religious issue for the antiabortion disciples. For example, Fox TV celebrity the Reverend Mike Huckabee says that the "unborn child" has a God-given right to life, life is a gift from God, and abortion is the sinful destruction of God's sacred creation. Yet those who oppose abortion seldom cite scripture to support their claims. Does God really oppose what the antiabortion zealots call the "murder of unborn children"? As the bible documentation in this section shows, God is not concerned about the destruction of either unborn or living children. Three primary categories of evidence are relevant: monumental massacres, major slaughters, and promised retribution for disobedience.

Three events of truly biblical proportions comprise the category of evidence labeled monumental massacres: the Noachian Deluge, Sodom and Gomorrah, and the Conquest of Canaan.

- In the Noachian Flood, God destroyed by drowning all living people (except eight adults), because they were deemed to be incorrigibly wicked (Genesis 6, 7, and 8).
- God destroyed by fire from heaven all living people (except three adults) in Sodom and Gomorrah and almost all surrounding cities and villages (Genesis 18, 19).
- God ordained the massacre of all residents of the cities and nearby towns ruled by thirty-three kings—not one person was left alive—in the Conquest of Canaan (Numbers 21, 31, 33; Deuteronomy 2, 3, 7, 20; and Joshua 6, 8, 10, 11, 12).

How many men, women, children, babies, and infants were killed in these three events? How many pregnant women and their unborn fetuses were murdered? The total numbers must be astronomical, because the death toll for the Conquest of Canaan alone is estimated to be between fourteen million and twenty million, based on Deuteronomy 7:1–2. The point that must be emphasized here and in the episodes listed below is that whenever the entire population of a city or nation or planet Earth is annihilated, it is a certainty that pregnant mothers-to-be and their "unborn children" are included among the victims. Are they properly regarded as "collateral damage" in God's quest for cosmic justice and a future kingdom?

At least twenty episodes compose the category of major slaughters, in which the biblical record states that every person was killed, oftentimes listing men, women, children, and infants, which includes of course pregnant women and their fetuses. These mass exterminations represent God's punishment of his people for disobedience or his rewarding of the Israelites for obeying him by destroying their enemies. Moreover, every event reported in the bible is an expression of God's supreme will, because he is an omnipotent being and thus is the author of human history.

- All the people of Zepath were massacred (Judges 1:17).
- The entire population of Bethel was slaughtered (Judges 1:25).
- King Jabin and all his people were destroyed (Judges 4:23–24).
- Abimelech captured Shechem, killed its people, and destroyed the city (Judges 9:45).
- Jepthah slaughtered Ammonites in twenty cities (Judges 11:32–33).
- All the people of Laish were killed and the city was burned to the ground (Judges 18:27).
- The Israelite army slaughtered the entire tribe of Benjamin, including men, women, and children (Judges 20:48).
- The Israelite army killed all the men, married women, and children of Jabesh-Gilead (Judges 21:10–14).
- Saul's army completely destroyed the entire Amalek nation, killing all men, women, and little children (1 Samuel 15:1–8).
- Doeg the Edomite killed eighty-five priests and their families, including men, women, children, and babies (1 Samuel 22:18–19).
- David and his men killed every person in the villages of the Geshurites, Girzites, and Amalekites (1 Samuel 27:8–9).
- David and his men massacred all the Amalekites, except 400 young men who escaped on camels (1 Samuel 30:17).

- The Philistines slaughtered the Israelites on Mount Gilboa (1 Samuel 31:1–6).
- Baasha killed all the descendants of Jeroboam (1 Kings 15:29).
- Zimri killed the entire royal family, as well as distant relatives and friends (1 Kings 16:11).
- King Menahem slaughtered the entire population of Tiphsah (Tappuah) and the surrounding area and ripped open the pregnant women (2 Kings 15:16).
- God's chosen people were completely destroyed for worshipping other gods and consulting fortunetellers (2 Kings 17:19–20).
- King Manasseh murdered great numbers of innocent people: Jerusalem was filled with the bodies of his victims (2 Kings 21:16).
- Enemy armies destroyed the nation of Judah because of the many sins of King Manasseh (2 Kings 24:2–4).
- Nebuchadnezzar slaughtered the residents of Jerusalem and destroyed the city (2 Chronicles 36:17–20).

The third category of biblical evidence addressing abortion, promised retribution for disobedience, subsumes a variety of situations and violations that come in good part from the prophetic literature. (Several of the items included here derive from a scholarly investigation by Gene Kasmar, *Why—The Brooklyn Center High School Bible Challenge* (1995). His work is gratefully acknowledged.)

- If a man accidently injures a pregnant woman causing her to abort the fetus, he must financially compensate the woman's husband. But if the woman dies, the man may be executed (Exodus 21:22–25). This suggests that the fetus is regarded as property, not as a person.
- If a man accuses his wife of adultery, she must submit to a priestly purity test that will cause her to abort the fetus if she is guilty (Numbers 5:11–31). This suggests that the fetus does not possess a right to life.

- For worshipping idols, God declared that not one of his people would live, not a man, woman, or child, not even babies in arms (Jeremiah 44:7–8).
- For worshipping other gods, Israel's children will die at birth, or perish in the womb, or never even be conceived (Hosea 9:10–12). Again, God will punish the Israelites by destroying their unborn children.
- For rebelling against God, Samaria's people will be killed, her babies dashed to death against the ground, and her pregnant women ripped open with a sword (Hosea 13:16).
- God enumerated his punishments (curses) for disobedience, including "cursed shall be the fruit of the body" (known as the curse of barren wombs) (Deuteronomy 28:18).
- God was petitioned to punish enemies by aborting their unborn children: "Their fruit shalt thou destroy from the earth" (Psalms 21:10).
- Isaiah prophesied doom for Babylon, including the murder of fetuses: "They will have no pity on the fruit of the womb" (Isaiah 13:18).
- Jesus did not express any special concern for fetuses during the anticipated end times: "Woe to pregnant women and those who are nursing" (Matthew 24:19) and "Blessed are the barren wombs that never bore and breasts that never nursed" (Luke 23:29).

The word *abortion* does not appear in most English versions of the bible. However, the Hebrew word *shakol*, which means aborting or miscarrying and is translated as *barren*, *loss*, or *bereave*, is found in a half-dozen verses (Exodus 23:26; Leviticus 26:22; Isaiah 47:8–9; Jeremiah 15:7; Ezekiel 5:17; Hosea 9:14). In no case is the practice of abortion prohibited or condemned, and it is often described as God's ordained punishment.

The overwhelming evidence indicates that the god of the bible does not oppose abortion. If he does, why didn't he just say so? Why didn't he authorize his spokesmen Moses, Jesus, and Paul to address the subject? Nor is there any support for the claim that fetuses possess a God-given right to life or that there is a biblical basis for assertions about the "sanctity of life." Antiabortion Christians have no legitimate justification for usurping God's supreme authority in these matters. When all his scores of homicidal rampages are tallied, the god of the bible is clearly the single greatest murderer of unborn children and the preeminent mass murderer of living people in all human history.

In conclusion, defenders of reproductive freedom should not allow the claims of biblical support for antiabortion dogma to go unchallenged. Pro-choice advocates must confront the Christian "pro-lifers" on the untruthfulness of their assertions about God's opposition to abortion. Moreover, we know that God causes *all* abortions, because he is omnipotent and therefore causes everything. Lastly, the right of religious refusal by antiabortion health professionals does not supersede the right of women to make reproductive decisions in accordance with *their* religious and moral convictions. Abortion rights supporters should insist that this principle be respected.

Addendum: Christian Antiabortion Terrorism in America

Over a span of two decades, twelve innocent medical personnel and patients were murdered by Christian antiabortion zealots. Six men committed eleven of the murders (the twelfth was never solved). They should be remembered for their terrible "pro-life" crimes: Robert Dear, Paul Hill, James Kopp, Scott Roeder, Eric Rudolph, and John Salvi.

Readers interested in examining the horrific history of Christian "pro-life" violence will find thorough analysis in these books:

Living in the Crosshairs: The Untold Stories of Antiabortion Terrorism, by David S. Cohen and Krysten Connon (2015).

The Street Politics of Abortion: Speech, Violence, and America's Culture Wars, by Joshua C. Wilson (2013)

The Wichita Divide: The Murder of Dr. George Tiller and the Battle Over Abortion, by Stephen Singular (2011)

Armed for Life: The Army of God and Antiabortion Terror in the US, by Jennifer Jefferis (2011)

THIRTY-FIVE

Who is History's Greatest Murderer of Unborn Children?

Christian fundamentalists constantly invoke their favorite definition of abortion: "the murder of unborn children." They often refer to advocates of women's reproductive rights using the epithets "baby killer" and "abortionist."

In the Austin, Texas, area, the Heidi Group claims that "God loves the unborn," the Georgetown Life Chain asserts that "Jesus forgives and heals," Texas Right to Life is "prayerfully building the Kingdom of God," and Lieutenant Governor Dan Patrick proclaims that "God forgives women who have aborted children through the blood of Jesus Christ."

These antiabortion zealots claim that scripture is the God-breathed, verbally inspired, perfect word of God, absolutely accurate in every verse and passage. In other words, everything in the bible comes straight from the mouth of God.

With this foundation, we can now ask: Who really is history's greatest abortionist? To answer the question, this chapter summarizes God's declarations and behavior taken directly from Holy Writ, which is properly regarded as God's personal diary.

- I declare that unborn children are property, not living persons (Exodus 21: 22–25).
- I will not cause pregnant mothers-to-be to abort their unborn children, if they worship me exclusively (Exodus 23:26).
- I will abort your unborn children as just punishment for committing adultery (Numbers 5:11–31).
- I assert that human lives are not sacred and will be destroyed as punishment for disobedience (Deuteronomy 28:18–24).
- I will murder your children and rip open pregnant mothers-to-be as punishment for disobedience (2 Kings 8:12).
- I will authorize leaders of my people to rip open pregnant mothers-to-be (2 Kings 15:16).
- I attest that the dead are happier than the living and those never born are the most fortunate (Ecclesiastes 4:2–3).
- I will murder the unborn children, infants, and living children of sinful Babylon (Isaiah 13:15–19).
- I reject all claims of sanctity of human life and will destroy my people for worshipping other gods (Jeremiah 44:4–14).
- I will murder unborn children in their mother's wombs, as well as living children, for Israel's sinful deeds and wickedness (Hosea 9:10–16).
- I will rip open pregnant mothers-to-be and dash infants to the ground for Samaria's sin of worshipping other gods (Hosea 13:16).
- I require the death penalty for sixty violations, but not for murdering an unborn child.
- I intentionally omitted the command "Thou shalt not abort an unborn child" from the Decalogue (Exodus 20:1–17).
- I drowned all living people on Earth, including pregnant mothers-to-be and their unborn children, except for eight adults (Genesis 6:7, 17; 7:21).
- I incinerated all living inhabitants of Sodom and Gomorrah and

nearby cities, including pregnant mothers-to-be and their unborn children, except for the residents of Zoar (Genesis 19:24–25).

- I massacred all people living in the hundreds of cities ruled by thirty-three kings during the Conquest of Canaan, including pregnant mothers-to-be and their unborn children (Joshua 10, 11, 12).
- I annihilated all living people, including pregnant mothers-to-be and their unborn children, in twenty major slaughters (Judges, 1 Sam, 1 Kings, 2 Kings, 2 Chronicles).
- I murder millions of unborn "persons" every year in the United States, because two-thirds of conceived embryos fail to implant or are spontaneously aborted after pregnancy is verified.

Four conclusions

The basic findings that emerge from the eighteen scriptural statements and one contemporary fact about abortion create four irrefutable conclusions.

1. God does not love unborn children, or their pregnant mothers-to-be, or living children, or adults. He is the greatest murderer of unborn children and the preeminent mass murderer of living people in human history.
2. The bible does not support the attack on women's reproductive health care. The fundamentalist antiabortion crusade is a dishonest political campaign that is thoroughly refuted by God's holy word.
3. God causes all abortions, spontaneous and elective, as well as the destruction of fertilized ova or "persons," because he is omnipotent and therefore is the cause of everything.
4. The antiabortion zealots' favorite epithets—"murderer of unborn children," "baby killer" and "abortionist"—apply accurately to their biblical God. He is history's greatest abortionist.

IX. Unscientific Biblical Creationism

THIRTY-SIX

Biblical Creationism Is Indefensible

Fundamentalist advocates of biblical creationism continue to pursue their century-long battle in America against the fact of evolution. Through their relentless efforts in state legislatures and boards of education, creationists have attempted to infuse the Genesis story into the public school science curriculum. Their failure to accomplish this goal can be credited to determined opposition by the science community, the federal courts, and mainstream Christianity. These three very different groups have thwarted creationist machinations to impose scriptural doctrine on science instruction.

Although biblical creationism proponents have repeatedly lost federal court battles to inject their literalist dogma into public school biology classes, they have not given up the fight. To the contrary, the anti-evolution zealots have renewed their efforts focusing on local school boards, state boards of education, and state legislatures. Their remarkable and thoroughly deceitful schemes include teaching the controversy, multiple viewpoints, equal treatment, alternate theories, weaknesses of theories, academic freedom, critical thinking, anti-Christian bias, religious freedom, promotion of atheism, and other highly imaginative ploys. The misnamed Louisiana Science Education Act adopted in 2008 illustrates just how damaging these forms of stealth creationism can be.

Unrelenting pressure from science deniers has caused many conservative politicians with national ambitions to pander to the creationist reactionaries. For example, Paul Broun, Ben Carson, Bobby Jindal, Rick Perry, Mitt Romney, and Marco Rubio have all voiced a literal belief in various versions of the Genesis stories. Carson, a retired brain surgeon, asserted that Satan inspired Charles Darwin and that evolution is a religion based on faith. Former congressman Paul Broun of Georgia, also a physician, stated that evolution is a lie straight from the pit of hell and that planet Earth is nine thousand years old. Former Louisiana governor Bobby Jindal, who was a Rhodes Scholar, demonstrates again that formal academic qualifications do not inoculate against intellectual infection with creationist viral nonsense.

Creationists have been appointed chairpersons of Senate Education Committees in Arizona and Indiana, and one has been appointed a state education commissioner in Maine. One of these appointees had previously recommended that his legislature pass a law requiring church attendance in the state, while another pledged to remove evolution from the state's science curriculum standards. Fortunately, they represent a minority of US adults, as polls have demonstrated.

There is actually much more good news for legitimate science education in the United States. In the past five years, more than a dozen attempts by state legislators to shoehorn creationism into public schools have failed. Pew Research Center surveys have determined that three-fourths of respondents under the age of thirty accept evolution, as well as solid majorities of Democrats and independents. Major textbook publishers have supported sound science education by refusing to put religious ideas into science texts. The Orleans Parish School Board in creationism-crazy Louisiana adopted a policy that prohibits science teachers from including creationism in their classes. Even the Rev. Pat Robertson has publicly rejected young-Earth creationists' claims!

Humanists and other advocates of science should know the basic facts about this movement in order to recognize the dishonest tactics and attempts to allow fundamentalist religion to creep into public school science curricula. It's also important to understand that creationists themselves can't agree on what constitutes biblical truth.

Not a Unified Theology

There are actually three major schools of biblical creationism promoted by zealous adherents in the United States. Brief descriptions of them indicate just how different they really are from one another.

1. Young-Earth creationists (e.g., Ken Ham of Answers in Genesis and John Morris of the Institute for Creation Research) believe that the universe is less than 10,000 years old, humans were created 6,500 years ago, and a worldwide flood occurred 4,500 years ago.
2. Old-Earth creationists (e.g., Hugh Ross of Reasons to Believe) accept the cosmological/geological timescale of a 13.5-billion-year-old universe and a 4.5-billion-year-old Earth, but believe humans were created 150,000 years ago and Noah's flood was not a global event.
3. Intelligent Design creationists (e.g., Philip Johnson and William Dembski of the Discovery Institute) exclude all references to God and the bible, claiming that Intelligent Design is a secular theory based on newly invented concepts like "irreducible complexity," "specified improbability," and the "law of conservation of information."

Although each one derives from the creation stories in Genesis 1 and 2, these three creationist theologies are mutually contradictory and therefore irreconcilable. Furthermore, untrue.

For example, in 2009, Hugh Ross expressed approval of federal court decisions that ruled that young-Earth creationism and Intelligent Design creationism were unconstitutional because they are religious explanations and therefore not legitimate science. Of course, proponents of the censured doctrines have vilified old-Earth creationism as heretical.

Two definitions are essential to understanding the factual conclusions about creationism that follow. Biblical inerrancy is the belief that the bible is without error and absolutely correct in every verse. Scientific evidence refers to information, data, or knowledge that derives from observation, demonstration, or experiment. Also, it should be noted that there are many non-biblical creation stories including Islamic, Hindu, and Confucian conceptions, as well as numerous creation narratives of native peoples. The three conclusions below certainly apply to all other versions of creationism.

Not Supported by Empirical Evidence

This conclusion is based on the professional judgments of three intellectual communities that represent very different domains of expertise: science, law, and mainstream Christianity.

First, every scientific organization in the world rejects biblical creationism. For example, in its 2008 publication *Science, Evolution, and Creationism*, the National Academy of Sciences (NAS) concluded that no scientific evidence supports any of the varieties of creationism and that creationist ideas lie outside the realm of scientific investigation.

Second, in the past forty-five years, two US Supreme Court decisions and six federal court decisions have ruled that biblical creationism is not science. For example, the 2005 decision by Judge John E. Jones III of the Pennsylvania Middle District Court in *Kitzmiller v. Dover Area School District* ruled that Intelligent Design creationism is not science because, among other things, it is not supported by any peer-reviewed research or publications. Several previous decisions rejected young-Earth creationism because it is a religious doctrine that does not satisfy scientific criteria.

Third, the mainline Christian denominations, including Catholic, Episcopal, Methodist, and Presbyterian, reject the literal reading of scripture and endorse the validity of the theory of evolution. For example, Pope John Paul II's 1996 encyclical "Truth Cannot Contradict Truth" concluded that because god is responsible for creation, evolution is God's creative mechanism, and thus evolution explains the development of humans over time.

Not Based on Naturalistic Causation

Naturalism is the doctrine that the physical or material universe is all of reality and there is nothing else. In contradistinction, supernaturalism is the belief that a divine agent exists outside or beyond nature and controls nature. To document the dependence of biblical creationism on supernatural belief, four creationist luminaries are quoted.

1. In *The Bible, Science, and Creation* (1991), Henry Morris issues ten postulates of creationism, which include the following: the Genesis creation account is accurate, Adam was the first human, God made dinosaurs, all living people are descendants of Noah, and death is not the end of human life. He labeled evolution "the devil's work."
2. In *Reason in the Balance* (1995), Philip Johnson lists seven foundational premises of supernaturalism, which include the following: God loves us, God created everything, Jesus is God's son, Jesus guarantees eternal life, and the bible is God's word. He called evolution "nature worship" and "naturalistic mythology."
3. In *The Design Revolution* (2004), William Dembski declared that "as Christians we know that naturalism is false." He said that Darwinian naturalism has prevented people from accepting Jesus and that Intelligent Design creationism would "revolutionize science." Scientific and legal evaluations of Intelligent Design creationism demonstrate Dembski's prediction of a scientific revolution was thoroughly unrealistic, if not completely delusional.
4. In *More Than a Theory* (2009), Hugh Ross asserts that the creator God must be the god of the Christian Bible. He believes that naturalism's stark answers to the "big questions of life fail to satisfy the soul's hunger for meaning, purpose, or hope." In *How to Think about God* (1980), philosopher Mortimer Adler disputes the claim that the creator God is the god of Judeo-Christian faith.

For biblical creationists, it is apparent that supernaturalism is an explicitly Christian theological dogma, and the creator god is their god. In contrast, supernatural causation is rejected by the entire scientific community. For example, the National Academy of Sciences asserts that science cannot investigate supernatural causation. In the *Dover* decision, the Pennsylvania court also declared that invoking supernatural causation violates the rules of science and is an inherently religious concept.

Not a Legitimate Scientific Discipline

Biblical creationism does not follow the accepted rules of evidence known as the scientific method. The key concept in the scientific method is the hypothesis, which is defined as a tentative proposal that can be subjected to empirical test. One essential requirement of scientific hypothesis testing is falsifiability. This means that it must be possible to disconfirm or refute the hypothesis. Because biblical creationism is held to be an undeniable truth, it cannot be falsified. In other words, creationism is unfalsifiable and thus irrefutable.

When truth is known a priori, scientific hypothesis testing serves no purpose. This is a major reason why these three communities of experts (science, law, and mainline Christianity) say that biblical creationism is not a legitimate discipline.

For example, the National Academy of Sciences notes that creationism rejects scientific findings and methods, and it is not a scientific theory because it cannot be tested. And in the *Dover* decision, the court concluded that Intelligent Design creationism distorts and misrepresents well-established scientific propositions and conducts no scientific research or testing.

The most devastating criticism of biblical creationism comes from the Botanical Society of America's 2003 Statement on Evolution, which demonstrated it to be utter pseudoscience:

1. Creationism has not generated any testable predictions;
2. Creationism has not made a single contribution to agriculture, medicine, conservation, forestry, pathology, or any other area of applied biology;
3. Creationism has yielded no classifications, no biogeographies, no underlying mechanisms, and no unifying concepts with which to study organisms or life; therefore
4. Creationism is a scientifically useless explanation.

Summary

It is not necessary for rational people to be able to recite the scientific details from anthropology, astronomy, botany, genetics, geology, paleontology, zoology, and the forty other specialties that constitute the overarching discipline of evolution science. Being knowledgeable about the definitive consensus judgments of the recognized communities of experts in science, law, and mainline Christianity is sufficient to reject biblical creationism. For those who prefer to be better acquainted with the overwhelming scientific documentation that supports human evolution, I recommend *The Ancestor's Tale* (2016) by Richard Dawkins and Yan Wong.

There are two essential conclusions about biblical creationism: It is a religious myth that reflects superstitions that emanate from our distant past dating back many millennia, and it is a continuing fundamentalist Christian menace to science education in America.

THIRTY-SEVEN

Biblical Creationism Is Unreasonable

I recently attended a multipart audiovisual program at the Palace Theatre in Georgetown, Texas, promoting biblical creationism as an alternative to neo-Darwinian evolution. The program, sponsored by the Main Street Baptist Church, consisted of a series of thirteen one-hour presentations delivered every other Sunday morning. The curriculum was developed by a fundamentalist Christian ministry located in California (with an Austin chapter) called "Reasons to Believe." A Christian apologist trained to deliver the curriculum presented the course, and the syllabus was composed of chapter-by-chapter critiques of the arguments and evidence summarized in prominent evolutionary biologist Richard Dawkins's book, *The Greatest Show on Earth.*

There are many problems with the assumptions, rationale, and logic of this curriculum.

Supernaturalism and Circularity

Reasons To Believe promulgates a comprehensive agenda of Christian apologetics that rejects all other belief systems and sacred texts. The theology is premised on two primary faith-based doctrines considered true beyond all doubt and immune from all criticism: the god of the bible is the only authentic deity, and the bible is his perfect word.

It follows that Reasons to Believe embraces supernaturalism as a valid mode of explanation of observed phenomena. According to it, the bible "describes reality beyond the natural world," and it possesses "supernatural accuracy." In plain language, God is responsible for everything. This position contradicts that of the entire scientific community, which accepts only natural causal mechanisms.

Reasons to Believe cannot be regarded as a legitimate scholarly endeavor, because it begins by asserting that the truth is known before any investigation is ever carried out. It does not propose hypotheses derived from the Genesis creation stories that can be tested and which are subject to empirical disconfirmation. The divine creation explanation cannot be refuted because it is assumed to be true a priori as an article of faith—a textbook example of circular reasoning.

Atheism and Materialism

Reasons to Believe's brochure briefly described some features of the curriculum that suggested an association between evolution and the philosophy of atheism. Specifically, a reference to "neo-Darwinian evolution as espoused by famed atheist Richard Dawkins" and the assertion that "Richard Dawkins is the face of atheism today" imply this connection, which is repeated throughout the program. In fact, evolution is not an atheistic doctrine.

The strongest argument against this unwarranted insinuation is that the vast majority of people who endorse evolution are religious believers. They are called "theistic evolutionists" and are typically devout Christians but also persons of other faiths who accept the scientific validity of evolution and regard the Genesis stories as possessing only poetic or metaphoric truth.

A related epithet creationist opponents invoke to stigmatize evolution is that it is "materialistic," meaning that spiritual factors are excluded from consideration. All scholarly disciplines are predicated on the assumption of philosophical naturalism, which holds that nonnatural explanations are beyond the realm of empirical investigation.

Inerrancy and Faith

The foundational postulate of the Reasons to Believe theology is that the bible is God's word and is therefore without error. This assumption is rejected by most Christian and Jewish denominations.

The bible contains hundreds of erroneous assertions and contradictory statements, which have been catalogued in numerous books. Furthermore, the well-known stories, including the Genesis creations, the Noachian deluge, the Mosaic decalogue, and the life of Jesus, were all adapted from earlier pagan folktales and legends. Also, the inerrantists cannot agree among themselves, with young-Earth advocates promoting a literal six-day creation and old-Earth proponents conforming their beliefs to the geological time scale.

The doctrine of inerrancy is accepted by adherents on the basis of faith, which entails a commitment or allegiance that reflects personal conviction alone. Because faith operates in the absence of evidence, or may even contradict evidence, it is by definition not a rational process. Hence, Reasons to Believe's self-descriptors, such as "scientific," "rational," "educated," and "thoughtful," are hardly warranted.

Spurious Strategies

The Reasons to Believe program is predicated on the fallacies of false equivalence and arguing from ignorance. The curriculum's criticisms of evolution are organized around the thirteen chapters in Dawkins's book. The underlying strategy assumes that identifying problems with evolution will enhance the case for biblical creationism. This premise violates two basic logical principles.

First, evolution and biblical creationism do not constitute "two sides of a debate." Evolution is a scientific fact that is supported by a monumental corpus of evidence generated by fifty disciplinary specialties, whereas Genesis creationism consists of two stories that total about 1,400 words and were adapted from two distinct Sumerian Babylonian creation myths. Counterpoising evolution against creationism entails a false equivalence, specifically that of equating and comparing evidence-based science with bible-based mythology. To suggest that creationism is a legitimate theory is a woeful misuse of language.

Second, the Reasons to Believe presumption that specifying difficulties in some lines of evidence will weaken the multidisciplinary argument for evolution and thereby establish support for Genesis creationism commits the fallacy of arguing from ignorance. This tactic would be valid only if there were just two acknowledged alternative explanations, only one of which was true. Neither of these requirements of the alternative syllogism is satisfied by the creationists.

Creationist Confusion

Biblical creationism is one of many religious creation myths that are sincerely believed by their adherents, including those from which the two Genesis stories were derived. Furthermore, the biblical creationists do not even agree among themselves, arguing for two very different time translations that differ by a factor or multiple of almost one million. In actuality, there are numerous creation stories, such as those of the Australian Aborigines and the native peoples of the Americas, as well as Islamic, Hindu, and Confucian conceptions.

Moreover, the stipulation that only one of the two alternative explanations can be true is violated by the position adopted by those Christians and Jews who are labeled theistic or God-directed evolutionists. These believers subscribe to the view that God implemented evolution as the process by which all life forms developed over time, including humankind. Clearly, this position accepts evolution as thoroughly compatible with the bible, finding different truths in each.

By devoting their energies to an ongoing attack on evolution, the proponents of biblical creationism also deflect attention from the major defect in their unrelenting mission of political advocacy. This is of course the complete lack of empirical evidence supporting their belief in the literal truth of the Genesis creation stories. Reasons to Believe even unbelievably asserts that "the appearance of design shifts the burden of proof to evolutionists." How ludicrous given that evolutionists have generated all of the evidence while creationists have not presented one iota of experimental evidence in support of their folk tales.

Human Evolution

The critical issue for old-Earth creationists is their belief that God created man and woman as adults 150,000 years ago exactly as described in the bible. They reject the overwhelming evidence that modern humans evolved from ape-like ancestors over a span of several million years. Creationists deny that our closest living cousins are chimpanzees, gorillas, and orangutans.

What explanation of human origins is favored by biblical creationists? They invoke their doctrine of "special creation" of humans, presented in three brief formulations in the two Genesis creation stories:

1. God created man and woman in his own image (Genesis 1:27).
2. God formed man from the dust of the ground and breathed life into him (Genesis 2:7).
3. God removed a rib from the man and made a woman (Genesis 2:21–22).

Do these declarations constitute a "rational creationist belief?" Have the Reasons to Believe scholars provided the "irrefutable, empirical, evidence" that they demand of evolution proponents to support their godly-image/dust-of-the-ground/woman-from-man's-rib "theory" of human origins? No, they have not done so. In their view, they don't have to conduct research because their postulation of scriptural inerrancy guarantees that the Genesis verses are historically and biologically accurate. Of course, we know that humans are not exempt from the laws of nature, regardless of what the bible says.

Undisclosed Information

The Reasons to Believe program is a carefully selected presentation of information and arguments designed to dispute the evidence supporting human evolution out of the erroneous belief that the case for Genesis creationism will be therefore enhanced. Creationists have battled to have their views included in public school science classrooms for the past forty years with virtually no success, despite reformulations as "scientific creationism" and "Intelligent Design."

Three factual conclusions not acknowledged by Reasons to Believe put the creationist endeavor in concrete perspective. First, every scientific organization in the world rejects creationist claims. Second, mainstream Christian and Jewish denominations reject biblical inerrancy and endorse human evolution. Third, eight US Supreme Court, federal appeals court, and federal court decisions have ruled that creationism cannot be taught in public school science classes because it is a religious doctrine.

The relentless effort of biblical creationism advocates to adduce reasons and assemble arguments to buttress their views demonstrates that they do not possess authentic faith. True faith does not require any justification, because faith *is* the unquestioning justification for all doctrinal beliefs. If there were reasons or evidence that supported Genesis creationism, then faith would not be necessary because creationism would be a valid scientific theory. The creationists' dogged search for reasons to believe betrays their claims of faith.

THIRTY-EIGHT

Does the Scientific Method Have Biblical Origins?

Hugh Ross is the founder and charismatic leader of a Christian ministry named Reasons to Believe that promotes old-Earth creationism. Although it has been active for twenty-five years, it holds the least popular creationist viewpoint among Christian fundamentalists and the least known among Christians of all persuasions. This is most likely because Reasons to Believe accommodates three major conclusions from mainstream science.

Specifically, its creationism stands apart from its creationist competitors (Answers in Genesis, Discovery Institute, and Institute for Creation Research) in adopting the 13.5-billion-year-old universe and the 4.5-billion-year-old Earth and rejecting the biblical worldwide flood. Reasons to Believe maintains that the Noachian Deluge was a regional flood that drowned all humans (except eight), since they all lived in a small area of the planet. Also, while endorsing the Adam and Eve narrative, Reasons to Believe dates the event to about 150,000 years ago. These postulates are anathema to the dominant young-Earth proponents, because they contradict the literal truth of the bible. Consequently, the other creationist groups consider Reasons to Believe creationism to be unbiblical.

What is overlooked by the critics of Reasons to Believe's old-Earth viewpoint is that the ministry unabashedly accepts almost all other standard inerrantist biblical beliefs. Examples are the reality of a supernatural realm and interventionist miracles, the existence of angels including Lucifer, the historic personage of Adam and Eve who lived in a God-designed Middle Eastern garden and are the ancestors of all people, the dominionist distinction between "soulish" animals and spiritual humans, eternal life for believers in a "new creation" with God and Jesus, and the doctrine that those who reject Jesus will be "removed from his presence."

The predominant themes in Ross's presentation of Reasons to Believe's old-Earth creationist conception are that it is derived from the bible, it is scientifically testable, and it is validated by virtually all scientific knowledge. He also claims that the bible contains exclusive truth and predicts scientific discoveries thousands of years ahead of time. Unless otherwise indicated, all statements are from Ross's 2009 book, *More Than a Theory: Revealing a Testable Model for Creation*.

Reasons to Believe's Biblical Foundation

Ross states explicitly that he is building Reasons to Believe's case for the god of the bible as the designer and creator of all nature—a supernatural, caring, intelligent designer—the one who embodies truth. Yet he continually invokes the terms *scientific integrity, scientific credibility, scientific merit, scientific value*, and *scientifically testable evidence* when favorably characterizing Reasons to Believe's creationism and castigating his creationist adversaries who make exactly the same theological assumptions he does. He even compares them to flat-Earth and geocentrism believers.

After severely criticizing the other biblical creationists for their lack of scientific credibility, Ross then contradicts himself by rejecting the widely accepted paleontological and molecular-genetic evidence documenting the evolution of humans from earlier primates, preferring instead the Adam and Eve story.

Ross's admiration for the bible includes the denigration of all other sacred books. He claims, for example, that the bible contains more scientific information than any other religious text; the bible uniquely predicts scientific discoveries; only the bible gives an abundance of specific, testable detail about cosmic events; the bible alone exhorts readers to objectively test before they believe; and, therefore, the bible is the best choice to build a scientifically testable theistic model.

Did Ross review all two dozen of the world's sacred religious texts? Or more appropriately, did he ask religious scholars from the other faith traditions to provide their independent opinions about his assertions of biblical superiority?

Scientific or Biblical Method?

Ross contends that the scientific method could more accurately be called the "biblical method." He repeats this claim in a dozen statements, including five listed here:

- Scripture is the source of the scientific method.
- The scientific method originated in scripture and in the development of Reformation theology.
- The benefits of the scientific age come from applying the testing process as set forth in scripture.
- The Genesis creation account reflects the classic scientific method.
- Historically, Christianity gave birth to both the scientific method and the scientific revolution.

Although these statements are clearly grandiose and some introduce extraneous issues, Ross's unequivocal claim is that the scientific method has its roots in the bible. What direct evidence does Ross provide to support his claim? Quite appropriately, he cites six verses from scripture that he believes document his case.

Six Bible Verses that Supposedly Established the Scientific Method

1. Acts 17:11–12. The Berean Jews received the message with great eagerness and examined the Scriptures every day to see if what Paul said was true. As a result, many of them believed.
2. Romans 12:1–2. Offer your bodies as a living sacrifice . . . do not conform to the pattern of this world, but be transformed by the

renewing of your mind. Then you will be able to test and approve what God's will is.

3. 1 Thessalonians 5:19–22. Do not quench the Spirit. Do not treat prophecies with contempt but test them all; hold on to what is good, reject every kind of evil.
4. 1 John 4:1–2. Do not believe every spirit, but test the spirits to see whether they are from God, because many false prophets have gone out into the world. This is how you can recognize the spirit of God: Every spirit that acknowledges that Jesus Christ has come in the flesh is from God.
5. Revelation 2:2–3. I know that you cannot tolerate wicked people, that you have tested those who claim to be apostles but are not, and have found them false. You have persevered and have endured hardships.
6. Job 34:4. Let us discern for ourselves what is right; let us learn together what is good.

(*All verses are from the New International Version (NIV), which is Ross's preferred translation.*)

The scientific method relies on observation, investigation, experimentation, and quantification to address questions about the natural world. Ross's six selected bible verses are concerned with false prophets, false apostles, Paul's truthfulness, and God's will. Four verses include the words *test* or *tested* but actually refer to the examination of prophecies, spirit messages, and teachings by applying some form of Christian litmus test. They do not constitute anything like a scientific investigation involving objective tests of observable phenomena in the natural world. Ross simply equates the words *test* and *tested* with scientific methodology.

The verse from Job is puzzling. God did collaborate with Satan in testing Job's faith in a gruesome story that illustrates wanton cruelty. However, the passage in Job 23:10, "When he has tested me, I will come forth as gold," would be more consistent with Ross's other choices. Ross failed to cite another verse that addresses testing: "Do not put the Lord your God to the test," which is found in both the Pentateuch (Deuteronomy 6:16) and the Gospel (Luke 4:12). Does this verse rule out all scientific investigation of theological questions?

Contradicting Ross's assertion about the "biblical method" is the consensus opinion of historians of science who locate the origins of modern science in the Greek Golden Age starting in 600 BCE and continuing for six centuries. Scientific inquiry was initiated in Ionian Greece, soon spreading to Athens and then to Alexandria. But the early precursors are found in Babylonia, Egypt, and Phoenicia several millennia before the advent of Greek science.

Prominent Greeks advanced knowledge about the natural world using the secular strategy of inquiry known as the scientific method. They made landmark discoveries leading to development of the modern disciplines of acoustics, anatomy, astronomy, botany, cartography, engineering, geometry, hydraulics, mathematics, mechanics, medicine, optics, pharmacology, physics, and zoology. Because the six previously listed New Testament verses were written sometime after 50 CE, they could not have influenced the genesis of the scientific method.

Ross also declared that Christian scholars throughout church history have asserted that the biblical narratives parallel the scientific method. However, he does not provide a single illustration. Ross makes other similarly remarkable claims, such as, "Every major Christian doctrine is either founded upon or linked to thousands of wide-ranging scientific details."

What should be recognized with respect to Ross's claim about the biblical origins of the scientific method is that the ancient Greeks were pagan polytheists who in succession worshipped a pantheon of Olympic gods, became attracted to the mystery (salvation) religions, and later embraced Epicurian and Stoic philosophies. However, the popular religions continued to be favored by Greeks. There is no indication that the bible influenced in any way early Greek scientists.

It should be mentioned that Ross cites three other items to buttress his claim: Galileo's alleged rebuke of Catholic theologians, an exposition about biblical faith, and reference to the writings of a Scottish theologian. Without any direct support from the bible or history, these ancillary points are not helpful to Ross's case.

The only reasonable conclusion to be reached is that this is an example of imaginative Christian revisionism associated with the fabrication of the pseudo-discipline called "theistic science."

Predicting Scientific Discoveries

Ross asserts that good science involves using models that make predictions that can be tested for validity. He states correctly that tests of predictive success are valued by the scientific community. However, Ross is referring to his own test of how well four creation and evolution viewpoints predict future scientific discoveries. He selected four competing models for his prediction test: Reasons to Believe old-Earth creationism, young-Earth creationism, theistic evolution, and naturalistic evolution. To accomplish the objective of a comparative evaluation of predictability, the critical activity was clearly the formulation of the predictions. Ross's project consisted of three steps.

First, Ross identified eighty-nine issues in three categories (simple sciences, complex sciences, social sciences) for which predictions would be developed. Examples of these issues are fine-tuning of physical laws, humanity's arrival in cosmic history, habitable zones for intelligent life, source of prebiotic molecules, diversity of early life, mass speciation events, human descent, occurrence of natural disasters, biblical inerrancy, creation of Adam and Eve, and the existence of the god of the bible.

Second, Ross formulated specific predictions about what scientists should discover in future research for each of the creation and evolution viewpoints for the eighty-nine issues. In what most people would regard as a wholly unscientific approach, Ross developed all predictions himself "while attempting to remain as neutral and objective as possible." His predictions are summarized in his 2006 book, *Creation As Science: A Testable Model Approach to End the Creation/Evolution Wars*.

Third, Ross evaluated the degree of success of his predictions for the four viewpoints on eighty-nine issues using a five-point scale: fulfilled, partly fulfilled, not yet fulfilled, partly falsified, and falsified. There was apparently no input from representatives of any other viewpoints. The results of Ross's one-man evaluation of the four viewpoints are shown in Table 2.

The outcome of this elaborate exercise should not be surprising to anyone, especially the monumental difference between Ross's old-Earth creationism and godless, naturalistic evolution. With a fulfillment rate of 78 percent versus 2 percent and a falsification rate of 0 percent versus 75 percent, some would construe these results as convincing evidence of

Reasons to Believe creationism's superiority over materialistic, ungodly evolution. Of course, this evaluation is not a legitimate demonstration of the relative merits of this particular variant of creationism and naturalistic evolution; it is instead just a contrived and meaningless expression of Ross's highly favorable opinion of his own biblically derived viewpoint and the corresponding abysmal failure of all others.

Ross summarized by declaring that Reasons to Believe creationism excels on predictive success and explanatory power and performs well on five additional "tests" he devised: censorship, stultification, integration, research passion, and destiny implications. He concluded that Reasons to Believe creationism has the power to change lives for the better because "the spiritual heart can rejoice with what the mind knows to be true."

Finally, Ross accuses evolutionists (and young-Earth creationists) of engaging in "ongoing purposeful attempts to ignore or shut out Reasons to Believe's claims." Considering how extreme the group's claims really are, it is understandable that the National Academy of Sciences, the Vatican Science Pontificate, and other scientific organizations would disregard its creationism

Table 2: Ross's Predictive Rates for Four Creation and Evolution Viewpoints

Judged Success	RTB	YEC	TE	NE
Fulfilled (or partly)	78%	25%	15%	2%
Falsified (or partly)	0%	51%	42%	75%

The labels are: RTB (old-Earth creationism), YEC (young-Earth creationism), TE (theistic evolution), and NE (naturalistic evolution).

The predictive rates were calculated from Ross (2009, p.244).

The columns do not add to 100 percent because the undetermined category (not yet fulfilled) was omitted.

Postscript: Scientific Method in the Bible?

Reader Nelson Hoffman suggested that a much more convincing piece of research for the biblical basis of the scientific method is the story of the prophet Daniel's controlled dietary experiment (Daniel 1:3–16, NIV), which dates to 530 BCE and might very well have influenced contemporary Greeks.

I replied that the Daniel episode illustrates a basic component of the scientific method, which is the comparison of groups of subjects to reach a conclusion about different conditions. It should be noted that the essential experimental requirement for randomization was absent from assignment of both participants and treatments to groups. Yet, this was a reasonable approach under the circumstances to address the question of benefits of a vegan diet.

Also, the precursors of scientific inquiry in Babylonia, Egypt, and Phoenicia predate the Greeks of the classical period by several millennia. Furthermore, as far as I know, there is no evidence that the Hebrew Bible impacted in any way early Greek scientists. The burden of historical documentation is on those who make the claim of biblical influence.

Moreover, the claim of biblical origins of the scientific method is disputed by Louis Liebenburg in his recent book, *The Art of Tracking: The Origin of Science*. The author argues that animal tracking skills and techniques constitute the foundation of scientific thought, including observation, hypothesis, evidence, prediction, and causal reasoning. Liebenburg asserts that this prehistoric development dates back 70,000 years! (Skeptical Inquirer, July/August 2016, p. 65)

THIRTY-NINE

Sorry, 'Theistic Science' Is Not Science

A recently published book documents the creationist misrepresentation of science called "theistic science." *Who Was Adam? A Creation Model Approach to the Origin of Humanity* (2015) consists of a reprint of a book of the same title published more than ten years earlier, followed by a thorough update that constitutes one-third of the text.

The authors are Fazale Rana and Hugh Ross, both executives and scholars with Reasons to Believe, a Christian ministry located in Southern California. They have graduate degrees in science (chemistry and astronomy, respectively) and have written many books that profess to put biblical creationism on a scientific foundation.

Rana and Ross's work focuses on the "scientific case for God's existence and the bible's reliability" and the "integration of scientific fact with biblical faith." Throughout *Who Was Adam?* they describe their creationist approach to human origins as science.

However, Rana and Ross also make clear their fundamental biblical premise: "We believe life's origin and history cannot be fully explained apart from the direct involvement of the Creator, who repeatedly intervened in Earth's history, initiating new life forms, including humans who alone were made in His image."

This premise reflects Rana and Ross's explicit statement that creation by supernatural intervention is the foundational assumption of Reasons to Believe's human origins model. The central presupposition of "theistic science" is operationalized in the repeated use of phrases such as "God's handiwork," "Creator's direct action," "work of the Creator," "God's creative work," and other causal behavior attributed to the biblical deity.

The Reasons to Believe strategy does not satisfy the basic requirements of a scientific endeavor, and in this chapter I explain why, giving numerous examples taken primarily from the ten-year update of *Who Was Adam?*

Creation Model

The Reasons to Believe human origins model is based on all bible verses that describe God's work in creating humans and that recount early human history. Six well-known assertions illustrate this creation model's testable propositions:

- God created Adam and Eve as the first humans (the primordial couple) through direct intervention.
- All humans came from Adam and Eve, who are the parents of humanity.
- Humans originated in a single geographical location, the Garden of Eden.
- A regional flood shaped early human history.
- Life spans of the first humans were once longer than 900 years but shortened after the flood.
- Humans are behaviorally distinct (in ways that reflect God's image) from the earlier hominids and the great apes.

The authors' stated objective is to demonstrate that a traditional biblical view of human origins has scientific credibility. They assert that the Reasons to Believe model recasts the biblical scenario into scientific terms. It is purported to be like all scientific ideas or models, in that it is poised to stimulate future scientific work. With this biblical model, Rana and

Ross argue that the concept of creation is testable and has entered the scientific domain. Not surprisingly, they claim that *Who Was Adam?* is primarily a scientific book.

Scientific Principles

Before listing concrete examples of Rana and Ross's approach to defending the Reasons to Believe's biblical view of human origins, I want to outline the major violations of scientific logic embodied in their work:

- Their creationist propositions are immune from refutation or falsification, because the Genesis account is held to be literally true. The premise of verbal inspiration or inerrancy of scripture contravenes the basic assumption of scientific hypothesis testing, which requires that negative evidence result in rejection of the tentative propositions that are formulated.
- The model is based on the alleged reality of supernatural causation, which is the core assumption of "theistic science." Rana and Ross continually invoke God's motives and actions in explaining scientific research findings or dismissing evidence that contradicts their creationist claims.
- One of the hallmarks of the scientific approach to knowledge discovery is objectivity. This means that independent evaluations of evidence are essential in making judgments about scientific claims. Yet Rana and Ross by themselves generate all conclusions about the validity of their model, even when their opinions are flatly contradicted by the scientific consensus.
- Rana and Ross repeatedly engage in circular reasoning in defending their human origins model against unsupportive or contradictory findings. Specifically, they regularly invoke ad hoc theological explanations, including common design (rather than common descent), the Noachian Deluge, and the mysterious life attribute of "soulishness."
- The false equivalence of biblical creationism and human evolution as scientific explanations is routinely advanced by Rana and Ross. This comparison is unwarranted because the former is faith-based

> while the latter is evidence-based. One is accepted by believers as God's truth while the other is subject to ongoing revision on the basis of abundant empirical data.

In what appears to be an inconsistency with their scriptural inerrancy assumption, Rana and Ross state that the Reasons to Believe model represents only one of many possible biblically derived models for humanity's origins. They explain that considerable freedom exists within their creation framework for adjustments, fine-tuning, revisions, refinements, and extensions. Of course, the authors' concession gives the biblical creationists a lot of flexibility or "wiggle room" in integrating scientific findings into the Reasons to Believe model.

The basis for this flexibility is the authors' declaration that the bible must be "properly interpreted and understood"—but who decides what constitutes proper interpretation? They do! For example, the authors accept the "day-age interpretation" of the first chapter of Genesis, which considers creation "days" to be long periods of time. Thus, they are able to embrace the true ages of the universe and planet Earth, while excoriating the young-Earth creationists as not scientifically credible.

Unscientific Reasoning

The following quotes from their book exemplify problems with Rana and Ross's scientific reasoning.

- "Unfortunately, the latest results show no direct evidence for the flood; however, this does not mean there is no evidence for the flood."
- "The popular interpretation of these salient discoveries challenges Reasons to Believe's prediction, but these interpretations are controversial and reasonable alternative explanations exist."
- "We would argue that God endowed some animals with soulishness and that chimp response to death reflects their soulishness, not a deep evolutionary connection to humans."
- "The high degree of human-ape genetic similarity is not problematic for Reasons to Believe's model; we view the similarity as reflecting shared designs, rather than shared descent."

- “Pseudogenes can legitimately be viewed as the work of the Creator who intentionally introduced these features into genomes for a specific purpose.”
- “Given the seriousness of this challenge to our model, we are unwilling to accept the results; we contend that the population sizes generated by these methods are merely estimates, not hard and fast values.”
- “We are not willing to abandon our conviction that mitochondrial Eve and Y-chromosomal Adam correspond to the biblical Adam and Eve.”
- “These events could be taken as evidence for the Creator’s role in designing the fusion. Perhaps God used a preexisting template to create hominids and human beings. Could not God be thought of as a divine genetic engineer?”
- “The substantial discrepancy between humanity’s origin and the emergence of agriculture could be explained by the first humans engaging in small-scale, mixed farming at levels that escape scientific detection.”
- “There are no 900-year-old human fossils because humans aged more slowly prior to Noah’s flood, long biblical life spans may only apply to a few people, and murder was rampant in the era before the flood.”
- “God created microbes for a variety of reasons, but He did not create corresponding human pathogens when He made humans; however, God did create beneficial microbes as part of His good creation.”
- “Even though most scientists interpret the genetic similarities between humans, Neanderthals, and apes as compelling evidence of common descent, we interpret these data as reflections of common design.”

In each of these examples, Rana and Ross argue against the majority scientific interpretation, or they simply reject the overwhelming scientific consensus. To buttress their contrary opinions, they always provide some kind of rationale, of which there are three types.

First, there are standard ad hoc theological explanations that have no basis in science. Second, there are vague criticisms. Third, there are non-specific objections.

Because they invoke common design so often in *Who Was Adam?* Rana and Ross argue that godly design is actually a respectable scientific concept. To accomplish this remarkable transformation from theology to science, they reached back in history to a pre-Darwin British biologist named Sir Richard Owen, who promoted a theistic explanation (One Cause, the Creator) that Rana and Ross refer to as an "alternate scientifically robust model that makes sense of biology." Thus, Reasons to Believe's biblical creation model employs this "scientific precedent to interpret shared features as a reflection of God's intent by repurposing common designs."

Rana and Ross's preeminent violation of scientific logic deserves special attention due to its ubiquitous presence in their book. This is the use of circular reasoning, which entails invoking theological concepts to defend the Reasons to Believe theistic model against nonsupportive or contradictory scientific findings. The bottom line for this logical fallacy: theological beliefs cannot legitimately explain away scientific evidence for the purpose of vindicating theistic propositions.

Evolution Criticism

Rana and Ross just can't seem to resist the impulse to attack human evolution, apparently believing that their criticisms strengthen the case for the Genesis creation narrative. In fact, the alleged difficulties with evolution, even if true, would not constitute evidence *in favor of* creationism. Here are six of their criticisms of evolution:

- "That human evolution occurred is as much a hypothesis as how it occurred."
- "This demonstrates just how tentative and speculative the central tenets of human evolution are."
- "It is eye-opening to realize how much uncertainty and speculation is associated with human evolution scenarios."
- "It is impossible to interpret the fossil record from an evolutionary perspective."

- "Evolutionary biologists' insistence that humanity emanated from a population (not two individuals) results in a theory-laden conclusion."
- "Confusion associated with the interpretation of hominid fossils from an evolutionary view supports Reasons to Believe's biblical creation view."

Contrast these severely critical remarks questioning the validity of human evolution with the circular ad hoc theological explanations, endless excuse-making, and outright denial of scientific consensus that Rana and Ross use to defend their human origins model. The last assertion above is especially noteworthy for illustrating the logical fallacy of arguing from ignorance.

Overall Evaluation

Rana and Ross claim that science affirms their human origins model in ten areas of research, for which they apply the following descriptors: "effectively accounted for," "new insights support," "in line with (but presents a problem)," "in accord with," "readily accommodates," "makes sense of," "expand the model," "a tour de force," "a fulfilled prediction," and "a reflection of God's intent by repurposing common designs." It is important to recognize that failure to contradict a claim does not constitute strong support for the claim. Only two of the ten descriptors are clearly affirmations, and the last is just one more ad hoc theological explanation.

The authors next identify five areas where science has challenged their model. First, they admit they were wrong about the dates for Adam and Eve but say their corrected dates still harmonize with scripture and, after re-interpreting two Genesis chapters, they conclude that Adam and Eve were created during the most recent ice age!

Contradicting Rana and Ross's prior position that modern humans and Neanderthals did not interbreed, strong evidence now shows that they did interbreed. However, the authors argue that from a Christian perspective, humans and Neanderthals are distinct products of God's creative activity and therefore this does not invalidate the Reasons to Believe model because the ability to interbreed is a manifestation of shared design, not common descent.

Rana and Ross characterize human-Neanderthal interbreeding as morally repugnant, sordid, salacious, sinful, distasteful, degenerate, and comparable to bestiality. Then they excuse this condemnable miscegenation by explaining that the bible and history testify to humanity's depraved nature after the Fall. They declare that it should not be surprising that humans interbred with Neanderthals, given the human propensity for intercourse with animals! Even after this admission, Rana and Ross assure us that their model can accommodate evidence for such degenerate behavior.

A key feature of this model centers on the idea that humans are uniquely created in God's image. Rana and Ross admit that the very large discrepancy of up to 100,000 years between the first appearance of humans and the emergence of symbolic capacity (reflecting God's image) is a potential problem and, after offering a partial explanation, they acknowledge some residual discomfort.

The authors concede that one of the most significant challenges leveled against their creation model relates to humanity's original population size. Was it several thousand people or just two individuals? They currently believe—even though almost all geneticists disagree—that their particular model can withstand this challenge.

After their detailed review of a variety of research studies that address the propositions of their human origins model, the book concludes by stating that "we trust that Adam's identity has been established as an image-bearer of his divine Creator." Thus, they achieve a theological conclusion that is independent of the scientific evidence. Not surprisingly, the conclusion follows directly from their faith-based premise that I summarized in the introductory section of this chapter.

Rana and Ross have produced creative and sometimes incredible arguments to provide people of faith with "reasons to believe" the alleged truth of the bible's creation narrative. For the reasons given, they don't accomplish their goal within the parameters of science. Can the biblical creation chronicle be reconciled with factual scientific knowledge? *Who Was Adam?* demonstrates that the answer is no. In other words, "theistic science" is not authentic science. Instead it constitutes a strategy for sustaining biblical faith.

Postscript: RTB's Continuing Assault on Science

On a Sunday morning in early February 2020, I attended a presentation at a local Baptist church titled "Science and Faith: Finding Truth in All Things." When leaving I received a complimentary copy of *Building Bridges : Presentations on RTB's Testable Creation Model*, the latest summary of the ministry's version of biblical creationism.

It's clear from the essays in this slim volume that Reasons to Believe is no longer attempting to achieve legitimacy in the mainstream scientific community, but rather has decided to direct their efforts to indoctrinating Christian believers in their idiosyncratic and incorrect view of science. Instead, they should publicly acknowledge that their work is entirely an expression of their sincere Christian faith and end their embarrassing misrepresentation of the philosophy and methodology of science. (Skeptical Inquirer, September/October, 2020, pp. 43–45.)

AFTERWORD
Biblical Truth Summarized

As a concluding overview, this section presents capsule summaries of the thirty-nine chapters that document the assertion that the Holy Bible is *not* a "Good Book."

1. Nine categories of basic bible facts, including universal jihad, patrilineal guilt, blood sacrifice, and eternal punishment, demonstrate that the strongest evidence against biblical inerrancy is the bible itself.
2. A critical examination of Christian fundamentalists' theopolitical positions on ten major sociocultural issues documents the allegation that these extremists intentionally misrepresent or distort what scripture actually says.
3. The Texas Republican Party platform constitutes a blueprint for implementing a fundamentalist theocracy in America based on zealotry, intolerance, hatred, denialism, bigotry, egocentricity, and unmitigated anger.
4. A review of twelve anchors of fundamentalist political theology, such as antiabortion, pro-Christian nationalism, anti-evolution,

pro-Decalogue displays, and anti-marriage equality, demonstrate that fundamentalism is a threat to American democracy.

5. A brief history of the first century of Christian fundamentalism in the United States exposes the foundations of a reactionary theology that persists in opposing mainstream developments in science, medicine, and human rights.
6. A personal journalistic report describes some minor annoyances as well as serious legal violations in an ultra-conservative Christian community, while illustrating that fundamentalists occasionally create unintended humor for nonbelieving residents.
7. There is no biblical sanctity of life principle, fetuses do not possess a God-given right to life, God doesn't love the unborn, and he is the greatest destroyer of human fetuses, according to his own perfect record.
8. The false claim that God loves children is refuted by numerous episodes of slaughtering innocent children, child sacrifice by parents, killing children with wild animals, beating infants to death, and parental cannibalism.
9. Obedience and subjugation of women is a dominant theme throughout the bible, including God's appraisal of women as less valuable than men and his depiction of women as dangerous, dishonest, manipulative, and untrustworthy.
10. The bible clearly condemns homosexuality as sinful and unforgiveable in both Hebrew and Christian testaments and sanctions several forms of marriage unions including polygyny.
11. Scripture is unequivocal in describing in gruesome detail the role that animal sacrifice fulfills in God's horrific theology of worship, which prefigures the blood sacrifice of his son, the "Lamb of God."
12. In stark contrast to his hateful behavior toward fetuses, children, women, homosexuals, and animals, God unambiguously endorses the institution of chattel slavery, as do his Christian spokesmen, Jesus, Paul, and Peter.

13. The terrible massacres described in the Pentateuch and Joshua document the ruthless, unforgiving, bloodthirsty nature of Yahweh's personality and his frightful theology of punishment.
14. The massacres, slaughters, and murders recounted in the Histories provide overwhelming evidence of insanely jealous Yahweh's propensity to kill all who disobey him.
15. The Prophets and Wisdom books reveal Yahweh's incomprehensible evil motivation and undiminished capacity for cruel infliction of pain and suffering on all living creatures.
16. A logical analysis of the God idea leads to the unequivocal rejection of believers' claims about the existence of thousands of territorial deities, as well as discrediting the untenable concept of a universal heavenly father.
17. Answers to ten questions from the gospels concerning Jesus's birthdate, atoning death, teachings, values, and "second coming," demonstrate that he is a composite mythical character derived from earlier savior god stories.
18. Jesus's obsession with hell is expressed in his detailed description of this abhorrent realm of unending torture and his enumeration of sixteen behavioral commandments that if violated ensure eternal punishment.
19. A careful analysis of Jesus's teachings in the four canonical gospels reveals an undeniable truth: he is *both* a prophet of peace and love *and* a purveyor of fear and hate, and therefore is not an exemplary role model for humanity.
20. The foundational belief of Christianity, which is that the killing of Jesus and his subsequent resurrection confers immortality on adherents, is based on the traditional conception of a ritual blood sacrifice of an innocent animal.
21. Most Christians don't know anything about Jesus's physical appearance, or that he was not executed on a cross, that he was wrong about prayer, and that the Shroud of Turin was not his burial garment.

22. Easter is the culminating event of Christian Holy Week, a completely unoriginal extravaganza that derives from numerous earlier celebrations and ritual practices, almost all of which incorporate crucifixion, resurrection, and everlasting life.
23. Exposing bogus Christian nationalism claims, reviewing the careers of ten prominent founders, and documenting the absence of Christian consensus on social issues, demonstrates that the US is not a Christian republic.
24. Christian Reconstructionist Herbert Titus was an early advocate of Christian nationalism's extreme views. including restricting office holders to Christian believers, posting the Decalogue in courthouses, and abolishing public schools and welfare programs.
25. The first declaration of "Christian Heritage week" dates back 25 years, when fundamentalist icon Mike Huckabee signed a proclamation that falsely identified four US founders as "Christian statesmen of calibre and integrity."
26. Sixteen reasons explain exactly why the Ten Commandments do not constitute an exemplary moral code and, if implemented, would actually produce an unjust, brutal society of religious fanatics.
27. The obsession with the Hebrew Decalogue will end when the commandments are incorporated into the US legal system and enforced in a manner consistent with God's will.
28. US Supreme Court Justice Neil Gorsuch believes that Ten Commandments monuments on public property are permissible or even desirable, because they communicate a "secular moral message," thereby demonstrating that he hasn't read the edicts.
29. For Christians, the infallibility of prayer is an article of faith that cannot be questioned, hence the typical responses to tragic prayer failures, such as "God has called him home" and "She has gone to be with Jesus."
30. The strongest empirical evidence against the claim that God answers prayer comes from five replicated, randomized clinical trials in which recipients of Christian prayer did not experience higher survival rates.

31. Christians have refused to accept the irrefutable scientific conclusion that God doesn't answer prayer, citing a variety of nonsensical excuses like "God is outside the domain of science" and "It's blasphemy to test God."
32. God's law mandates the death penalty for sixty specific offenses, including adultery, apostasy, astrology, blasphemy, false prophecy, homosexuality, idolatry, mediumship, perjury, Sabbath-breaking, sorcery, and unchastity.
33. Biblically approved methods of executing violators include beating, beheading, burning, burying, consuming, dropping, drowning, envenoming, impaling, infecting, mauling, ripping, scraping, stabbing, stoning, and suffocating.
34. Three important facts about abortion are that most Americans support women's reproductive rights and reject the dogma of fetal personhood, while many abortion opponents endorse an exception for severe fetal abnormality.
35. Scripture demonstrates that the antiabortion zealots' favorite epithets, "murderer of unborn children" and "baby killer," accurately describe their biblical God, who is truly history's greatest abortionist.
36. Biblical creationism is a fundamentalist myth and a menace to science education, represented by three mutually contradictory versions that are unanimously rejected by science, law, and mainstream Christianity, yet accepted as true without evidence by devotees.
37. Old-Earth creationism, which is promoted by the Christian ministry Reasons to Believe, denies the bible-based claims of a 9,000-year-old universe and a world-wide flood, thereby incurring the wrath of opposing ministry Answers in Genesis.
38. Simultaneously, Reasons to Believe advances two astounding false claims itself, that the scientific method originated in the bible and its version of creationism is vastly superior to naturalistic evolution in predicting scientific discoveries.

39. The foundational premise of all creationist approaches to life's origins is the perversion of legitimate science called "theistic science," which embodies the faith claim of supernatural or Godly causation, for which there is absolutely no evidential support.

In conclusion, the numerous grandiose claims made by bible believers are *not* justified. The bible is *not* a compendium of humankind's collected moral wisdom, nor does it contain unsurpassed ethical guidelines for living a responsible life. In fact, it is a collection of cruel ideas and brutal traditions that emerged several thousand years ago in Middle Eastern cultures. Again, the Holy Bible is *not* a "Good Book."

Academic Recognition and Contributions

Brian Bolton, Ph.D. (University of Wisconsin–Madison), was University Professor of Rehabilitation and Adjunct Professor of Psychology at the University of Arkansas–Fayetteville from 1971 to 2002. He was an Assistant Professor of Psychology at the Illinois Institute of Technology from 1968 to 1971. He is a Fellow of the Division of Evaluation, Measurement, and Statistics (1978) and Fellow of the Division of Rehabilitation Psychology (1980) of the American Psychological Association, Fellow of the Society for Personality Assessment (1980), and Fellow of the American Psychological Society (1989). He received the Burlington Northern Foundation Faculty Achievement Award for Scholarly Research from the University of Arkansas in 1986, the Roger Barker Distinguished Research Award in Rehabilitation Psychology from the American Psychological Association in 1988, the Distinguished Career in Rehabilitation Counseling Research Award from the American Rehabilitation Counseling Association in 1989, an Alumni Achievement Award from the University of Wisconsin in 1996, and a Distinguished Reviewer Award from the Buros Mental Measurements Institute in 2005. He received twelve research project awards from the American Rehabilitation Counseling Association, including the first place awards in 1975, 1996, and 2000. He is a licensed psychologist, Humanist minister, Karate black belt, and Distinguished Toastmaster. His ten edited and authored books include *Handbook of Measurement and Evaluation in Rehabilitation* (4th ed.), *Psychology of Deafness for Rehabilitation Counselors*, *Psychosocial Adjustment to Disability*, *Rehabilitation Counseling Research* (2nd ed.), *Rehabilitation Client Assessment*, *Vocational Adjustment of Disabled Persons*, *Rehabilitation Counseling: Theory and Practice*, and *Special Education and Rehabilitation Testing: Current Practices and Test Reviews*. He contributed twenty chapters to the *Encyclopedia of Clinical Assessment*, the *Annual Review of Rehabilitation* (Vols. 2 & 4), *Functional Psychological Testing*, *Hearing and Hearing Impairment*, *Handbook of Multivariate Experimental Psychology*, *Rehabilitation Counseling: Basics and Beyond*, *Rehabilitation Outcomes: Analysis and Measurement*, *Vocational Rehabilitation of Persons with Prolonged Psychiatric Disorders*, *Psychology for Health Science Students*, *Improving Assessment in Rehabilitation and Health*, and *Counseling Theories for Rehabilitation Health Professionals*. He has written forty test reviews for the eighth, ninth, eleventh, twelfth, thirteenth, fourteenth, and fifteenth *Mental Measurements Yearbooks* and *Test Critiques* (Vol. 1, 2, 3, 4, 5, 6, 7, 8, 9, 10, & 11). He authored 100 articles in psychology and rehabilitation journals, presented ninety papers to psychology conferences, and wrote sixty book reviews for psychology journals. His assessment instruments include the Work Personality Profile, Employability Maturity Interview, Vocational Personality Report, Work Temperament Inventory, and Functional Capacities Report. He was editor of the *Rehabilitation Counseling Bulletin* and *Rehabilitation Education* and consulting editor to the University Park Press and the Test Corporation of America and served on the editorial boards of *Rehabilitation Psychology, Multivariate Experimental Clinical Research, Rehabilitation Counseling Bulletin, Computers in Human Behavior*, and *Assessment in Rehabilitation and Exceptionality.* He was president of the Society for Applied Multivariate Research in 1975–76, 1992–93, and 1997–1998 and president of the Northwest Arkansas ACLU from 1996 to 2002.

Original Publication Sources

1. American Atheist, First Quarter 2016, pp. 24–28.
2. Free Inquiry, June/July 2019, pp. 36–44.
3. American Rationalist, January/February 2017, pp. 6–7.
4. Humanist, March/April 2017, pp. 20–23.
5. American Rationalist, March/April 2012, pp. 3–4.
6. Freethought Today, May 2016, p. 3.
7. American Atheist, Third Quarter 2016, pp. 6–9.
8. American Atheist, Second Quarter 2017, pp. 8–11.
9. American Atheist, Third Quarter 2017, pp. 26–27.
10. Freethought Today, June/July 2019, pp. 14–15.
11. Freethought Today, March 2017, p. 17.
12. American Atheist, First Quarter 2018, pp. 22–26.
13. American Rationalist, July/August 2015, pp. 5–7.
14. American Rationalist, September/October 2015, pp. 6–8.
15. American Rationalist, November/December 2015, pp. 2–5.
16. American Rationalist, September/October 2016, pp. 6–7.
17. Freethought Today, December 2006, p. 14.
18. American Rationalist, November/December 2014, pp. 5–8.
19. American Atheist, Fourth Quarter 2017, pp. 16–18.
20. Not previously published.
21. Not previously published.
22. Freethought Today, March 2013, p. 15.
23. Free Inquiry, December 2019/January 2020, pp. 18–28.
24. American Rationalist, May/June 2017, pp. 2–3.
25. Freethought Today, March 1995, p. 17.
26. Freethought Today, January/February 2005, p. 12.

27. American Atheist, First Quarter 2017, pp. 18–21.
28. Not previously published.
29. Freethought Today, April 2006, p. 8.
30. American Rationalist, May/June 2007, pp. 7–8.
31. Free Inquiry, December 2018/January 2019, pp. 20–25.
32. American Rationalist, May/June 2015, pp. 2–6.
33. American Atheist, Second Quarter 2016, pp. 18–21.
34. American Rationalist, January/February 2015, pp. 2–5.
35. Freethought Today, January/February 2019, p. 5.
36. American Atheist, Fourth Quarter 2016, pp. 16–19.
37. Skeptical Inquirer, May/June 2012, pp. 8–11.
38. Skeptical Inquirer, March/April 2016, pp. 53–56.
39. Skeptical Inquirer, May/June 2018, pp. 50–53.

Index